Bonnie Stern, beloved teacher and bestselling cookbook author, wants nothing more than for you to feel like she's in the kitchen cooking beside you.

In her latest cookbook, *Don't Worry, Just Cook*, written with her daughter Anna Rupert (who has, in fact, been in the kitchen cooking beside Bonnie her whole life!), Bonnie and Anna are here to help cooks of all experience foster comfort and connection through food.

With her trademark encouraging style and attention to detail, Bonnie writes recipes that are consistently delicious, widely appealing, and, as always, timeless. Like all of her cookbooks, *Don't Worry, Just Cook* doesn't simply give instructions to create a dish, it also shares stories, lessons, and kitchen wisdom that will build your cooking technique and confidence in the kitchen.

In this new book, you'll find easy-to-follow recipes for all-day breakfasts, soups, starters, and side dishes, as well as breads and vegetarian, fish, and meat mains. And, for those wanting something sweet, Bonnie and Anna have included plenty of desserts! You'll be amazed by how quickly such special dishes

like Jeweled Roasted Salmon with Herbs and Sheet Pan Chicken with Lemon and Olives come together. The simplicity and beauty of dishes like Ja'ala Herb Salad with Lemon Honey Dressing and Roasted Cauliflower Steaks with Tahini and Z'hug will impress even the cook! And the desserts, like the Pavlova Cake with Lemon Curd and Berries, Bonnie's Rugelach, and S'mores Chocolate Bark have never been so fun or delicious.

Bonnie and Anna have also provided notes and variations to help you modify dishes for special diets, and have sprinkled in essays on topics that will resonate with all of us, from things not worth worrying about, to a love of leftovers and what to do with them. Bonnie and Anna's warm voices and subtle humor come through on every page. With 125 enjoyable and thoughtful recipes, and stunning photography, home cooks will turn to this instant classic time and time again to nourish themselves and the people they love.

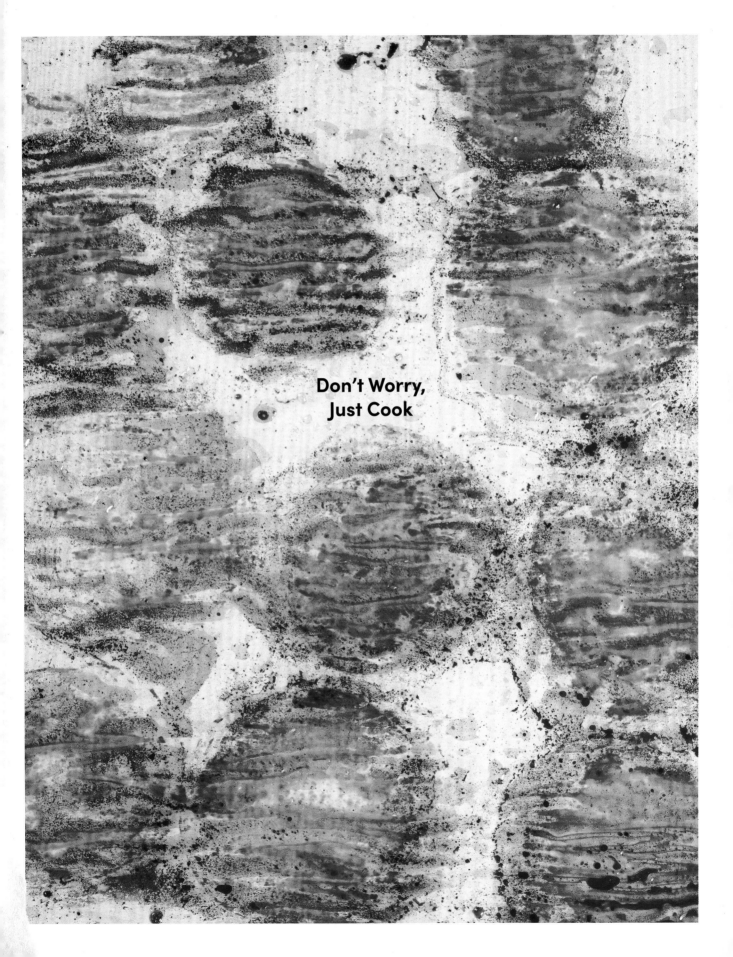

Don't Worry,
Just Cook

Don't Worry, Just Cook

Delicious, Timeless Recipes for Comfort & Connection

Bonnie Stern & Anna Rupert

appetite
by RANDOM HOUSE

Appetite by Random House® and colophon are registered
trademarks of Penguin Random House LLC.

Library and Archives of Canada Cataloguing in Publication
is available upon request.

ISBN: 9780525611585
eBook ISBN: 9780525611592

Cover and book design by Kelly Hill
Photography by Tyler Anderson
Additional photos provided by Mark Rupert and Anna Rupert
Food styling by Olga Truchan
Printed and bound in China

Published in Canada by Appetite by Random House®,
a division of Penguin Random House LLC.
www.penguinrandomhouse.ca

10 9 8 7 6 5 4 3 2 1

appetite
by RANDOM HOUSE

Penguin
Random House
Canada

To everyone we call family, who helps us
with our worries and helps us to not worry.
Thank you for letting us be in your life,
and letting us try to do the same for you.

Contents

Foreword by Yotam Ottolenghi

Preparing food is the most blissful activity, second only to serving it to a home crowd, happy to express their joy and gratitude. I get this kind of kick in abundance, both in my restaurants and when feeding friends and family at my dining table. The process of cooking and nurturing (yourself and others) is fundamental to being human yet, somehow, in the modern world, it doesn't always come naturally. For some, it could even be a source of anxiety.

Paradoxically, to get over such worries, and capture the full potential for joy that cooking can give you, you simply need to start doing it. There really is no other way. Luckily, there are people like Bonnie Stern around, a teacher at heart, and her daughter, Anna, to hold your hand when you need it, guide you through the process, and supply you with a bunch of home dishes that withstood the test of time in the Stern-Rupert family, all of them as comforting as they are reassuring.

I have known Bonnie for years and have been a huge fan of her rugelach, her vast knowledge and her amazing skill at connecting people around food. Everyone knows her and everyone loves her, precisely because she so naturally uses food to disarm and defuse, to pave ways and lead people on their culinary journeys.

There are so many fantastic dishes in this book, all of which you'd probably want to add to your repertoire. The most important takeaway, though, could only come from Bonnie and Anna and it is printed on the cover: Don't worry, just cook. I toast to that.

A Note from Bonnie

I have always felt like a social worker in the kitchen. Although I trained as a chef, it was teaching people about cooking and supporting them in their everyday lives that resonated with me. Nothing makes me happier than helping someone cook, and feeling like I am right there in the kitchen with them. I love hearing things like "Your rice pudding saved my marriage!" "Your Cuisinart book gave me the courage to take it out of the box." "Your HeartSmart recipes meant my dad didn't have to give up flavor when he had to change his diet." "*Friday Night Dinners* helped bring our family together." This is what makes all the hard work (and public speaking, which, believe it or not, terrifies me!) worthwhile. Food has the power to make our lives better in so many ways, both seriously and joyfully, and cooking has the ability to connect us—to ourselves, our families, our friends, and our communities.

Over the years I've connected with people through many channels: my cookbooks, newspaper columns, newsletters, and TV and radio appearances. But the one I loved the most was my cooking school, which I ran in Toronto for 37 years. I always love when people talk to me about their experiences and memories of the school; it makes me feel very proud of everything we accomplished there together. The wonderful thing about the school was that it was personal—it was about our lives and relationships, and you were there in the room with me. At the school we didn't just teach people how to make a recipe; we also gave them reasons to

make it and stories about how the dish came to be. In that way, it is similar to how I write about food, but I was able to immediately hear from my students, which cemented that feeling of connection and helped me understand what they needed to succeed. We could adapt the recipes to suit them. People shared their stories with me about making my recipes, what they wanted to see in the instructions, and how the recipes became part of their families—it's made my career so rewarding.

Closing the school in 2011 was an immensely difficult decision. I knew it was the right time to do it, but I didn't expect to feel like I had lost such a big part of myself—in fact, this is the first cookbook I've written since then. In the years that followed, I continued to teach cooking through small, private classes in my home, and, thankfully, I was able to continue working with a number of people from the school. I marveled at how our connections to food and cooking have changed as the world has evolved. And then, of course, came 2020 and the COVID-19 pandemic, when I started teaching over Zoom! I also began to use social media more (or I should say, my son, Mark, started helping me use social media more). Everyone was cooking at home, and having all sorts of feelings about what was going on in the world and in their lives. I wanted to find a way to connect with people and to help—and teaching cooking was the best way I knew how. I started posting simple recipes as often as I could. I started going through my cookbooks and refreshing classic recipes I hadn't made in a while. I got to hear your stories again and learn from your questions. And hearing that people appreciated the recipes and the posts made a tremendous impact on me, and helped me during that time too.

I didn't know if I had the confidence to write another cookbook until my daughter, Anna, offered to work on it with me. Cooking has always been a strong bond between us, and I value her input and trust her judgment completely. Together, we've each brought our own strengths to this project: I have the years of experience in teaching and recipe development, and Anna knows how the next generation thinks about food and cooking, loves writing, and is an expert communicator. And when we stop to consider why we love cooking together so much and why we wanted to write this book, it always comes down to one thing: food is a way to bring people together. It's been my message my whole career. In a world that is constantly changing and full of uncertainty, I think it's wonderful that food can be a source of stability and comfort, something that grounds us and reminds us of what matters most.

As Anna and I were writing together, she often wondered out loud what the title of the book should be. One day she asked me if we had any family sayings or what advice I always give.

And I answered, "I guess I tell people 'Don't worry, just cook! It will be fine!'" We both laughed, because if you know me, you know it's true. I tell everyone not to worry all the time. But if you really know me, you know I'm the biggest worrier on the planet. (We've since realized just how often I give this advice, including in almost every recipe in this book! Don't worry, it's been edited.) I tell you not to worry because I've done all the worrying for you! And I hope that as you cook through this book, you'll keep that in mind, and draw as much comfort and connection from these pages as I have.

Bonnie

Love, Bonnie

A Note from Anna (Banana)

When I was little, I dreamt that, one day, my mom and I would have a cooking show called *BonANNA's in the Kitchen*. Or *Bananas in the Kitchen*. (I never decided whether there would be an apostrophe or not, i.e., whether it was a show about *me* in the kitchen with Bonnie or the fact that when my mom and I do things together, it is often hilarious, if not totally . . . bananas.) Although this show was never made, and no one went for it as the title of this book, I've clearly been working on making this collaboration happen since I was 6 years old. And at my mom's end, I suspect that this book may have started out as a ploy to spend more time with me, so we're both guilty of wanting this to happen very badly.

But otherwise, why am I involved in *Don't Worry, Just Cook*? Well, cooking with my mom is one of my favorite things in the world to do. And I love to write. Writing has always been part of my professional life in healthcare and research, but I love to write personally as well. And years ago, I started helping friends, colleagues, and family with editing and writing. My brother, Mark, is the real genius in social media, but we did notice that I'm quite good at channeling what Bonnie would say, and how she would say it. I kinda just get her.

I also understand how much she cares about what she does—supporting so many people to successfully cook at home, and feel confident doing it. I have listened to her take countless phone calls, even on Friday while we're making our Friday night dinner, to coach someone through making their own. I have watched her struggle to google something for a caller because the person on the other end of the line is struggling more to google that something. And I have seen her scour her library of cookbooks for that recipe the caller knows they once saw in that other chef's cookbook back in 1987 and can't find the recipe, but maybe Bonnie knows of it and what book it's in and can tell them how much sugar is called for. Really.

My mom and I also have this unofficial custom that has been going on for years. At some point midweek, the two of us discuss and plan the menu for Friday night dinner and any other special meal that is coming up. I've been menu planning and assisting in recipe development since . . . forever. I think it's in my blood. I am also quite handy in the food memory department (although my mom's food memory is also extremely well developed!). Doesn't everyone have a separate memory specifically for the dishes they ate once 7 years ago in that distant country at that restaurant recommended by Mitchell Davis? (It's always Mitchell.) My dad marvels at this every time he sees it in action.

I am so grateful my mom thinks highly enough of me to include me in this process with her, to name me as a co-author. And to trust my opinion on what she is the ultimate master of: creating delicious, easy, accessible recipes for people to cook at home no matter their experience level. Cooking is one of the things that connects my mom and me best, and I get to witness daily the impact that connecting with you has on her too. I hope you love this book as much as I loved helping to write it.

Anna

Love, Anna

Pantry
Ingredients, Utensils, Spice Blends & Sauces

In this section, you'll find a list of the basic kitchen staples and utensils, spice blends and sauces that I love and find incredibly useful, even out of the kitchen. I was once asked what my favorite piece of kitchen equipment is, and the answer was easy: tongs. One of the reasons I love tongs so much is because I'm short and, in the past, when I pulled up to a parking lot with a ticket dispenser, I couldn't reach the ticket! Once I started keeping tongs in the car, I never had a problem again. Unfortunately, it didn't make me a better driver, but at least it gave other drivers one less reason to become impatient with me.

Ingredients

Salt

So many different salts are available now, and basically salt is salt, but here are my top picks. For general cooking, I use Diamond Crystal kosher salt. Kosher salt tastes less salty than table salt because per measure it's a larger grain. It doesn't have any additives and has a texture that makes it easy to pick up with your finger-tips. Overall, I recommend choosing one salt as your everyday salt so that you get used to its saltiness and learn how much to add when cooking. Maldon salt from England and Falk salt from Sweden are both flaky sea salts and saltier than table salt and kosher salt. I use these as seasoning salts and for garnish. Plus, you can see the flakes and they're beautiful.

Tomato paste

I avoided tomato paste for years because I found it bitter. It wasn't until I tried Mutti tomato paste and fell in love with its sweet and intense tomato flavor and umami goodness that I started using it again.

Cooking oils

About 95% of the oil I use is extra virgin olive oil. It's a naturally flavored delicious oil, and I use the same medium-flavored extra virgin olive oil for cooking, baking, dipping, and eye-makeup removing (kidding, but not). I would rather add fresh flavors to a basic oil than open lots of bottles of specialty flavored olive oils (lemon, rosemary, etc.) that will eventually go bad if not used in time. In olive oil–producing countries, people use extra virgin olive oil for all purposes, including frying, and so do I. The other 5% of the time, I use a neutral unflavored oil like safflower or sunflower oil because it is completely unflavored.

Herbs

I love using fresh herbs and I grow many of them in my garden, which makes using them in summer extra special. I love the bright fresh taste they bring to food. I generally don't recommend substituting dried herbs when a recipe calls for fresh—I would tell you instead to substitute another fresh herb—but if you are going to use dried herbs, use just a little. With fresh herbs, use lots! And when I call for fresh herbs, I'm generally referring to using the leaves and tender stems, and if I specify just leaves, it's usually because it's a garnish.

Chilies

Chilies vary in spiciness, even within the same variety (e.g., jalapeño), and often you can't tell until it's too late. A trick is to cut off the stem end and run your finger over the white part, then taste it carefully from your finger—you should be able to tell how spicy the chili is. If it's really spicy, use just a little of it, depending on your heat tolerance, and if it isn't spicy, use it all. Also, if you remove the ribs (the spiciest part) and seeds, it will be less spicy. Remember, you can never trust a chili.

Chipotle chilies are smoked and dried jalapeños. I usually buy them in a can with adobo sauce, puree them, and keep them in a preserving jar in the refrigerator—ready for use whenever needed. It will keep that way for months, but if you want to keep them longer, you can put the puree in a resealable plastic bag, flatten it, freeze, and then break off pieces as needed. I generally use it 1 tsp at a time, and label it well because it is very hot!

Harissa is a hot sauce that originated in Tunisia and is now easy to find in grocery stores. I use it in many recipes. Each brand of harissa is different—some contain just hot chilies and some contain chilies and spices, so be sure to taste test the one you are using to judge how much you should add for your heat tolerance.

I usually use Belazu rose harissa, which is on the milder side and includes a variety of spices.

Milk and Yogurt

Throughout the book, when I call for milk, I am using 2% regular or lactose-free organic cow's milk. I encourage people to use the ingredients they feel comfortable with; however, substitutions may impact the recipe slightly.

My go-to yogurt is 2% plain organic yogurt. Thick yogurt has become very popular, though. When recipes call for thick yogurt, you can use Greek yogurt or labneh, or you can make your own thick yogurt (called pressed yogurt or yogurt cheese). Labneh reminds me of the yogurt cheese I used to make all the time, using the strainer I sold at my store (the Donvier yogurt cheese maker, which you can find online), where you simply put your favorite yogurt into a small container with a sieve to drain and, depending on how thick you want it, it's ready in anywhere from a few hours later to overnight. But labneh is saltier and more tart than regular yogurt, so if you're making your own that way, add a little lemon juice and salt. It's usually made with rich cow's, goat's, or sheep's milk. Now, like many ingredients, labneh is becoming much easier to find. And to share a piece of Israeli wisdom passed on to Anna (who learned the hard way), labneh is brilliant at soothing sunburns.

Vinegars

It's very hard to find a good red wine vinegar, so I use sherry vinegar instead. Most sherry vinegar is good quality because it isn't usually mass-produced, and I think it is worth the investment. I also think it's worth investing in a good-quality balsamic vinegar. Usually, the price is an indication of how good it will taste. If balsamic is called for in a marinade, I'm not as concerned with the quality, but if you're using it on a salad or in a dipping sauce, buy the best you can afford. I like to have a few other mild vinegars on hand, including apple cider vinegar and rice vinegar. Know too that you can use fresh lemon juice instead of vinegar in most dressings for a refreshing, light acidity.

Nuts

I generally use roasted nuts for cooking because they add much more flavor than raw nuts. When I buy nuts, I usually buy more than I need, roast them, and then keep them in the freezer to have on hand.

To roast, spread nuts in a single layer on a baking sheet and place in a preheated 350°F oven on the middle rack for 15 to 20 minutes. Remove one and taste to see if it's ready (they should be lightly browned with a deeper flavor), and watch carefully, as they can burn easily. Cool and use, or freeze. An exception to this is hazelnuts: once they're out of the oven and cooled, rub them in a clean tea towel to remove the skins (don't worry if some skin remains). Pine nuts and coconut chips should be roasted for only 4 to 8 minutes, or until lightly browned—watch closely as both burn easily.

We are so lucky now that many nuts (almonds and hazelnuts especially) can be bought ground (often called almond flour and hazelnut flour respectively). You can also grind the nuts yourself. If you want a roasted flavor, use roasted nuts. Be careful when grinding: If you grind too many nuts at one time, or grind them for too long, they can turn into nut butter, which is delicious but will not work as flour when baking! If you use an electric grinder, depending on its size, grind about ¼ cup at a time. In a food processor, grind about 1 cup at a time. With either method, always pulse on/off rather than letting the motor run continuously.

Vanilla

Vanilla beans, pure vanilla extract, and pure vanilla paste have all become very expensive because of a worldwide shortage. You can make your own vanilla extract from vanilla beans by chopping up the vanilla beans and soaking them in vodka for at least 2 weeks. The longer you soak them, the more flavorful it will be. But if you don't have weeks to soak vanilla beans and/or don't have vanilla extract or paste, I recommend using another flavoring, like grated lemon or orange peel, lime juice, a liqueur, orange blossom water, or rosewater—or any concentrated flavor that is natural. You can also use vanilla beans many times. Rinse and dry them, and store them in your sugar canister for a vanilla-sugar taste.

Chocolate

Any time someone tells Anna she makes great chocolate chip cookies she says, "No, I just use great chocolate." (She shops at her mother's house—but she does make great cookies.) As with most ingredients, the better quality the chocolate, the better the results. There are so many brands available, but Valrhona has always been my favorite to bake with, as well as Cacao Barry. Both come in pellets or discs, so you don't even have to chop.

Hints for melting chocolate:

- Always use a clean, dry bowl and utensils for melting chocolate. Even a tiny amount of liquid can cause the chocolate to seize. If the chocolate seizes, it becomes dull, grainy, and hard to stir. You can rescue it by gently stirring in a little bit of unflavored oil until it smooths out.
- It is always best to melt chocolate in relatively evenly sized pieces.
- Chocolate burns easily, so always use indirect heat. Conventional methods to melt the chocolate are in a bowl set over a pot of simmering water, or in the microwave on medium-high at 30-second intervals.
- If melting chocolate along with a significant amount of liquid, heat the liquid so that it's very hot before pouring over the chopped chocolate, let the mixture rest, and then stir it until melted.

A Note on Dietary Needs and Modifications

I've always been aware of dietary needs and modifications because of my husband Ray's lactose intolerance and because as a host I always like to try to make people feel comfortable and enjoy themselves. When Anna started following a gluten-free diet about 12 years ago, it meant I learned quite a bit about gluten-free cooking and baking. There are now many different gluten-free flour blends available that can be substituted cup for cup in place of all-purpose flour in most recipes. Our favorite brand is Cup4Cup, and we love using it because people never notice a difference. You can use a blend like this substituted for regular all-purpose flour in most recipes in this book (except those that include yeast, like for bread or pizza dough), and you may find pastry doughs a little harder to roll out with this substitution until you get used to it. The other common substitution we make to accommodate those who are gluten-free is tamari for soy sauce, and there are gluten-free versions of many sauces (like hoisin sauce) now available in stores. So many other products can be substituted to accommodate different diets, like vegan marshmallows, vegetarian Worcestershire sauce, and vegan plant-based eggs, to name just a few. As for lactose intolerance, it's fairly easy now to find lactose-free dairy products, including lactose-free cheese, milk, whipping cream, and yogurt. For other diets, including vegetarian, vegan, and/or kosher, I've tried to make suggestions for how the recipes can be modified in various ways, provide alternative ingredients, and point out that many ingredients are optional. But you know your health and sensitivities/allergies best (as well as the people you're cooking for), so when considering my suggestions, please take that into account first and foremost.

Utensils

Hand mixer

Even if you have a stand mixer and especially if you don't, a hand mixer is a valuable piece of equipment in your kitchen. I like the Breville hand mixer because it has three sets of beaters, a light, and a timer.

Whisk and Danish whisk

Whisks are very important to me. I have lots of whisks in all different shapes and sizes (and I think you should too), including a Danish dough whisk, which I've been enjoying because it helps me mix all the ingredients together and the dough doesn't get stuck in it as easily as with a traditional whisk.

Mini tongs

I used to have tongs hanging off the door of my oven, but when we got a puppy, we had to find them a new home. I have tongs that are different sizes and shapes, coated and uncoated. But mini tongs are a new favorite. I use them all the time for serving (they make the best salad servers), they're easy for small hands, and, in a pandemic, everyone can have a set of their own to dish out their food.

Microplane

The microplane started out as a wood-working tool and ended up being indispensable in the kitchen. I use it for grating citrus peel and ginger, and it has now replaced my previously beloved garlic press. (I feel bad for the garlic press for even writing that.)

Instant-read thermometer

Stephen Alexander, owner of Cumbrae's butcher shops in Toronto and Dundas, Ontario, always used to say that given that meat is so costly, having an instant-read thermometer is essential to make sure your meat is cooked properly, instead of leaving it to chance! It's also a helpful tool to check the temperature of cakes, breads, and other baked goods. Thermapen is my favorite brand.

Quarter baking sheet (9 × 13 inches)

Throughout the book when I reference a baking sheet, I'm referring to a typical baking sheet that is 12 × 18 inches (half the size of a professional baking sheet). Quarter baking sheets—9 × 13 inches—are helpful for roasting different vegetables that have different cooking times; prepping and assembling ingredients; baking small batches of cookies; and fitting into smaller ovens. Ray has even adopted one as his breakfast tray. He says it reminds him of the university cafeteria—I just hope the food's better.

Mini masher

I tend to not like gadgets, and so my love of my mini masher doesn't make sense. It's technically an avocado masher, but I use it for small batches of mashed root vegetables and applesauce.

Pepper mill

The best-selling item in my store was the PepperMate pepper mill. People still ask me for it. It's easy to load, you can adjust the grind, and you can see how much pepper you're using before adding it in. Perfect!

Scrapers and bench scrapers

Plastic flexible scrapers are extremely helpful for cleaning out bowls of dough, and smaller non-flexible scrapers are wonderful for scraping pots. Metal bench scrapers are essential for cleaning dough off work surfaces and are handy for transferring chopped foods from your cutting board to the frying pan.

The 35-year-old spatula that you will never part with

You know, the one that is no longer available and that, despite being broken, you'll never throw away.

Whisk and Danish whisk

Microplane

Tongs

Beloved spatula

Spice Blends & Sauces

BAHARAT

Makes about ¼ cup

Baharat is one of the most commonly used spice blends in Middle Eastern cooking. The blend varies from one country to another, even from one spice shop to another, and depending on the purpose. This is the blend I usually make and keep in the freezer. It's delicious with chicken, beef, or lamb.

2 tsp ground cardamom

2 tsp ground cinnamon

1½ tsp ground allspice

1½ tsp ground ginger

½ tsp ground nutmeg

1 tsp ground coriander, optional

½ tsp ground cumin, optional

½ tsp freshly ground black pepper, optional

1. Combine the spices. If not using immediately, store in a tightly covered jar in the freezer where it will keep for months.

Sauces from top: Herb Salsa Verde, Charmoula, Preserved Lemon Paste, Vietnamese Peanut Sauce, Basic Tahini Sauce, Z'hug

DUKKAH

Makes about 1½ cups

Dukkah is an Egyptian nut and spice mix. The most common way to serve it is alongside extra virgin olive oil, where bread is first dipped in the olive oil and then into the dukkah. You can also sprinkle it on roasted vegetables, grilled poultry, meat, or fish, or mix it into labneh for a spread. There are many variations, and it deserves its growing popularity.

½ **cup roasted hazelnuts,** skinned (see page 6) and finely chopped

½ **cup roasted almonds,** finely chopped

3 **Tbsp sesame seeds,** lightly toasted

1 **Tbsp whole coriander seeds,** lightly toasted and coarsely ground

1 **Tbsp cumin seeds,** lightly toasted and ground

1 **tsp kosher salt**

¼ **tsp freshly ground black pepper**

1. Combine all the ingredients. Store in a tightly covered jar in the freezer where it will keep for months.

HAWAIIJ

Makes about ⅓ cup

This Yemenite spice blend comes in two versions: a savory one for soups and meat, and a somewhat sweeter one for coffee. Cumin isn't usually included in the blend for coffee, so that's a good way to differentiate the two.

3 **Tbsp cumin seeds**

2 **Tbsp coriander seeds**

1 **Tbsp whole black peppercorns**

1 **Tbsp whole caraway seeds**

1 **tsp ground cardamom**

1 **tsp ground ginger**

1 **tsp ground turmeric**

½ **tsp ground allspice**

½ **tsp ground cinnamon**

1. Place the cumin seeds, coriander seeds, peppercorns, and caraway seeds in a heavy-bottomed skillet set over medium heat. Shake constantly to prevent burning. Once the spices are fragrant, 2 to 3 minutes, transfer to a small baking sheet or plate to cool.

2. In a small spice grinder, grind the toasted seeds until fine. Add the cardamom, ginger, turmeric, allspice, and cinnamon and blend together. Store in a tightly covered jar in the freezer.

SWEET AND HOT SRIRACHA BUTTER

Makes one 4 oz stick of butter

Compound butter is back. I have always said to hang on to everything you love because inevitably these things will come back in style. (This is usually said in response to Ray criticizing my preference to hold on to everything from the past, and thank goodness time keeps proving me right.) Compound butters were a big deal when I was in chef training, then they seemed to disappear for a while. But these days, with such a diversity of cuisines and available ingredients, it's fun to see their comeback, this time often incorporating different flavors. This butter is delicious on top of a grilled steak, lamb chops, or shrimp. To use as a sauce, cut the stick of butter in about ¼-inch-thick slices so it melts quickly; cut a slice that's a little thicker if you're using it as a garnish. (You could even have four or five—or more—different compound butters in your freezer at the same time and ask guests which sauce they would prefer.)

½ **cup butter,** room temperature

2 Tbsp sriracha

1 Tbsp honey

1 garlic clove, minced or grated

1 tsp finely grated lemon peel

1 Tbsp finely chopped fresh flat-leaf parsley or cilantro or chives

1. Combine the butter with the sriracha, honey, garlic, lemon peel, and herbs. This can be done with a wooden spoon, handheld mixer, or blender, or in a food processor.

2. Spoon or pipe the butter mixture onto a piece of waxed or parchment paper or plastic wrap into a stick shape about 1 inch thick and 4 to 6 inches long. Roll it up tightly in the paper or plastic wrap, twisting the ends so it forms a tight cylinder without too many air pockets. Refrigerate if using soon or freeze for months.

Z'HUG

Makes about 1 cup

This Yemenite spicy sauce is delicious and goes with everything. I put it on hummus (page 24) and chirshi (page 26), and on fish, chicken, steak, or vegetable steaks, as well as in chicken soup (page 46), rice, and so much more. The z'hug my Israeli friends make is so hot! But I usually make this less spicy quick version because not all of my family members can take the heat. Feel free to use more (or many more) chilies. (See page 5 to learn how to tell how hot your chili is.) I also sometimes make this without the cardamom, cumin, and cloves as a general cilantro pesto.

2 cups packed fresh cilantro (about 1 bunch)

1 cup packed fresh flat-leaf parsley (about ½ bunch)

1 or 2 jalapeño or serrano chilies, coarsely chopped with ribs and seeds for more spiciness

2 large garlic cloves, coarsely chopped

1 tsp kosher salt

½ tsp ground cardamom

½ tsp ground cumin

¼ tsp ground cloves

½ cup extra virgin olive oil + more as needed

1. In a blender or food processor or by hand, coarsely chop the cilantro, parsley, chilies, and garlic. Transfer to a bowl and stir in the salt, cardamon, cumin, and cloves. Add the olive oil in a steady stream while mixing to make a paste. Store in a tightly sealed jar in the refrigerator for up to 1 week or freeze it flat in a resealable plastic bag (to break off what you need) for up to a few months.

HERB SALSA VERDE

Makes about 1½ cups

This Italian version of salsa verde will become your go-to summer/autumn sauce, salad dressing, and dip all in one.

1 small shallot, coarsely chopped

1½ cups coarsely chopped fresh flat-leaf parsley

¼ cup coarsely chopped fresh green onions

2 Tbsp fresh mint leaves

2 Tbsp fresh tarragon leaves

2 Tbsp fresh dill, torn

2 Tbsp capers, drained and rinsed

2 anchovies, chopped, **or 1 Tbsp anchovy paste,** optional

Grated peel of 1 lemon

2 Tbsp fresh lemon juice or sherry vinegar

½ cup extra virgin olive oil + more as needed

Kosher salt and freshly ground black pepper

1. Place the shallot, parsley, green onions, mint, tarragon, dill, and capers in a food processor, blender or a bowl for an immersion blender. Pulse until they are as finely chopped as you wish. (If you do not have a food processor or blender, simply chop everything on a cutting board.)

2. Add the anchovies, lemon peel and lemon juice. Pulse. Add the olive oil and pulse to combine. If you want a smooth paste, puree. Adjust seasoning to taste with salt and pepper.

NOTE: I know some people avoid anchovies, but use them if you can, because they add umami—a real boost of flavor without being overpowering. If you open a tin, just freeze the remaining anchovies for another time.

VIETNAMESE PEANUT SAUCE

Makes ½ to ⅔ cup

For those of us not allergic to peanuts, everyone loves a peanut sauce. This one is perfect for dipping salad rolls into or coating noodles, or use it as a dressing for a salad. For a peanut-free version, use tahini.

3 Tbsp hoisin sauce

3 Tbsp peanut butter

3 Tbsp coconut milk or cream

1 Tbsp fresh lime juice or rice vinegar

1 small garlic clove, grated

¼ tsp sriracha or other hot sauce

About 3 Tbsp boiling water

1. Whisk the hoisin sauce and peanut butter together gently.

2. Whisk in the coconut milk, lime juice, garlic, and hot sauce. Whisk in enough boiling water to thin the sauce to a dipping consistency.

3. Taste and adjust to balance.

CHARMOULA

Makes about 1 cup

Traditionally, charmoula is a spicy Moroccan sauce that is olive oil–based and often used on fish. I, on the other hand, make it this way and use it on everything.

1 cup mayonnaise

1 garlic clove, minced or grated

2 Tbsp chopped fresh cilantro

2 Tbsp fresh lemon juice

1 tsp pureed chipotle chilies (see page 5) **or Tabasco Chipotle**

½ tsp ground cumin

½ tsp smoked paprika

Kosher salt and freshly ground black pepper

1. Combine the mayonnaise with the garlic, cilantro, lemon juice, chipotles, cumin, and paprika. Season to taste with salt and pepper.

Appetizers
& Spreads

Hummus

Freshly made hummus is a treat. If you are used to store-bought refrigerated hummus with long expiry dates, you should make this recipe right away—it might change your life. In Israel, many people don't even make their own hummus, especially if they live near a hummuseria that makes fresh hummus all day long. They just buy what they need and then buy it again fresh the next day.

After leading 10 culinary tours to Israel, I have learned that everyone who makes hummus makes it a bit differently and that everyone has their own special secrets. Here are some of the secrets that have been shared with me over the years:

- Be sure to puree the chickpeas while they're warm.
- Be sure to puree the chickpeas while they're cold.
- Puree in a food processor.
- Never puree in a food processor.
- Remove the chickpea peels before pureeing.
- Do not bother to remove the chickpea peels before pureeing.
- Always start from dried chickpeas.
- Canned chickpeas will work just fine.

And so it goes. One important secret that everyone agrees on, though, is to use good-quality tahini. If you're not sure about the quality of the tahini you have, taste it on its own. It should not have a bitter aftertaste and it should be delicious enough to spread on bread and eat like peanut butter.

In this recipe, I use the "secrets" I like the most, and after you make it a few times, you'll have your favorites too. There are many ways to make and serve hummus, but this is my go-to basic recipe. Serve it as is or with some of my favorite toppings: a drizzle of extra virgin olive oil or pure tahini; a sprinkle of smoked paprika or chopped fresh cilantro or flat-leaf parsley leaves; dots of harissa or cilantro pesto (see the z'hug recipe on page 13); or roasted cherry tomatoes (see page 87), sautéed mushrooms, roasted peppers, or any seasonal vegetables, spooned into the center.

Serve hummus at room temperature. (I know—I also eat it cold from the refrigerator; there's nothing better when you are really hungry!) Serve with pita bread, challah, or vegetables for dipping.

CHIRSHI

Makes 2½ to 3 cups

I first learned about chirshi, the delicious Tunisian and Libyan pumpkin spread, from my friend, Israeli food journalist and author Gil Hovav. He makes it very spicy and garlicky (like it is supposed to be), but it is very versatile and can be adapted in so many ways that it will surely become a family staple, as it is in mine. It is a perfect vegetarian/vegan appetizer and also makes a great vegetable side dish. Serve it as is, or sprinkled with pumpkin seeds, cilantro, pomegranate seeds, goat or feta cheese, or drizzled with tahini, thick yogurt, or labneh. I also love it drizzled with z'hug (page 13), or sprinkled with Aleppo pepper or sweet paprika. Serve with challah, pita, tortilla chips, or raw vegetables. Leftovers can be made into soup (add broth or water) or pancakes (add eggs and flour). If I haven't convinced you of the wonders of chirshi yet, I'm not sure what will.

2 Tbsp extra virgin olive oil

1 Tbsp tomato paste

1 tsp kosher salt + more to taste

1 lb butternut or buttercup squash, peeled and cut into 1½-inch chunks (see note)

1 lb sweet potatoes, peeled and cut into 1½-inch chunks

1 or 2 garlic cloves, grated

⅓ cup pure tahini

2 to 3 Tbsp fresh lemon juice, to taste

1 Tbsp fresh thyme leaves

1 tsp to 1 Tbsp harissa or other hot sauce + more to taste

½ tsp smoked or sweet paprika

Freshly ground black pepper

1. Preheat the oven to 375°F and line a baking sheet with parchment paper. In a small bowl, combine the olive oil with the tomato paste and salt. Place the squash and sweet potatoes on the lined baking sheet and toss well with the olive oil mixture to coat. Roast for 30 to 40 minutes, or until tender and lightly browned. Let cool on the baking sheet. Transfer vegetables to a bowl and mash with a potato masher or fork if you like it slightly chunky like I do, or puree coarsely or until smooth in a food processor.

2. Mix in garlic, tahini, lemon juice, thyme, harissa, and smoked paprika. Season to taste with salt and pepper.

3. Spread on a platter and serve as is, or sprinkle with pumpkin seeds, cilantro, pomegranate seeds, or any ingredients mentioned in the recipe introduction.

NOTE: When a recipe calls for pumpkin, I usually use a winter squash like butternut or buttercup instead.

RICOTTA WITH BASIL PESTO AND ROASTED TOMATOES

Serves 6 to 8

This delicious appetizer can also be made with buffalo mozzarella—either the Italian-made one (expensive but so delicious) or a Canadian one (Bella Casara is my favorite). Use a firm ricotta but not the dried type for grating. If your ricotta is wet, place it in a strainer lined with cheesecloth or paper towel set over a bowl to drain. When tomatoes are in season, don't bother roasting them, just cut them up coarsely and serve them raw, which is especially great if you are in a hurry.

Tomatoes

2 cups cherry tomatoes (or other ripe tomatoes cut into chunks)

2 Tbsp extra virgin olive oil

½ tsp kosher salt

1 sprig fresh rosemary

1 sprig fresh thyme

Pesto

1 bunch fresh basil (about 1 cup packed) **+ sprigs** for serving

1 garlic clove

½ tsp kosher salt + more to taste

⅓ cup extra virgin olive oil + more for drizzling

8 oz ricotta

Flaky sea salt

Good-quality balsamic vinegar

Crusty bread or focaccia

1. Preheat the oven to 425°F and line a baking sheet with parchment paper.

2. For the tomatoes, combine the tomatoes with the olive oil, salt, and sprigs of rosemary and thyme. Spread on the lined baking sheet and roast for about 15 minutes, or until juicy and lightly browned. Discard the dried sprigs. Cool.

3. For the pesto, chop the basil with the garlic and ½ tsp salt until finely minced. Place in a bowl and add ⅓ cup olive oil. Add more salt to taste.

4. To serve, place the cheese on a serving plate. You can mold it into a small loaf or round, if you like. Sprinkle with flaky sea salt and sprigs of basil. Drizzle with the balsamic vinegar and pesto. Spoon the tomatoes around the cheese and drizzle with olive oil. Serve with crusty bread.

ELIZABETH'S CHERRY TOMATO TARTES TATIN

Makes 24 tarts

Every year, our friends Elizabeth Pizzinato and Richard Paquet hold an incredible holiday open house in their beautiful home. Not only is the food all homemade and so delicious, it's a jaw-dropping spread. There are items that repeat every year, and I am honored that my lamb chops (from *Friday Night Dinners*) are one of them. Richard has become such an expert at making them, it's got to the point now that when I am making them myself, I call Richard for advice. But this recipe for Elizabeth's cherry tomato tartes tatin is one of my favorite things they serve at the party.

⅓ **cup butter**

2 shallots, finely chopped (about ¼ cup)

3 Tbsp balsamic vinegar

2 Tbsp light brown sugar

3 cups cherry tomatoes (about 1 lb/500 g), halved

Kosher salt and freshly ground black pepper

24 tiny sprigs fresh thyme

½ **lb puff pastry** (see note)

1. Melt the butter in a large skillet set over medium heat. Add the shallots, balsamic vinegar, and sugar. Cook for a few minutes, or until the shallots are tender, then add the tomatoes. Season to taste with salt and pepper. Cook until the tomatoes are caramelized and starting to collapse, about 5 to 8 minutes.

2. Butter or spray a 24-cup mini-muffin pan. (If you don't have a mini-muffin pan, make these double the size in a regular-size 12-cup muffin pan.) Preheat the oven to 400°F.

3. Place a sprig of thyme in each muffin cup. Add 2 or 3 tomato halves and some of the juices. Let the tomatoes cool in the pan to room temperature.

4. Roll out the puff pastry on a lightly floured work surface to a thickness of ¼ inch or thinner. Using a 2½-inch round pastry cutter, cut out 24 rounds. Gently press the rounds into the muffin cups on top of the tomatoes.

5. Bake for 15 to 20 minutes, or until browned. Cool for 5 minutes on a wire rack. Scoop and turn the tartes tatin out of the muffin pan one at a time using a fork and spoon, so that the tomatoes are on top. Serve warm or at room temperature.

NOTE: Puff pastry makes these very special, but in a pinch you can use regular pastry. You can use store-bought puff pastry, or try this quick homemade version that I learned from pastry chef Nick Malgieri. Cut 1¼ cups cold butter into ¼-inch cubes and refrigerate for 30 minutes. Also refrigerate ⅔ cup water. Place 2 cups all-purpose flour in a food processor with ¾ tsp kosher salt, add ¼ cup (2 oz) of the diced cold butter and pulse 8 times. Add the remaining diced butter and pulse twice, just to distribute into the flour. Drizzle the cold water over the flour and pulse 5 or 6 times. Turn the mixture out (it will be crumbly) and gather into a rough rectangle. Flour a work surface and roll the rough dough into a 12 × 18-inch rectangle. Fold into thirds lengthwise, and roll up from the short end and press into a rough square. Wrap well and refrigerate for a few days or freeze.

Potato Pancakes

Potato pancakes, also known as latkes, are delicious all year round, but are traditionally eaten on the Jewish holiday of Hanukkah, when it is customary to eat foods cooked in oil. Every family knows that the way they make latkes is the right way. For example, my family knows that latkes made right are thin and crispy. Whereas your family might know for certain that latkes made right are thick and pudgy. Just as people can be particular about what a bagel should be, or the appropriate consistency of a matzo ball, they can also be particular about latkes.

The problem I have every year is that I want to make the traditional foods everyone loves best, but I also like trying new recipes. (And it is the oil we celebrate, not the potato, so anything fried in oil is fair game.) A few years ago, I made sweet potato latkes. They were so delicious! Half of our Hanukkah party guests were delighted. The other half (the traditionalists) were disappointed, asking "Where are the latkes we look forward to all year?" I felt terrible! Because I can't change the fact that I will always want to try something new but understand the importance of tradition and comfort in doing things the way they've always been done, I started a new tradition with Anna: at Hanukkah now we always serve two types of latkes. We serve the traditional latkes like the ones my mother made, plus something new we want to try out. We've made latkes with sweet potato, beets, and even one massive potato pancake that we cut into wedges. Here I've included the two recipes we like best.

OUR TRADITIONAL POTATO LATKES

Makes 20 to 24 latkes

This is the recipe that the traditionalists (but really all of us) like to have at our Hanukkah dinner. I like to eat latkes as my main course so that I can eat lots without feeling too guilty, but many people serve them as a side dish or appetizer. A few years ago, when we instituted the "two types of latkes" tradition, Anna thought it would be fun to make a latke bar. We cooked both types of latkes as guests arrived and set them out as the appetizer on platters, with all the toppings placed in bowls around them. For toppings, we tried to please everyone. We had sour cream and applesauce (traditional), smoked salmon (sort of traditional), labneh and guacamole (has become traditional for us). Everyone loved the latke bar, and now it's part of the tradition too.

2 lb russet potatoes or Yukon Gold potatoes, scrubbed or peeled

1 large onion, cut into chunks

2 eggs

⅓ cup all-purpose flour, cornflake crumbs or matzah meal

1 tsp kosher salt

⅛ tsp freshly ground black pepper

½ cup unflavored vegetable oil + more as needed

Toppings of your choosing (see recipe intro)

1. Using a cut-resistant glove (if you have one), grate the potatoes and onion on the coarse side of a box grater (the side you would use for cheddar cheese) or similar-size grater of a food processor. Using your hands or a clean tea towel, squeeze the moisture out of the potato mixture, a handful at a time. The onion juice will help keep them from discoloring.

2. If you are doing this by hand, in a large bowl combine the eggs, flour, salt, and pepper. Chop half of the grated potato mixture into very short pieces and add them to the egg mixture, then stir in the remaining grated potato mixture that is still in larger pieces. If you are using a food processor, dry the bowl (no need to wash it) and replace the grating disc with the main chopping blade. Add the eggs, flour, salt, and pepper, and blend. Add half of the grated potato mixture and pulse until it is chopped into even smaller pieces. Transfer the mixture to a large bowl, then add the remaining grated potatoes still in their longer strands. Stir to combine.

3. In a large skillet, heat the oil over medium to medium-high heat. Line a baking sheet with paper towel and set aside. Add the batter to the hot oil by generous spoonfuls and gently flatten with the back of a spoon. Don't crowd the pan—you'll need to cook these in batches. Cook the latkes for 3 to 4 minutes, or until brown and crisp, then flip and cook for another few minutes on the second side. The thinner the latkes, the less time they will need to cook through. When the latkes are cooked through, transfer them to the lined baking sheet. Adjust the heat and add more oil to the pan between batches as necessary. Try to remove any bits of batter from the oil between batches, if you can. Repeat until all the batter is used. Serve immediately with your choice of toppings, or keep warm in a preheated 275°F oven, or cool and freeze.

SWEET POTATO LATKES

Makes about 24 latkes

Anyone who says that they only like regular potato latkes will reluctantly admit that these ones are pretty special. They're perfect for a Hanukkah party, but try making large ones topped with shredded leftover brisket for dinner, or poached or fried eggs for brunch.

2 eggs

½ tsp pureed chipotle chilies (see page 5)**, chipotle sauce, or preferred hot sauce,** optional

2 green onions, finely chopped

¼ cup chopped fresh cilantro or flat-leaf parsley

⅓ cup all-purpose flour

1 tsp kosher salt

½ tsp baking powder

½ tsp ground cumin, optional

1¼ lb sweet potatoes, scrubbed or peeled

¼ cup vegetable oil + more as needed

Suggested Toppings

Sour cream or thick yogurt

Pure tahini or tahini sauce (page 17)

Herb Guacamole (page 25)

1. Beat the eggs together in a large bowl with the chipotles, green onions, and cilantro. In another bowl, combine the flour, salt, baking powder, and cumin.

2. Grate the potatoes on the coarse side of a box grater (the side you would use for cheddar cheese) or similar-size grater of a food processor. Using your hands or a clean tea towel, squeeze as much liquid out of the grated sweet potatoes as you can, a handful at a time. (Some sweet potatoes contain hardly any water and some contain lots, so try your best and don't worry. I'm just now noticing how often I tell you not to worry!)

3. Add the grated sweet potatoes to the egg mixture, and stir. Add the flour mixture and mix together well.

4. Heat the oil in a large skillet set over medium to medium-high heat. Line a baking sheet with paper towel and set aside. Add the batter to the hot oil by generous spoonfuls and gently flatten with the back of a spoon. Don't crowd the pan—you'll need to cook these in batches. Cook the latkes for 3 to 4 minutes, or until brown and crisp, then flip and cook for another few minutes on the second side. Drain on the lined baking sheet. Adjust the heat and add more oil to the pan between batches as necessary. Try to remove any bits of batter from the oil between batches, if you can. Repeat until all the batter is used.

5. Serve with your choice of toppings.

SMOKED EGGPLANT WITH TAHINI, LEMON, AND POMEGRANATE MOLASSES

Serves 6 to 8

The wonderful smoky taste in certain eggplant dishes comes from roasting the eggplants on an open flame. It is a bit messy on a gas stove, but the taste is so delicious! Anna puts aluminum foil around her burners to protect them (somewhat), a trick she learned from Yotam Ottolenghi's *Plenty*. You could also roast the eggplants on a barbecue (preferably over charcoal, but gas works too), or you can cook them under the broiler. When choosing eggplants, make sure they have shiny skin, and choose ones that are lighter rather than heavy. It's also important to use good-quality tahini (see page 17).

2 oval-shaped eggplants (about 1½ lb total)

1 tsp kosher salt

1 to 2 Tbsp fresh lemon juice

⅓ to ½ cup pure tahini

1 to 2 Tbsp pomegranate molasses

2 Tbsp pomegranate seeds

2 Tbsp chopped fresh cilantro leaves

Focaccia, pita, or your favorite bread to serve

1. Place the eggplants directly on one or two gas burners set over medium-high heat and cook for 15 to 18 minutes, rotating the eggplants with tongs, or until the skins are black and blistered and the eggplants have collapsed and are cooked through. You could also blacken the skins, transfer the eggplants to a baking sheet, and bake in a 425°F preheated oven for 10 to 15 minutes, or until the eggplants have collapsed.

2. Cool the eggplants slightly, then carefully peel off the skins using a paring knife or your hands (but don't worry about getting every bit of skin off) and cut them open lengthwise. Place the eggplants in a colander or sieve set over a bowl and drain for about 15 to 20 minutes. Remove and discard the strips of eggplant seeds if they are very large.

3. Coarsely chop the eggplants and spread on a serving plate.

4. Sprinkle with salt, and drizzle with lemon juice, tahini, and pomegranate molasses to taste.

5. Sprinkle with pomegranate seeds and cilantro. Serve with bread or pita.

TUNA POKE

Serves 8

Poke, originally from Hawaii, is now popular around the world. There are all sorts of poke with different fish (raw or cooked) and sauces. My version is a riff on the famous ahi tuna poke dip at the Kahala Resort in Honolulu, where I first tried it. This also makes a great main-course salad, sandwich filling, topping on a rice bowl, or filling for sushi rolls. Chopped cooked shrimp works well in place of the tuna.

½ cup mayonnaise

1 Tbsp fresh lime juice

1 Tbsp soy sauce

¼ cup coarsely chopped fresh cilantro

3 Tbsp coarsely chopped pickled ginger (sushi ginger)

½ tsp toasted sesame oil

¾ lb raw sushi-grade tuna, cut into small cubes

½ ripe avocado

1 tsp nigella seeds or chopped toasted nori, optional

Little gem lettuce cups or tortilla chips, for serving

1. Combine the mayonnaise with the lime juice and soy sauce, followed by the cilantro, ginger, and sesame oil.

2. Add the tuna and refrigerate until ready to serve.

3. Dice the avocado and gently stir into the poke just before serving.

4. Serve in lettuce cups or on tortilla chips.

HOT SWEET SHRIMP

Serves 4 to 6

This is my slightly less dramatic version of a crab dish from Chef Erez Komarovsky, a super-star in Israel. He made this for one of the groups I took to Israel on a culinary tour. His were on fire! Literally. These ones are only smoking hot. It's a bit messy to eat shrimp in the shell, but I think it's fun and extra delicious. Serve them as a "get your hands dirty" appetizer. If you make them without the shells, they are great in a lettuce wrap or cup, or served over rice for a main course.

It is always important to have your ingredients ready for when you start to cook, but shrimp cook quickly, and in this recipe, it is essential to be organized.

1½ lb extra-large (12 to 16 count) shrimp, shells on and deveined

1 whole star anise or ½ tsp ground

1 tsp coriander seeds, crushed, or ¼ tsp ground

1 tsp kosher salt

2 Tbsp butter

1 Tbsp + 1 Tbsp honey

1 long red chili, thinly sliced into rounds

1 jalapeño, seeds and ribs removed if desired, diced small

2 garlic cloves, finely chopped

2 Tbsp extra virgin olive oil

2 Tbsp tamarind paste thinned with 2 Tbsp water (see note)

1 Tbsp fresh lime juice

1 Tbsp light brown sugar

3 green onions, sliced

¼ cup chopped fresh cilantro + sprigs for serving

1. Pat the shrimp dry with paper towel and set aside in the refrigerator. Place the whole star anise and coriander seeds in a hot, dry skillet, and toast over medium-high heat for 30 to 45 seconds. Let cool, then grind the spices in a mortar and pestle or in an electric spice grinder. Or skip this step entirely and use spices already ground.

2. Combine the ground star anise, ground coriander, and salt in a small ramekin. Have the butter, honey, chilies, garlic, olive oil, tamarind, lime juice, brown sugar, green onions, and cilantro in separate ramekins close to the stove.

3. Set a cast iron or heavy-bottomed skillet over medium heat to get very hot.

4. Increase the heat to medium-high, and when the pan is extremely hot, add the shrimp to the dry pan in a single layer. Let the bottom side of the shrimp brown for 1 to 2 minutes. Add the butter, drizzle with 1 Tbsp honey, scatter the chilies overtop, and sprinkle with half of the salt-spice mixture. Using a large metal spatula, flip the shrimp over. Brown on the second side. Add the garlic, remaining spice mixture, 1 Tbsp honey, olive oil, tamarind, lime juice, and brown sugar and toss together. Add the green onions and cilantro, and cook only until the shrimp are opaque. This dish cooks quickly, so don't get distracted.

5. Serve with cilantro sprigs scattered on top.

NOTE: If you don't have tamarind paste, substitute an additional 2 Tbsp fresh lime juice mixed with 2 Tbsp light brown sugar.

Soups

Yemenite Chicken Soup

We like to say that Hanoch Drori is my Israeli son and I am his Canadian mother. We met many years ago on the set of my television show, when he had just moved to Canada. He was hired to do my hair and makeup, and he has been part of our family ever since. The first time I had Yemenite chicken soup I was in Israel at his actual mother's house in Rishon LeTzion, just south of Tel Aviv. It was delicious and I realized then why Hanoch always said my Ashkenazi chicken soup was nothing like his mother's (i.e., not as flavorful). (He never said that, but mothers know.) I was so inspired I put my first version of this soup in my *Friday Night Dinners* cookbook.

The second time I had it in Israel was with my good friend Mitchell Davis (a brilliant cook, author, leader, and changemaker—a description that doesn't even begin to do him justice—as well as the funniest and nicest person I know). When Mitchell and I are together, we run around and eat everything in sight. We happened to be in Israel at the same time and we spent his last day in Tel Aviv trying everything he hadn't tasted yet. The Yemenite chicken soup in Carmel Market was one of the most delicious things we tried— and reminded me of Hanoch's mother's soup. It was served as a main course with whole pieces of chicken (bones and skin and all), chunks of beef, and marrow bones. I knew my kids would be more inclined to love it if it was served a little

more like the chicken soup they were raised on. So when I wanted to adapt my original recipe, I came up with this version. I feel sad that my parents never got to taste it.

A Note on Matzo Balls

When you serve the soup, you can add potatoes, or even cooked rice, noodles, or matzo balls. My sister, Jane, makes the best matzo balls in the world. They are so light and fluffy, just like our mother, Ruthie, made them. You can use a matzo ball mix to get light and fluffy matzo balls or you can add ½ tsp baking powder for each cup of matzo meal in your own recipe and your matzo balls will be light and fluffy too. (Baking powder is now generally approved for Passover use, but check with your own local rabbinical authority if you are worried.)

A Few Other Thoughts

Use good-quality chicken to make your soup. Kosher, free-range, or organic are great choices. If you're using chicken pieces, remember, dark meat has the most flavor. People often ask what the best pot is for making soup. My first choice is always the old pot my mother used. Aside from that, I like to use a pasta pot that has an insert where you can just lift what you're cooking out of the larger pot and it's strained (not perfectly, but pretty well). You don't want a pot that is too heavy or you won't be able to lift it with the soup and chicken in it! And lastly, the Yemenite herb paste, z'hug, is a must for this recipe. It's a shot of flavor not to be missed. There is another Yemenite condiment that is commonly served with this soup called hilbe, a fenugreek paste, but honestly, I haven't warmed up to it yet. Next book maybe.

YEMENITE CHICKEN SOUP

Serves 8 to 10

4 to 5 lb chicken, whole or cut up (or equivalent weight pieces of chicken)

2 marrow bones or a few pieces of beef shoulder, brisket, or short ribs (about 1 lb total), optional

3 to 4 quarts (12 to 16 cups) water

1-inch piece fresh turmeric root, scrubbed or peeled, **or ½ tsp ground turmeric**

1-inch piece fresh ginger, scrubbed or peeled

4 garlic cloves, peeled

2 onions, skin-on and halved

4 carrots, whole, scrubbed or peeled

2 ribs celery or 4 oz peeled celeriac (celery root), roughly cut into 2-inch chunks

1 parsnip, whole, scrubbed, or peeled

1 bunch fresh cilantro (with stems and roots) **+ chopped leaves** for serving

2 tsp hawaiij spice blend + more to taste (page 11), optional

1 Tbsp tomato paste

Kosher salt

Z'hug, for serving (page 13)

1. Place the chicken and the marrow bones, if using, in a large pot and cover by about 3 inches with cold water. Bring to a boil over medium-high heat. Scum will rise to the surface; reduce the heat to medium-low, skim, and discard. Add the turmeric, ginger, garlic, onions, carrots, celery, parsnip, and cilantro, and bring to a boil. Add the hawaiij, tomato paste, and 2 tsp salt. Skim again if necessary. Reduce the heat to low, and cook gently for 3 to 4 hours or longer, partially covered, or until the chicken and vegetables have given you all they have to give.

2. Strain the soup into a bowl and set on a wire rack. If not serving right away, let it cool to room temperature, then put in the refrigerator to chill completely. Discard the fat that solidifies on the surface or save and freeze it to use as seasoned schmaltz. The soup will keep in the refrigerator for at least 1 week or for a few months in the freezer.

3. Remove the chicken from the bones to add when serving the soup (discard skin and bones, as well as turmeric, ginger, garlic, cilantro, and the skin of the onions). If using marrow bones, remove the marrow, cut into pieces and set aside to add to the soup when serving. If using chunks of beef, cut into smaller pieces and add to the chicken. Cut the vegetables into smaller chunks.

4. If you're serving right away, reheat the strained soup with the chicken, meat, if using, and vegetables. Season to taste. Serve with z'hug or chopped fresh cilantro, and marrow, if using.

A NOTE ON SERVING: On a quick trip to visit Mitchell in New York, I tasted his version of the soup we had in Tel Aviv, meat on the bone with skin and all, and it took me right back to the Yemenite quarter of the market. He served it as a soup course with a freshly cooked drumstick and root vegetables in each bowl. He's such a wonderful cook, and it was outrageously delicious. You can make and serve it this way too.

ICY COLD BEET BORSCHT

Serves 4

I'll tell you the truth: I never really liked cold soup. That is, until we had the hottest summer ever and I revived this one. When I was little, my parents loved borscht and ate it all the time, but to me it was just gross. I guess it is true what they say—we become our parents. Roasted beets have a much more intense flavor and color than boiled beets, but they do take longer to cook. You could always roast a whole bunch of beets and keep them in the refrigerator or freeze them for future soups and salads. If you have any cooked potatoes or hard-cooked eggs, they would also make great toppings for this soup.

2 red beets (12 oz total)

½ cup ice water

½ cup plain yogurt (Greek or regular)

1 Tbsp sherry vinegar or good red wine vinegar

1 Tbsp fresh lemon juice

¾ tsp kosher salt + more to taste

Suggested Toppings

½ cup Greek yogurt or sour cream + ice water if necessary

⅓ cup diced cooked beets

1 Persian cucumber, diced

2 green onions or handful of fresh chives, thinly sliced on the diagonal

2 Tbsp chopped fresh dill

1. Preheat the oven to 400°F.

2. Wash the beets and pat them dry. You do not have to peel or even trim them—by leaving them whole, all the sweet juices will stay inside. Wrap the beets in aluminum foil and roast on a baking sheet for 1 to 1½ hours, or until tender when pierced with a knife. Unwrap the beets carefully—beware of steam—and let them cool enough to be able to handle. Trim the ends and rub off the skins, or use a paring knife to peel it away. (Wear gloves to avoid staining your hands, if you care.) Let the beets cool completely, then dice and reserve about ⅓ cup for the topping.

3. Place the remaining beets in a food processor or blender, and add the ice water and yogurt. Puree. Add the vinegar, lemon juice, and salt. If the soup is too thick, add a few tablespoons of ice water, until it reaches a creamy consistency. Season to taste and ladle into individual bowls.

4. For the topping, stir the yogurt and add ice water, if necessary, until the yogurt is about the same consistency as the soup. Place a spoonful on the soup in each bowl and sprinkle with the reserved diced beets, cucumbers, green onions, and dill.

NOTE: For Hot Beet Borscht, sauté 1 chopped onion in 2 Tbsp extra virgin olive oil and cook until lightly browned. Add diced roasted beets (or use peeled and chopped raw beets) and 1 cup water. Cook for 10 minutes (or 30 minutes if the beets are raw). Puree in a food processor or blender. Stir in the yogurt, vinegar, lemon juice, and salt to taste. Heat but do not boil. Thin with hot water if necessary and season to taste. Top with any or all of the suggested, toppings if you like.

HARIRA (MOROCCAN MEAT AND VEGETABLE SOUP)

Serves 8 to 10

On a trip to Israel, Hanoch took me to a restaurant he loved that served only soup (I promise we do other things together aside from just eating soup!). I was so overwhelmed by how many options there were, I became paralyzed by indecision, but the woman at the next table told me that if I didn't get the Moroccan lamb soup called harira, I would be making a big mistake. She was right. I have been making my version of that delicious soup ever since. Traditionally it includes meat but many people now make it vegetarian or vegan, see note below.

2 Tbsp extra virgin olive oil

1 lb lamb or beef shoulder or boneless, skinless chicken thighs, cut into 1-inch pieces

1 large onion, chopped

2 garlic cloves, finely chopped

1 carrot, scrubbed or peeled and diced

1 rib celery, diced

1-inch piece fresh ginger, peeled and chopped

¾ tsp ground cumin

¾ tsp ground turmeric

¼ tsp cinnamon

1 Tbsp tomato paste

1 tsp harissa or other hot sauce

2 cups cooked chickpeas (canned or freshly cooked, see page 24)

⅓ cup red lentils, picked through for small stones and rinsed

One 28 oz/796 mL can plum tomatoes, chopped or pureed

5 cups meat or chicken broth, or water + more as needed

Kosher salt and freshly ground black pepper

1 Tbsp fresh lemon juice

1 tsp honey

⅓ cup orzo or other small pasta, or basmati rice rinsed until the water runs clear

3 cups baby kale or chopped Swiss chard leaves

¼ cup coarsely chopped fresh cilantro + more for serving

1. Heat the olive oil in a large saucepan or Dutch oven set over medium heat. Add the meat and brown on all sides.

2. Add the onions and cook until they brown slightly. Add the garlic, carrot, celery, and ginger and cook gently for another few minutes, or until fragrant but not browned. Add the cumin, turmeric, and cinnamon. Cook, stirring constantly, for about 30 seconds. Stir in the tomato paste and harissa. Cook, stirring constantly, for another 30 seconds. If the pan seems dry, add ¼ cup water. Add the chickpeas and lentils, and cook for a few minutes longer, stirring to combine well.

3. Add the tomatoes and broth and bring to a boil, then reduce the heat to a simmer. Simmer gently for 45 minutes to 1 hour, or until the meat is tender and the soup has thickened slightly from the lentils.

4. Season partially with salt and pepper. Add the lemon juice and honey, bring the soup to a boil, and then add the orzo, reduce the heat to medium, and cook for 8 to 12 minutes, or until the pasta is very tender. The soup will thicken even more—add more broth or water as you like.

5. Add the kale and ¼ cup cilantro and cook for 3 to 5 minutes, or until just wilted. Season to taste and serve with cilantro.

NOTE: This soup can be made vegetarian or vegan by omitting the meat and using vegetable broth or water.

LENTIL SOUP WITH CARROTS AND HARISSA

Serves 6 to 8

Even Mark, Anna, and Ray, who have never been especially keen about lentils, go crazy for this soup. Adding more carrots than I usually do ramps up the sweetness and the color, and the tomato paste increases the umami factor. I like using red lentils because they dissolve when cooked and thicken a soup or stew without having to puree it. If you want lentils to keep their shape—for instance, in salads, side dishes, and certain soups and stews—use green lentils or the tiny black or French lentils.

2 Tbsp extra virgin olive oil

1 leek, white and light green part only, cleaned and chopped (see note on page 110)

1 garlic clove, finely chopped

4 large carrots, diced

1 tsp ground cumin

1 Tbsp tomato paste

1 to 2 tsp harissa, depending on your heat tolerance

1 cup red lentils, picked through for small stones and rinsed

5 cups water or chicken or vegetable broth + more as needed (see note)

1 tsp kosher salt + more to taste

¼ tsp freshly ground black pepper

2 Tbsp fresh lemon juice, optional

Suggested Toppings

½ cup plain yogurt or thick coconut milk

Basic Tahini Sauce (page 17)

1 tsp harissa or paprika mixed with 2 Tbsp extra virgin olive oil

½ cup chopped spinach or kale

2 Tbsp chopped fresh cilantro or flat-leaf parsley

Lemon rounds, thinly sliced

1. Heat the olive oil in a large saucepan or Dutch oven set over medium heat, then add the leeks and garlic. Cook gently for 8 to 10 minutes, or until fragrant and translucent but not browned. Add the carrots and cook gently for about 5 minutes. Add the cumin, tomato paste, and harissa, and cook for another 1 to 2 minutes. Add the lentils and stir well. Add the water or broth, 1 tsp salt, and pepper, and bring to a boil. Reduce heat to medium-low and cook gently for 25 to 30 minutes, or until the vegetables and lentils are tender.

2. Transfer half of the soup to a blender or food processor and puree (or use an immersion blender to partially puree right in the pot). Return the pureed mixture to the pot and stir in the lemon juice. Thin with more water or broth if necessary and re-season to taste. You'll especially need to do this if you've made the soup ahead, as it will thicken more.

3. Serve the soup with any of the suggested toppings: dollops of yogurt, tahini sauce or swirls of coconut milk, drizzles of harissa oil, greens, herbs, and/or lemon rounds.

> **NOTES:** If you are using chicken or vegetable broth that is salted, do not add salt until you taste the finished soup. Or do what I do: dilute a salted broth half and half with water before using. If you want the soup to be vegan, use vegetable broth or water, and drizzle with tahini sauce or coconut milk or dairy-free yogurt to serve.

ROASTED CAULIFLOWER SOUP

Serves 6 to 8

On a sunny but chilly winter day in Oslo, my close friend Mitchell Davis and I had a free day while on a press trip and decided to take an open boat cruise around the fjords. What were we thinking? Although it was a beautiful day, we were completely frozen by the time we disembarked. On the advice of our amazing guide, Kirsti Svenning, we rushed to the nearby, cozy restaurant Kolonialen, where we discovered the meaning of "hygge" in the form of roasted cauliflower soup. It's a soup I'd eat in any season.

1 head garlic

1 large head cauliflower, broken into about 2-inch chunks

Extra virgin olive oil

Kosher salt

1 onion, chopped

5 cups chicken or vegetable broth, or water

Freshly ground black pepper

½ cup cream or coconut cream, optional

Suggested Toppings

Reserved roasted cauliflower florets

Baby arugula, kale, or spinach, or fresh dill, coarsely chopped

Chopped roasted hazelnuts

1. Preheat the oven to 400°F. Cut off the top quarter of the head of garlic and brush with 1 tsp of the olive oil. Wrap in aluminum foil. Bake for 45 to 60 minutes, or until very soft. Meanwhile, line a baking sheet with parchment paper.

2. Toss the cauliflower with 2 Tbsp olive oil and 1 tsp salt. Spread in a single layer on the lined baking sheet and roast for 25 to 35 minutes, tossing once, or until the cauliflower has browned and is tender. You should have 4 to 5 cups of roasted cauliflower. Reserve about ½ cup florets if using as a topping.

3. Heat 2 Tbsp olive oil in a large saucepan or Dutch oven over medium heat and cook the onions for 5 to 8 minutes, or until they just start to brown. Squeeze in the roasted garlic, and add the roasted cauliflower and broth and bring to a boil. The broth should just cover the cauliflower. Add 1 tsp salt (but be careful to not over-season if the broth is already salted) and pepper, to taste. Reduce the heat to low and cook for 20 minutes longer.

4. Remove the pan from the heat and puree the soup with an immersion blender, or in blender or food processor. Return the soup to the heat. Add cream, if using, and adjust seasoning to taste.

5. To serve, top the soup with the reserved roasted cauliflower, greens, and/or hazelnuts, if you wish.

ISRAELI ORANGE SOUP WITH CILANTRO AND ROASTED PUMPKIN SEEDS

Serves 6 to 8

This is a popular vegetarian/vegan soup in a country where many people are vegetarian or vegan. It is often served for Friday night dinner or Jewish holiday meals instead of the matzo ball soup that many Ashkenazi Jews are used to. I always make it with water or vegetable broth and freeze any leftovers just in case any unannounced vegetarians or vegans come over for dinner. You could roast the squash, sweet potatoes, and carrots first to intensify their flavor. Sometimes I add a little curry paste instead of the harissa, sometimes I swirl z'hug (page 13) on top when serving, sometimes I add sautéed spinach or baby kale as a topping, or sprinkle the soup with chopped roasted nuts instead of seeds. And sometimes I even add mini matzo balls if it's for a Jewish holiday dinner.

2 Tbsp extra virgin olive oil

1 small onion, chopped

1 garlic clove, finely chopped

1-inch piece fresh ginger, scrubbed or peeled, minced or grated

1 tsp chopped fresh turmeric root or ½ tsp ground turmeric

1 Tbsp tomato paste

½ to 1½ tsp harissa, depending on your heat tolerance, **or ½ tsp chipotle sauce**

½ tsp smoked or sweet paprika

1 lb butternut squash, peeled and coarsely chopped (about 2 to 2½ cups)

1 lb carrots, coarsely chopped (about 2 to 2½ cups)

1 lb sweet potatoes, scrubbed or peeled, and coarsely chopped (about 2 to 2½ cups)

5 cups vegetable broth or water + more as needed

1 tsp kosher salt + more to taste

½ cup coconut milk, optional

1. Put the olive oil, onions, garlic, ginger, and turmeric (if using fresh turmeric) in a large saucepan or Dutch oven set over medium heat, and cook gently until tender but not browned, about 5 to 8 minutes. Add the tomato paste, harissa, and paprika (and turmeric, if using ground) and cook 1 minute.

2. Add the vegetables, and stir to combine with the onion mixture. Add the broth and bring to a boil. Add 1 tsp salt. Cover, reduce the heat to medium-low, and cook gently for 25 to 30 minutes, or until the vegetables can be crushed with the back of a spoon.

3. Remove the pan from the heat and puree the soup with an immersion blender, or in a blender or food processor, until smooth. Return to the heat. If the soup is too thick, add more broth a little at a time, until it reaches the consistency you like. Add the coconut milk, if using, and season with salt to taste.

4. Serve drizzled with coconut milk, if you like, and/or topped with cilantro leaves, roasted pumpkin seeds, and a sprinkling of paprika.

SUGGESTED TOPPINGS
½ cup coconut milk
½ cup coarsely chopped fresh cilantro leaves
¼ cup roasted pumpkin seeds
½ tsp smoked or sweet paprika

WILD MUSHROOM SOUP WITH COCONUT CREAM

Serves 6 to 8

Even just a small amount of dried wild mushrooms elevates a classic mushroom soup to a new level, especially since many of the fresh "wild" varieties are now actually cultivated, not wild. I usually use cremini for the fresh mushroom base, as they are the most reasonably priced and have lots of flavor (they are baby portobellos). Other types available are oyster, shiitake, hen of the woods, enoki, and king (trumpet), which I sometimes sauté and use as a garnish. Any time you are soaking dried mushrooms, make sure to save the soaking liquid—it's packed with flavor and can be used in other soups or in any braised dish and can be frozen for later use.

½ **oz dried wild mushrooms**

1 **cup boiling water**

3 **Tbsp extra virgin olive oil**

1 **onion,** chopped

1 **leek,** white and light green part only, cleaned and chopped (see note on page 110)

1 **lb mixed fresh wild mushrooms or cremini mushrooms,** well rinsed and chopped or sliced

1 **garlic clove,** finely chopped

4 **cups vegetable broth or water**

1½ **tsp kosher salt**

⅛ **tsp freshly ground black pepper**

½ **cup unsweetened coconut milk or cream** (see note)

Suggested Toppings

Drizzle of coconut cream or whipping cream

Sautéed mushrooms, fresh or wild

Chopped fresh chives or tarragon leaves (or a combination)

1. Place the dried wild mushrooms in a bowl and cover with boiling water. Rest for 20 to 30 minutes, or until the mushrooms have softened. Line a sieve with a paper towel or cheesecloth, set it over a bowl or measuring cup, and drain the mushrooms, reserving the soaking liquid. Squeeze or press down on the mushrooms as much as possible, to get as much flavorful liquid out as you can. Rinse the mushrooms well (they are usually quite sandy) and finely chop. Set both the mushrooms and the liquid aside.

2. Meanwhile, heat the olive oil in a large saucepan or Dutch oven over medium heat. Add the onions and leeks, and cook until softened, about 10 minutes. Add the fresh mushrooms and reserved soaked, dried mushrooms. Cook until any liquid in the pan has evaporated. Add the garlic and cook for 1 to 2 minutes.

3. Add the broth and the reserved mushroom soaking liquid. Bring to a boil, then add the salt and pepper. Cook gently, uncovered, for 25 to 30 minutes. Remove the pan from the heat and partially puree the soup with an immersion blender, or in a blender or food processor—the soup should still have some texture. (Or puree completely, if you prefer.) Return the soup to the heat.

4. Stir in the coconut milk and heat thoroughly. If the soup is too thick, add a little water. Taste and adjust seasoning—it will probably need more salt. Serve as is or with any of the suggested toppings.

NOTE: Coconut cream is becoming more readily available. Alternatively, you could refrigerate a can of full-fat coconut milk and use the cream that thickens and rises to the top. It adds flavor and richness to the soup while allowing it to remain vegan, kosher, lactose-free, and gluten-free.

Salads

JA'ALA HERB SALAD WITH LEMON HONEY DRESSING

Serves 6 to 8

One night at Mashya, an innovative and beautiful restaurant in Tel Aviv, I fell in love with a salad. It seemed simple, with its bed of leafy greens, leaves of fresh herbs, and dried fruits and nuts scattered on top, yet somehow it managed to be so special. I learned that this salad is named after the Yemenite custom of serving a variety of roasted nuts and dried fruits as a snack when people drop by. This is my favorite version, but feel free to make up your own.

6 cups mâche or other leafy mild lettuce (see note)

¼ cup whole or coarsely chopped fresh cilantro

¼ cup whole or coarsely chopped fresh dill

¼ cup whole or coarsely chopped fresh mint

¼ cup whole or coarsely chopped fresh flat-leaf parsley

1 Tbsp chopped fresh tarragon

2 green onions, thinly sliced

¼ cup dried cherries

¼ cup Medjool dates, pitted and sliced (see note page 208)

¼ cup chopped dried apricots, preferably dried sour apricots

⅓ cup coarsely chopped roasted cashews, almonds, or hazelnuts (or a combination)

2 Tbsp roasted sunflower seeds or pumpkin seeds (or a combination)

Lemon Honey Dressing

⅓ cup extra virgin olive oil

2 Tbsp fresh lemon juice (about ½ juicy lemon)

1 Tbsp honey

½ tsp kosher salt + more to taste

1. Lightly toss the mâche with the herbs and green onions. Arrange on a shallow serving platter.

2. Sprinkle the greens with the dried fruit, then with the roasted nuts and seeds. If not serving right away, cover with a damp paper towel or a clean damp tea towel.

3. When ready to serve, dress the salad by drizzling it with the olive oil, lemon juice, and honey. Sprinkle the salt overtop. Gently toss and serve.

NOTE: Mâche is a tender green sometimes called lamb's lettuce. At the best of times, it can be hard to find. You can use watercress, butter lettuce, arugula, or any other tender leaf lettuce you like.

ROASTED DELICATA SQUASH AND GRILLED HALLOUMI SALAD

Serves 4 to 6

Delicata squash is not just delicious. It has the prettiest scalloped edges, as if created by a fashion designer. Anna jokes that she's abandoned all other squash because she loves the flavor and texture of delicata squash so much, and adds it to salads of all kinds. We came up with this salad together, and decided to add halloumi, the celebrity of Greek cheeses, because adding it can easily make this dish a vegetarian main course. Halloumi is a semi-hard fresh cheese that is salty like feta and can be grilled, seared, or roasted, making it crispy, soft, chewy, and everything else that makes this cheese special. When I roast delicata squash, I don't peel it first, as the skin is thin and edible, and the same goes for butternut squash.

2 delicata squash (about 1 lb)

1 small butternut or honeynut squash (about 1 lb)

2 Tbsp + 1 Tbsp extra virgin olive oil + more for brushing

1 tsp + ½ tsp kosher salt

Freshly ground black pepper

1 Tbsp + 1 tsp maple syrup

3 sprigs fresh thyme

1 small head broccoli (about 1 lb)

12 oz halloumi cheese

2 cups baby arugula

2 or 3 fresh figs, cut into wedges

¼ cup roasted hazelnuts, coarsely chopped

Lime Honey Dressing

⅓ cup extra virgin olive oil

3 Tbsp fresh lime juice

1 Tbsp honey

½ tsp kosher salt + more to taste

1. Preheat the oven to 425°F and line two baking sheets with parchment paper.

2. Cut the delicata squash in half crosswise and use a spoon to scoop out all the seeds. Then slice into rounds about ½ inch thick. Cut the neck of the butternut squash into rounds about ½ inch thick (use the rest for soup, puree, or mash). If the rounds are very large, cut them in half. Place the squash on one of the lined baking sheets and toss with 2 Tbsp olive oil, 1 tsp salt, some pepper, and 1 Tbsp maple syrup. Place the sprigs of thyme over the squash. Roast for 30 to 35 minutes, or until tender and browned around the edges. Cool.

3. Remove the tough stalks from the broccoli and cut into medium-sized trees with florets and some stalk. Arrange on the second lined baking sheet and toss with 1 Tbsp olive oil, 1 tsp maple syrup, ½ tsp salt, and pepper. Roast for 20 to 25 minutes, then cool.

4. For the dressing, whisk together the olive oil, lime juice, honey, and salt. Adjust seasoning to taste.

5. Just before serving, slice the halloumi into pieces about ½ inch thick, pat dry with paper towel, and brush with olive oil. Sear in a hot, dry nonstick skillet for 1 to 2 minutes per side, or until browned.

6. Assemble the salad by arranging the arugula on a platter and topping with roasted squash, broccoli, halloumi, and figs. Drizzle with the dressing and sprinkle with hazelnuts.

CURLY ENDIVE SALAD WITH GREEN OLIVES AND ROASTED FENNEL

Serves 6 to 8

Curly endive is delicious cooked or raw. The fennel can be thinly sliced and served raw if you prefer, or roast in slices or wedges as instructed in the recipe. When fennel is cooked, it becomes milder and loses a lot of its licorice flavor—people who say they don't like fennel (Anna) usually love it roasted (she does).

2 bulbs fennel, trimmed and cut into wedges or slices

2 Tbsp extra virgin olive oil

1 Tbsp honey, optional

1 tsp kosher salt

2 sprigs fresh thyme or oregano

1 large bunch curly endive or escarole, cut into 1-inch pieces

1 small bunch radishes, thinly sliced

½ cup large green olives, gently smashed and pits removed

Dressing

½ cup extra virgin olive oil

3 Tbsp sherry vinegar or good red wine vinegar

Kosher salt and freshly ground black pepper

1. Preheat the oven to 425°F and line a baking sheet with parchment paper.

2. Toss the fennel with the olive oil, honey, if using, salt, and thyme. Arrange in a single layer on the lined baking sheet and roast for 20 to 25 minutes, or until tender and browned. Cool.

3. Place the curly endive in a shallow salad bowl and top with the radishes, olives, and roasted fennel.

4. To dress the salad, drizzle with the olive oil and vinegar, then sprinkle with salt and pepper to taste.

HERB "TABBOULEH" SALAD WITH SEEDS AND BERRIES

Serves 6 to 8

Although tabbouleh salads always contain lots of herbs, this one uses even more. I always have leftover herbs in the refrigerator or taking over my garden, and this is a great way to use them up. Instead of using the usual bulgur (cracked wheat) or other grains typically found in tabbouleh, this version uses pumpkin and sunflower seeds and fresh berries. It really tastes like summer. This recipe was inspired by Yossi Elad, a founding chef of Machneyuda in Jerusalem and Palomar in London. Instead of (or along with) the sunflower and pumpkin seeds, you could add 1 cup of cooked quinoa, rice, or bulgur. For the herbs, just use the leaves and tender stems.

1 bunch fresh flat-leaf parsley

1 bunch fresh cilantro

1 bunch fresh dill

1 small bunch fresh mint leaves

1 bunch green onions, thinly sliced

¼ cup roasted sunflower seeds

¼ cup roasted pumpkin seeds

¼ cup chopped roasted almonds

1 mild or medium-hot red chili, seeded and chopped

2 cups fresh berries (blueberries, sliced strawberries, raspberries, pitted cherries, and/or husked cape gooseberries)

Lemon Dressing

1 lemon

¾ tsp kosher salt

⅛ tsp freshly ground black pepper

⅓ to ½ cup extra virgin olive oil

1. Combine the parsley, cilantro, dill, and mint, and coarsely chop. Add the sliced green onions. Spread over a shallow salad bowl or serving plate.

2. Sprinkle with the sunflower and pumpkin seeds and almonds, chilies, and berries.

3. To dress the salad, just before serving, squeeze the juice from ½ of a lemon (about 2 to 3 Tbsp) over the salad, sprinkle with salt and pepper, and drizzle with ⅓ cup olive oil. Toss and add more of any of these ingredients to taste.

ANNA'S QUINOA SALAD

Makes 5 to 6 cups

Years ago, Anna came up with this dish that's perfect for traveling—but she makes it all the time at home too. It's gluten-free, vegan, and light but filling, and you can add or subtract anything you like or don't like (or don't have). Instead of the quinoa you could use cooked rice, lentils, or chickpeas; if it doesn't have to be gluten-free, you can use cooked grains like rye or wheat berries, bulgur, barley, spelt, freekeh, or farro. You could also add 1 cup diced firm tofu (vegan) or diced goat cheese or feta (vegetarian), or ½ cup coarsely chopped roasted nuts. If traveling, squeeze the seeds and juices from the cherry tomatoes so that the salad doesn't get soggy.

1 cup quinoa (see note)

2 cups boiling water (or amount needed as per package directions)

1 cup cherry tomatoes, halved or quartered

1 cup cooked corn kernels

1 cup cooked and coarsely chopped sweet potatoes, carrots, or squash

1 cup cooked chickpeas (canned or freshly cooked, see page 24)

¼ cup chopped fresh cilantro, flat-leaf parsley, or dill (or a combination)

2 Tbsp roasted sunflower seeds

2 Tbsp roasted pumpkin seeds

3 to 4 Tbsp fresh lemon juice

1 tsp kosher salt + more to taste

¼ to ⅓ cup extra virgin olive oil

1 cup crumbled goat cheese, optional

NOTE: Quinoa can be bitter if its natural coating isn't rinsed off. Most quinoa now comes pre-rinsed, but if the package directions say to rinse the quinoa before cooking, place it in a fine-mesh sieve and rinse it a few times with cold water.

1. Place the quinoa in a medium saucepan and cover with boiling water. Bring to a boil, cover, and cook gently for 15 to 20 minutes. Fluff with a fork, then spread on a baking sheet lined with parchment paper to cool.

2. In a large bowl, combine the tomatoes, corn, sweet potatoes, chickpeas, cilantro, sunflower seeds, and pumpkin seeds. Add the quinoa and toss gently.

3. Stir in 3 Tbsp lemon juice, salt, and ¼ cup olive oil. Taste and adjust seasoning. Scatter the crumbled goat cheese overtop, if using.

GRILLED CORN SALAD WITH CAULIFLOWER AND BROCCOLI

Serves 6 to 8

When corn is in season, we make this salad over and over again and never seem to get tired of it. One year we started including roasted vegetables like cauliflower and broccoli, and it only seemed to get better. Try adding roasted carrots or celery root, parsnips, sweet potatoes, cherry tomatoes—whatever you and your family like. The dressing is similar to the charmoula sauce we love so much, but the seasoning is more intense to highlight all the ingredients.

5 ears corn, husked

1 small head cauliflower, broken into 1-inch chunks (florets and core)

2 Tbsp + 2 Tbsp extra virgin olive oil

1 Tbsp + 1 Tbsp maple syrup or honey

½ tsp + ½ tsp kosher salt

Freshly ground black pepper

1 head broccoli, stems trimmed and sliced into ½-inch rounds, and florets cut up to 1 inch

Smoky Paprika Dressing

½ cup mayonnaise

1 garlic clove, minced or grated

1 tsp pureed chipotle chilies (see page 5) **or Tabasco Chipotle** + more to taste

½ tsp smoked paprika

½ tsp ground cumin

2 Tbsp fresh lime juice

¼ cup + ¼ cup coarsely chopped fresh cilantro + more to taste

½ cup grated smoked cheddar cheese, optional

1. Grill the corn on the barbecue over medium-high heat—no need for butter, oil, or seasonings. Cook for a few minutes, turning often, or until nicely browned and charred in a few spots. If you have a gas stove, you can grill it over the flame or use a hot grill pan or broiler. (And recently I saw someone use a kitchen blowtorch to grill corn.)

2. To remove the corn from the cob, break or cut the cob in half crosswise so you can stand it up on the cut flat end. Place it on a rimmed baking sheet, holding it securely at the top. Then cut the kernels off the cob from top to bottom. Transfer kernels to a large mixing bowl.

3. Preheat the oven to 425°F and line two baking sheets with parchment paper. Place the cauliflower in another large bowl and toss with 2 Tbsp extra virgin olive oil, 1 Tbsp maple syrup, ½ tsp salt, and a pinch of freshly ground black pepper. Spread on one of the lined baking sheets and roast on the bottom rack of the oven for 15 to 20 minutes, or until tender and browned. Repeat with the broccoli, then combine the roasted vegetables with the corn. You can roast the cauliflower and broccoli on the same baking sheet if there's space, but if the pan is crowded, the vegetables will be more likely to steam and not brown.

4. For the dressing, whisk the mayonnaise with garlic, chipotles, paprika, and cumin. If you like it spicy, add more chipotle. Stir in the lime juice, ¼ cup cilantro, and grated cheese, if using. Toss the dressing with the vegetable mixture, and season to taste.

5. Place in a serving bowl and scatter ¼ cup cilantro overtop.

NOTE: For a vegan version, use vegan mayo in the dressing or substitute the mayo with ⅓ cup extra virgin olive oil.

CHICKEN SALAD WITH PEANUT AND LIME DRESSINGS

Serves 4 to 6

This salad is truly a family favorite, and every time I make it, I add something new that livens it up. You can cook it all according to the recipe, or use leftover or rotisserie chicken and/or leftover roasted vegetables to speed things up. Anything goes. Sometimes I add roasted poblano chilies, grilled asparagus, roasted broccoli or cauliflower, or cherry tomatoes (roasted or raw). The constants are the two dressings and, if you ask Anna, the crushed corn tortilla chips.

1½ lb boneless, skinless chicken breasts or thighs

3 Tbsp extra virgin olive oil

1 Tbsp chopped fresh rosemary

1 tsp kosher salt

Salad

6 cups chopped little gem or Romaine lettuce (or any greens you like)

3 ears corn, grilled and kernels removed (see step 2 on page 66)**, or 2½ cups cooked corn kernels**

2 carrots, shaved or grated

2 cups sugar snap peas, trimmed and strings removed, boiled or steamed for 3 to 4 minutes, or until bright green and crisp

⅓ cup coarsely chopped fresh cilantro

2 cups broken corn tortilla chips or toasted corn tortillas cut into strips

¼ cup roasted salted peanuts or cashews

Lime Dressing

3 Tbsp fresh lime juice

1 Tbsp honey

1 small garlic clove, minced or grated

½ tsp kosher salt

3 Tbsp extra virgin olive oil

Peanut Dressing

3 Tbsp peanut butter

2 Tbsp honey

3 Tbsp soy sauce

2 to 3 Tbsp water

1. Preheat the oven to 400°F. In a bowl, combine the chicken with the olive oil, rosemary, and salt. Brown the chicken on both sides in an ovenproof skillet brushed with olive oil on medium-high heat, then transfer to the preheated oven. Cook chicken breasts for 15 minutes and thighs for 25 minutes or, in both cases, until an instant-read thermometer registers at least 165°F when inserted into the thickest part. Cool and slice. (If you like, the chicken can be grilled instead.)

2. Meanwhile, make the lime dressing by whisking the lime juice with the honey, garlic, and salt. Whisk in the olive oil. For the peanut dressing, whisk together the peanut butter and honey until combined, then slowly and gently whisk in the soy sauce and then water.

3. For the salad, place the lettuce in a large bowl, then top with the corn kernels, carrots, peas, chicken, cilantro, tortilla chips, and peanuts. Drizzle with both dressings and toss at the table before serving.

ROASTED BEET AND ORANGE WINTER SALAD WITH POMEGRANATE DRESSING

Serves 6 to 8

In the winter it can be hard to come up with festive-looking, delicious salads that celebrate the season. That is why I love this salad as a vibrant, fresh centerpiece to balance heavier winter dishes. You could add roasted squash or carrots, if you like.

2 lb red beets, scrubbed or peeled and cut into about ⅓-inch-thick slices

2 lb yellow beets, scrubbed or peeled and cut into about ⅓-inch-thick slices

1½ Tbsp + 1½ Tbsp extra virgin olive oil

½ tsp + ½ tsp kosher salt

Freshly ground black pepper

½ Tbsp + ½ Tbsp honey or maple syrup

2 oranges (navel, cara cara, blood, or a combination)

3 cups baby arugula

2 Tbsp roughly torn fresh mint leaves

2 Tbsp roughly torn fresh cilantro leaves

½ cup roasted whole pecans or walnuts, optional

⅓ cup pomegranate seeds, optional

Pomegranate Dressing

⅓ cup extra virgin olive oil

2 Tbsp pomegranate molasses

2 Tbsp honey + more to taste

1 Tbsp fresh lemon juice

1 tsp kosher salt + more to taste

¼ tsp freshly ground black pepper

1. Preheat the oven to 425°F and line two baking sheets with parchment paper.

2. In separate bowls, toss the red and yellow beets each with 1½ Tbsp olive oil, ½ tsp salt, a pinch of pepper, and ½ Tbsp honey. Spread in a single layer on the lined baking sheets. Roast for 30 to 40 minutes, or until tender. Cool.

3. Peel the oranges by cutting off the tops and bottoms. Holding the orange in place on one cut flat end, cut off the peel from top to bottom. Cut the peeled oranges into rounds crosswise.

4. Arrange the arugula on a large platter. Scatter the mint and cilantro overtop. Top with the beets and oranges (and any other vegetables you're using; see recipe intro). Sprinkle with nuts and pomegranate seeds, if using.

5. For the dressing, combine the olive oil, pomegranate molasses, honey, lemon juice, salt, and pepper using a whisk or blender. Adjust seasoning to taste with more honey or salt. Drizzle the dressing over the salad to taste just before serving.

If you buy bunches of beets with the stems and leaves on, chop the stems and sauté in a little olive oil until tender (usually about 5 minutes) and then add the leaves and cook until they wilt. Season with salt and pepper. It's fantastic as a side dish or omelet filling, or in a wrap.

SHRIMP AND POMELO SALAD WITH THAI DRESSING

Serves 4 as a starter or 2 as a main

I was so excited when I bought my first pomelo. The only problem, I realized, was that I didn't know how to open it. But the internet quickly helped me solve that challenge! Peeling pomelos is a process, but they are definitely worth it. And I actually find it pretty fun. You can eat them plain or use in fruit salads, but using them in this Thai salad is especially delicious. Serve for lunch, a light dinner, or as part of a spread.

1 peeled pomelo or 2 red or pink grapefruits

½ lb cooked shrimp, shells removed and deveined, whole or halved lengthwise

3 little gem lettuces, leaves separated

⅓ cup fresh cilantro leaves, whole or coarsely chopped

2 Tbsp shredded fresh Thai or regular basil leaves

1 Tbsp shredded fresh mint leaves

1 medium-hot green or red chili, very thinly sliced

½ cup roasted coconut chips

Crispy shallots (see note)

Thai Dressing

¼ cup fresh lime juice

2 Tbsp fish sauce or soy sauce

2 Tbsp light brown sugar

½-inch piece fresh ginger, peeled and grated

1 small glove garlic, grated

1. Combine the peeled pomelo segments, shrimp, lettuce leaves, cilantro, basil, and mint in a shallow salad bowl.

2. For the dressing, in a small bowl, combine the lime juice, fish sauce, sugar, ginger, and garlic. Drizzle over the salad.

3. Top with chilies, coconut chips, and crispy shallots, if using.

NOTE: Crispy shallots can be purchased at some Asian markets, but they are easy to make. Make more than you need, because they keep for up to 1 month and are delicious on everything. Thinly slice 4 peeled shallots by hand or using a mandolin (wearing a protective glove!). Place about 1 cup vegetable oil and the shallots into a medium saucepan set over medium heat and cook, stirring often, until golden brown. Strain through a sieve set over a metal or heatproof bowl. Cool and refrigerate the cooking oil for use in salad dressings. Spread the shallots on a baking sheet lined with paper towel. Sprinkle with salt. Once cool, store in an airtight container at room temperature.

HOW TO OPEN A POMELO: Start by making four cuts through the skin and pith (there is so much pith!) from top to bottom but not so deep that you hit the flesh. This allows you to start peeling away the skin and pith from the bottom, working toward the top. This is when you realize the edible part of a pomelo is about half the size you thought it would be. Next, insert your thumbs into the opening at the bottom of the pomelo and gently but firmly pull it apart. Unlike other citrus, you will want to peel the membranes off each segment, as they are quite thick and tough. Do this with your fingers or a paring knife.

SMOKED TROUT AND HARD-COOKED EGG SALAD (OR SPREAD)

Makes about 2½ cups

This combination is so delicious, whether you have it as a main-course salad or turn it into a spread for sandwiches or crackers. If serving this as a salad, leave the trout and eggs in large chunks and serve on a bed of mâche, watercress, or arugula. You could add roasted or boiled potatoes for an even heartier main-course salad. If making it as a spread, flake the trout and grate the eggs—and caramelized onions would be a wonderful addition!

8 oz smoked trout, flaked or in chunks (see note)

3 hard-cooked eggs, grated or cut into chunks (see below)

2 green onions, thinly sliced

1 medium-hot red or green chili, very thinly sliced

½ cup mayonnaise

1 Tbsp finely chopped pre-served lemon peel, rinsed (or more to taste) **or 1 Tbsp fresh lemon juice**

1 small garlic clove, minced or grated

1 Tbsp chopped fresh tarragon

Fresh chives, cut into 1½-inch lengths

1. Gently combine the trout, eggs, green onions, and chili in a large bowl.

2. In another bowl, combine the mayonnaise, preserved lemons, garlic, and tarragon, then add to the trout mixture. If serving as a salad, combine gently and mound ingredients onto a bed of greens. If serving as a spread, gently mash the mayonnaise mixture with the trout until spreadable but still chunky. Taste and adjust seasoning with lemon, tarragon, and salt. Sprinkle with chives as a garnish just before serving.

NOTE: Smoked trout is now much easier to find than it used to be—you can even buy it already deboned and skinned. Keep it in the freezer for last-minute meals or snacks. Other hot-smoked fish, like whitefish, can be used instead of trout, but not cold-smoked fish like smoked salmon. Most of the smoked salmon in eastern Canada is cold-smoked at low temperatures and has that soft silky texture and mild smoke flavor you're used to eating on a bagel. That's why it doesn't flake like smoked trout or whitefish. Hot-smoked salmon, though not as readily available, is cooked at a higher temperature, resulting in a firmer, flakier texture and a stronger smoke flavor, and can be used in this recipe.

HOW TO HARD-COOK EGGS: Bring a large pot of water to a boil and add 1 tsp salt. The salt seals the shells if they crack when adding to the water and prevents too much of the egg white from escaping. Lower the eggs gently into the water and cook, uncovered, for 9 minutes after the water returns to a boil. Transfer the eggs to a bowl of ice water, crack shells gently against the side of the bowl, and allow to cool in the water. Peel and cut in half.

THAI GRILLED STEAK SALAD

Serves 4

The idea for this beautiful and delicious Thai steak salad came from a salad I ate in Copenhagen. I love that the presentation of this is so different and that, despite being a steak salad, it highlights the tomatoes. You could also make this using flank steak—marinate, cook it rare, slice thinly, and top with the tomatoes and dressing. If you are not eating red meat, this would also be delicious with chicken, fish, or a vegetable steak.

Four 6 oz boneless ribeye or filet steaks, ½ inch thick

1 tsp flaky sea salt

Freshly ground black pepper

Thai Steak Dressing and Marinade

¼ cup fresh lime juice

¼ cup hoisin sauce

¼ cup extra virgin olive oil

3 Tbsp soy sauce

2 Tbsp honey

2 Tbsp rice vinegar

2 Tbsp boiling water

1 Tbsp fish sauce or soy sauce

1 tsp toasted sesame oil

½ tsp sriracha

Salad

2 cups salad greens (e.g. curly endive, escarole)

4 large ripe red heirloom tomatoes, sliced about ¼ inch to ⅓ inch thick

Freshly ground black pepper

¼ cup coarsely chopped fresh cilantro

2 Tbsp coarsely chopped fresh Thai or regular basil

2 Tbsp coarsely chopped fresh mint

1. Remove steaks from the refrigerator while preparing the dressing.

2. For the dressing, combine the lime juice, hoisin, olive oil, soy sauce, honey, vinegar, boiling water, fish sauce, sesame oil, and sriracha. Brush ¼ cup dressing (in total) over both sides of the steaks. Set the remaining dressing aside. Marinate the steaks for 30 minutes at room temperature or for a few hours in the refrigerator. Just before cooking, season the steaks on both sides with flaky sea salt and pepper.

3. Preheat your barbecue to very high (or preheat a grill pan or cast iron skillet over high heat). Cook the steaks for 2 to 3 minutes per side, depending on their thickness and the heat of the grill—you may need to add a bit more time. They should be browned well but rare in the center.

4. Line the plates with the salad greens, place the steaks on top, and spoon 1 Tbsp of the remaining dressing over each. Arrange the sliced tomatoes over the steaks, almost to cover, drizzle with the remaining dressing, and sprinkle with pepper and then herbs.

GRILLED FLANK STEAK AND POTATO SALAD NIÇOISE

Serves 6

When I started my cooking school in the '70s, a steak meant filet, rib, tenderloin, New York sirloin, or strip steak. Hanger, flank, skirt, tri tip, and other delicious, so-called alternative cuts weren't well known. And everyone thought that if you were going to cook one of these, you had to marinate it overnight to tenderize it. I remember cooking a flank steak on a popular morning show, *Canada AM*, and brought one that had been marinated and cooked. I had another for my on-air demo that had only been marinated for about 1 minute before I cooked it. After the show, while the hosts, crew and I were eating the steak, I explained that the demo steak would probably be too tough because it wasn't marinated long enough. I sliced it anyway and it was delicious and very tender and we finished that one too. I have loved these alternative cuts ever since, and of course now with the price of beef where it is and supporting the nose to tail philosophy, alternative cuts are the stars.

Niçoise Dressing and Marinade

1 large garlic clove, minced or grated

3 Tbsp sherry vinegar

3 Tbsp fresh lemon juice

2 Tbsp balsamic vinegar

1 Tbsp honey

1½ tsp Dijon mustard

1 tsp kosher salt

⅛ tsp freshly ground black pepper + more to taste

1 cup extra virgin olive oil, or to taste

1. For the dressing, whisk together the garlic, sherry vinegar, lemon juice, balsamic vinegar, honey, mustard, salt, and pepper. Whisk in the olive oil, and keep whisking until the dressing becomes creamy—this can also be done in a blender or food processor.

2. Place the steak in a large, heavy, resealable plastic bag or shallow baking dish and add about ⅓ cup dressing. Turn the steak over and marinate for 1 hour at room temperature or up to overnight in the refrigerator.

3. About 30 minutes before you're ready to cook, remove the steak from the refrigerator (if you have time and remember). Sprinkle steak with flaky sea salt. Preheat the barbecue on high, then cook the steak for about 4 minutes per side for medium rare or until an instant-read thermometer registers between 125°F and 130°F when inserted into the thickest part. Remove from the heat and let rest for about 5 to 10 minutes before carving. The steak can also be cooked in a scorching-hot cast iron skillet for 4 minutes per side as above.

continued . . .

Salad

2 lb flank steak

1 tsp flaky sea salt

2½ lb baby Yukon gold or fingerling potatoes, cut in half if large

1 Tbsp + 1 Tbsp chopped fresh tarragon or flat-leaf parsley

½ lb green beans

3 cups arugula or little gem lettuce

1 to 2 cups cherry tomatoes, raw or roasted, optional

4 hard-cooked eggs (see note on page 73)

½ cup pitted black olives

4. Meanwhile, preheat the oven to 450°F and line a baking sheet with parchment paper. Toss the potatoes in ¼ cup of the dressing and spread in a single layer on the lined baking sheet. Cover the baking sheet tightly with aluminum foil. Roast for 20 minutes, then remove the aluminum foil. Reduce the oven temperature to 425°F and roast the potatoes for another 20 to 25 minutes, or until well browned and crisp. Toss with another ¼ cup dressing and 1 Tbsp tarragon.

5. To blanch the green beans, trim the beans, and bring a skillet of water to a boil. Prepare a large bowl of ice and water for the blanched beans. Cook the beans for 4 to 5 minutes, or until bright green and just tender, drain in a colander, and place in the ice water to stop the cooking and set the color. Drain the beans, and pat dry with paper towel or a clean tea towel.

6. When ready to serve, slice the steak thinly against the grain (see note on page 149). Arrange the arugula on a large platter, then add the roasted potatoes, beans, tomatoes, eggs, steak, and olives. Drizzle everything with ½ cup dressing, sprinkle with 1 Tbsp tarragon and serve warm or at room temperature. Any leftover dressing will keep for up to 1 week stored in the refrigerator in an airtight container, and is delicious on everything.

NOTE: Instead of flank steak, you can use any of the alternative cuts mentioned in the recipe intro, chicken, or fish (using canned tuna or even sliced grilled tuna steaks makes it more of a traditional Niçoise). Or omit meat or fish completely, grill some tofu, and serve it vegetarian or vegan (without the eggs).

Things Not Worth Worrying About

I was born a worrier. You should have met my father. It's taken me a long time to learn there are some things not worth worrying about.

Perfection

Perfection is overrated. Home cooking is not about the food being perfect. It's about nurturing yourself and nurturing your family (however you define that), and, if you're having people over, it's about the atmosphere being warm and inviting. This is a lesson I have to keep telling myself, especially when chefs come over for dinner. And when my tahdig sticks to the pot, the glass in my oven door explodes (seriously), or when my fruit tart is especially "rustic." If you've ever wished your desserts looked like they came from a bakery, guess what? Many bakeries now want their desserts to look homemade. And just because something doesn't seem perfect to you, that doesn't mean it isn't perfect to someone else. I remember when Mark was about 10 years old, I tested a variation of my chocolate souffle cake and he told me, "Mom, don't change a thing. It's perfect."

Best-Before Dates

My husband, Ray, once called Heinz on me because he noticed that our ketchup was past the best-before date and I refused to replace it (I will admit it was a few years past). Before these dates even existed, my mother kept a bottle of ketchup for about 15 years. My sister and I were discriminating (fussy) eaters and never liked ketchup, so the bottle was there for when our friends came over. No one ever got sick! I'm not suggesting you keep the same bottle of ketchup for 15 years—we should probably have bought a new bottle much sooner than that—but use common sense and remember that, in most instances, the dates are best-before dates and an indication of peak freshness, not safety (which are noted with expiry dates).

Hot and Cold

Most of the time I don't worry about whether food is served very hot or very cold. When I first started cooking professionally, it was somewhat typical for diners at restaurants to complain if their food wasn't steaming hot, and they would send it back. When I started my cooking school, some of my students would say their partners would complain if their food at home wasn't as hot as it would be if they were eating in a restaurant, and would ask me how to keep it at that temperature. Warm the plates, of course, but also have a staff of people helping you rush the hot food to the table. Think about it—in a restaurant there are six people working on your dinner, but at home you alone may be working on six dinners! After traveling in Europe and seeing platters of food served safely at room temperature, I began to relax and realized that the flavor of food is actually more pronounced when it isn't really hot or really cold. However, I don't take health risks; always consider the temperature of the room, length of time the food sits out, and how perishable the type of food is.

The 5-Second Rule

If food falls on the floor, I use common sense as to whether to eat it or not. For your information, the 5-second rule is not scientific. It is a widely known food-hygiene myth that makes us all feel better about eating the cookie we dropped. Ray says the trick about the 5-second rule is just to never talk about it.

Unsalted Butter

When my sister, Jane, was a little girl, one of the few things she ate with joy was toast ordered at the Woolworth's counter. No matter how my mother made toast for her at home, it was never the same. When Jane married Wayne, they lived with my parents for a few months until they found a place of their own. Although my mother always used unsalted butter, Wayne grew up with salted butter and she changed to that for him. The first time my mother made them toast for breakfast, my sister said, "What did you change!? It finally tastes like Woolworth's." After 20 years!

For many years I used unsalted butter for everything. In chef training, I learned that it burned less quickly than salted butter when cooking on direct heat and was usually fresher. During that time, I used salted butter in one specific cookie only—a shortbread cookie that I make to this day (page 250). Although I tried the cookies with unsalted butter, even adding extra salt, they never tasted as good. Eventually, I switched over to salted butter for all my baked goods. Although most cookbooks call for unsalted butter, I've never had a problem eating something made using salted butter instead. I guess what I'm trying to say is, in my opinion, when a recipe calls for unsalted but you only have salted, unsalted is not worth running to the store for.

As a Born Worrier, Though, There Are Still Many Things I Worry About . . .

- I believe in being careful and cautious with poultry: cleaning utensils, your hands, and work surfaces well when they've come in contact with raw poultry, and using an instant-read thermometer to make sure it's cooked to 165°F.
- And on that note, I believe in instant-read thermometers! Meat and poultry are expensive, so why leave cooking it properly to chance when a thermometer can tell you when it's perfectly done? Plus, a thermometer tells you when your breads and cakes are ready too!
- Using fresh and healthful ingredients is important to me. And so I worry about everyone's access to quality ingredients, and fresh and healthful food in general.
- I worry about processed foods and the impact of diet culture, because I believe in eating in moderation and not telling yourself that certain things are not allowed.
- I believe in being respectful of knives. Never leave a knife in the sink to wash later. Wash it and then put it away immediately. And if you use a mandolin, you MUST wear protection.
- I feel very strongly about wearing shoes in the kitchen (ask my kids). In fact, I also worry about you wearing dangly jewelry and, worst of all, cooking naked. Don't do it!
- I try my best not to waste food but still waste too much. I'm working on this.
- I worry about climate change, food sustainability, and hunger.
- And I try to spend as much time as I can with the people I love.

I could go on, but we all have enough to worry about, so I'll stop here.

Sides

SHEET PAN ROASTED CHERRY TOMATOES WITH HERBS AND GARLIC

Serves 4 to 6

When cherry tomatoes are roasted, they taste especially wonderful. The roasting process evaporates some of their liquid, which intensifies their flavor, and salt, olive oil, and herbs maximize their taste. These tomatoes can be used in so many ways: tossed with pasta; chopped and used as a salsa; used as a topping for risotto or polenta, or for fish, chicken, or burgers; or served with ricotta, labneh, or hummus as an appetizer—and they're delicious served hot or at room temperature. When tomatoes are in season, I sometimes combine roasted tomatoes with fresh ones for a gorgeous tomato salad—use different varieties from your garden, a neighbor's garden, or the supermarket to make this recipe even more personal.

2 lb cherry tomatoes, a variety of colors and sizes

4 garlic cloves, peeled

1 jalapeño, sliced into rounds about ¼ inch thick (see page 5)

1 tsp kosher salt

⅛ tsp freshly ground black pepper

3 Tbsp extra virgin olive oil

2 sprigs fresh thyme

2 sprigs fresh basil

2 sprigs fresh oregano

2 sprigs fresh rosemary

1. Preheat the oven to 425°F and line a baking sheet with parchment paper.

2. Leave the cherry tomatoes whole, and if you are using any larger tomatoes, cut them into ½-inch- to 1-inch-thick slices or chunks. Arrange in a single layer on the lined baking sheet. Nestle the garlic cloves and jalapeños in and around the tomatoes.

3. Sprinkle the tomatoes with salt and pepper. Drizzle with olive oil. Arrange the herbs overtop. (If the tomatoes look too delicious to cook, drizzle with balsamic vinegar and eat them now. Then start again.)

4. Roast on the bottom rack of the oven for 15 to 20 minutes, or until the tomatoes are tinged with brown and the herbs are dried. Discard the stems and any large, dried pieces of the herbs. (Don't forget to dip some bread into the pan juices as the chef's treat.)

MASHED SWEET POTATOES AND CARROTS WITH BROWN BUTTER

Serves 6 to 8

Brown butter is a chef's secret ingredient. I learned to make it in chef training many years ago, when it was called by its traditional name, beurre noisette, because it smells and tastes like roasted hazelnuts. It is popular again today with chefs, bakers, and home cooks alike. It takes sautéed or roasted fish or vegetables to a new level—and then even higher levels when it's topped with roasted almonds or hazelnuts. It is also delicious in mashed cauliflower or mashed potatoes.

2 Tbsp extra virgin olive oil

1 leek, white and light green part only, cleaned and chopped (see note on page 110), **or 1 onion,** chopped

1 garlic clove, finely chopped

1½ lb carrots, peeled and diced (see note)

1½ lb sweet potatoes, peeled and cut into chunks

1 tsp kosher salt + more to taste

⅓ cup butter

Freshly ground black pepper

1 Tbsp chopped fresh flat-leaf parsley leaves, optional

1. Heat the olive oil in a large saucepan on medium heat. Add the leeks and garlic, and cook gently for 10 to 15 minutes, or until lightly browned.

2. Add the carrots and sweet potatoes and cover with boiling water. Add the salt. Bring to a boil, then reduce the heat to medium-low and cook gently for 20 to 30 minutes, or until the carrots and sweet potatoes are very tender.

3. Meanwhile, make the brown butter by cutting the butter into evenly sized small cubes and place them in a heavy-bottomed medium saucepan (use stainless steel or a light-colored pot, to be able to see the color of the butter cooking). Melt the butter over medium-low heat, never higher. Once melted, reduce the heat and cook gently, stirring often, until nutty-smelling (like roasted hazelnuts) and browned. Watch more closely if you're using salted butter, which can burn more quickly than unsalted. This could take 15 to 20 minutes. When ready, pour the butter into a bowl to stop the cooking.

4. When the vegetables are ready, drain, return to the pot, and mash with a potato masher so that the mixture is coarse rather than pureed. Mash in about ¼ cup of the brown butter (or more to taste). Season with salt and pepper. Sprinkle with parsley, if using.

NOTE: I cut the carrots smaller than the sweet potatoes, as they usually take a bit longer to become tender.

FREEKEH WITH ROOT VEGETABLES

Serves 6 to 8

Freekeh (pronounced either "freek-ah" or "freek-ee") is green wheat, harvested when unripe and roasted over fire to give it a smoky taste. It has gained popularity in North America and is now considered a superfood, which has made it easier to find. Read the package directions to see if you have to rinse it before using—usually no longer necessary, as it is often commercially processed. Rice or quinoa can be substituted, for a gluten-free adaptation.

2 Tbsp + 1 Tbsp extra virgin olive oil if needed

1 onion, chopped

¾ lb celeriac (celery root), peeled and diced (about 2 cups)

¾ lb carrots, scrubbed or peeled and diced (about 2 cups)

2 garlic cloves, finely chopped

1 tsp baharat spice mixture (store-bought or see page 10)

1 Tbsp tomato paste

2 cups freekeh

4 cups chicken or vegetable broth, or water

1½ tsp kosher salt (+ more or less to taste, depending on if the broth is salted)

2 Tbsp butter, optional

Toppings

¼ cup roasted chopped almonds

¼ cup roasted pine nuts

¼ cup fresh flat-leaf parsley leaves, torn

1. Heat 2 Tbsp olive oil in a large saucepan or medium Dutch oven over medium heat. Add the onions, celeriac, and carrots. Cook, stirring occasionally, until the vegetables are tender and beginning to brown, about 10 minutes. Add the garlic and baharat. Cook, stirring, for 1 minute, then add the tomato paste and cook for 1 minute longer.

2. Add the freekeh and also 1 Tbsp olive oil if the pan seems dry, and cook for 1 to 2 minutes, stirring. Add the broth and salt, and bring to a boil. Reduce the heat, cover, and cook gently for 20 minutes.

3. When the freekeh is tender and the liquid is absorbed, add the butter, if using, and season with salt to taste. Transfer to a serving dish and sprinkle with the nuts and parsley.

ROASTED TURNIPS WITH ZA'ATAR AND LABNEH

Serves 6

Erez Komarovsky is the person who brought artisanal bread to Israel in the form of his bakery-cafés, Lehem Erez. ("Lehem" is Hebrew for bread.) But he's brought other foods into my life too. The first time I tried roasted turnips was at Erez's house in Mattat, Israel, and they were incredibly delicious. Honestly, I wasn't even sure which root vegetable I was eating. He welcomes groups for cooking classes with a big spread of appetizers and breads on huge inviting platters, and it's all so hard to resist that we are full before the class even starts. Anna laughed at me for saying that I used to confuse turnips with rutabagas. However, 2 minutes later we discovered that she thought that rutabaga was just another name for celeriac. For the record, turnips are white and purple, with a white interior, and are smaller and more tender than rutabagas, which are large-ish, yellow and purple on the outside, and yellow on the inside. This recipe comes out best using turnips, not rutabagas, and can also be made with beets, carrots, kohlrabi, celeriac, or squash. This is delicious as a side dish or an appetizer but also wonderful over arugula or microgreens with grilled halloumi cheese (or ricotta or feta) and a simple lemon dressing.

2 lb turnips (not rutabagas), scrubbed or peeled, trimmed, and cut crosswise into halves or rounds

2 Tbsp + 1 Tbsp extra virgin olive oil + more to drizzle

1 tsp + 1 tsp honey

½ tsp + ½ tsp kosher salt

1 tsp za'atar

1½ cups labneh or thick yogurt

2 handfuls of arugula

Suggested Toppings

¼ cup chopped roasted hazelnuts or almonds

1 Tbsp fresh lemon juice + more to taste

Fresh chopped chives

Edible flowers, if available

Watermelon radish, if available, thinly sliced

1. Preheat the oven to 425°F and line a baking sheet with parchment paper.

2. Toss the turnips with 2 Tbsp olive oil, 1 tsp honey, ½ tsp salt, and za'atar. Spread in a single layer on the lined baking sheet, and roast on the bottom rack of the oven until browned and tender, 25 to 30 minutes depending on the size of the turnips.

3. Stir 1 Tbsp olive oil, 1 tsp honey, and ½ tsp salt into the labneh and spread over the bottom of a serving platter. Arrange the arugula over the labneh and top with the roasted turnips (warm or at room temperature and be sure to admire the beautiful pattern on their cut surfaces). Drizzle with more olive oil, then add any of the suggested toppings: sprinkle with hazelnuts and lemon juice, and scatter chives or flowers and watermelon radishes overtop.

CHARRED SWEET POTATOES WITH MISO SESAME DRIZZLE

Serves 6 to 8

Sweet potatoes are much more popular now than they used to be. I could never understand why no one seemed to like them as much as I did. So I'm glad everyone has caught on! (We might have sweet potato fries to thank for that, but who knows—at least we got here.) This dish can be served warm or at room temperature—perfect for barbecues or picnics, as well as for dinner parties. The sweet potatoes are delicious on their own, and the sauce can be used separately as a dip or spread, or as a dressing on other roasted vegetables. Any extra sauce keeps refrigerated in an airtight container for about 1 week.

3 lb sweet potatoes, scrubbed

3 Tbsp extra virgin olive oil

2 Tbsp maple syrup or honey

1 tsp kosher salt

⅛ tsp freshly ground black pepper

3 sprigs fresh thyme

Miso Sesame Sauce

¼ cup white miso

¼ cup pure tahini

3 Tbsp rice vinegar

2 Tbsp ice water

1 to 2 Tbsp maple syrup or honey, to taste

1 Tbsp toasted sesame oil

1 Tbsp finely chopped sushi ginger, optional

½ tsp gochujang or other hot sauce to taste, optional

1 garlic clove, finely chopped

1. Preheat the oven to 425°F and line a baking sheet with parchment paper.

2. Cut the sweet potatoes into halves lengthwise, large chunks, or long wedges and place on the lined baking sheet. Drizzle with the olive oil and maple syrup, then scatter the salt, pepper, and thyme overtop. Turn over to coat well. Roast, cut side down, on the bottom rack of the oven for 25 to 40 minutes (depending on the size of the sweet potatoes), or until they are very tender and charred in spots. Turn the sweet potatoes over halfway through cooking time or once the bottoms are browned.

3. Meanwhile, for the miso sesame sauce, in a medium bowl, whisk together (or blend) the miso with the tahini, vinegar, and ice water until smooth. Whisk in the maple syrup, sesame oil, ginger, gochujang, and garlic. Adjust seasoning to taste.

4. Place the sweet potatoes (warm or at room temperature) cut side up on a platter, and drizzle with the sauce.

NOTE: This is a delicious side dish or vegan/vegetarian main course. If serving as a main, you could roast the sweet potatoes in halves, sprinkle with cooked chickpeas or black lentils for more protein, and then drizzle with the sauce.

JANNA'S GREEN RICE

Serves 8

Janna Gur is a wonderful cook, cookbook author, and friend. She is the founder of Israel's premier food magazine, *Al Hashulchan*, and whenever I am in Israel, she cooks for me, shares her recipes, and answers my millions of questions about Israeli food! I first had this dish at her house along with incredible beef kebabs (see page 157) and have been making these two recipes ever since. This meal was also the first time I had ever been to Janna's house, and that year in Israel I was with Anna, Mitchell, and Nathan Goldstein (our close friend and Mitchell's husband). Mitchell is a much braver driver than I am and insisted that we rent a car. No matter where we went, the GPS misguided us. When driving to Janna's home for Shabbat dinner we arrived at an open field with a picnic table, and we knew we had been misguided once again. Luckily with some help from passersby, we finally made it to dinner.

3 Tbsp extra virgin olive oil

1 large onion, finely chopped

6 cardamom pods, lightly crushed

½ tsp ground cumin

3 cups basmati rice, rinsed until the water runs clear

1 cup fresh cilantro, chopped

1 cup fresh dill, chopped

1 cup fresh flat-leaf parsley, chopped

2 tsp kosher salt + more to taste

¼ tsp freshly ground black pepper

4½ cups boiling water

3 Tbsp butter, optional

1. Heat the olive oil in a large, heavy-bottomed saucepan. Add the onions and cook over medium heat for about 10 minutes, or until golden. Add the cardamom pods and cumin, and cook for 1 minute, or until fragrant. Add the rice and cook for about 2 minutes, or until coated with the onions and oil.

2. Stir in half of the fresh herbs, along with the salt, pepper, and water. Bring to a boil (increase the heat if necessary). Cook over medium heat for 5 to 8 minutes, or until the surface water is absorbed. Cover and cook over low heat for an additional 10 minutes. Rest the rice, covered, for 10 minutes off the heat.

3. When you lift the lid, you should see the 6 cardamom pods on the surface. Remove and discard them. If you don't see them, look for them as you serve, and alert your guests. Stir in the remaining fresh herbs, and butter, if using. Season with salt to taste.

RICE PILAF WITH CRISPY ONIONS AND CHICKPEAS

Serves 6

Pilaf is a wonderful method for cooking rice. When I learned this technique in chefs' school, we used plain long-grain rice. We didn't even know about basmati rice, which now is the go-to long-grain rice for many. This recipe makes for a delicious side dish and a great vegetarian or vegan main course, and is also wonderful with two fried or poached eggs on top.

¼ cup extra virgin olive oil

3 large onions, sliced

1½ cups basmati rice, rinsed until the water runs clear

1 Tbsp chopped preserved lemon peel (see page 16) or grated fresh lemon peel

1 cup cooked chickpeas (canned or freshly cooked, see page 24)

¼ tsp saffron threads, optional

2½ cups boiling water or chicken or vegetable broth

1 tsp kosher salt + more to taste

2 Tbsp butter, optional

2 Tbsp chopped fresh cilantro leaves, optional

2 Tbsp dukkah (page 11), optional

1. Heat the olive oil in a wide, deep saucepan over medium heat. Add the onions and cook until well browned, about 20 to 30 minutes or longer, depending on the heat and the type of pan. Stir often but not constantly, to allow the onions on the bottom of the pan to brown. Remove about half of the onions and spread out on paper towel to drain and crisp up.

2. Add the rice to the remaining onions in the pan and cook for a few minutes, stirring to coat the rice well with the onions and oil. Add the lemon peel and then the chickpeas. Cook for another 1 to 2 minutes. Place the saffron in a glass measuring cup or bowl and crush with the back of a spoon. Add ½ cup boiling water and 1 tsp salt and let the saffron infuse for at least 5 minutes, or until using. Add to the rest of the boiling water. Pour the water into the rice, bring to a boil, cover, and simmer gently over low heat for about 15 minutes, or until the rice is tender and the water has been absorbed.

3. Once the rice has absorbed all the liquid, stir in the butter, if using. Season with salt to taste. Top with the reserved crispy onions, and the cilantro and dukkah, if using.

NOTE: To make this with brown rice, cook the brown rice separately in a large pot of boiling salted water until tender (25 to 35 minutes), drain, and combine with the cooked onions in the pan. Heat thoroughly, add the lemon peel and chickpeas but omit the saffron, and then continue with step 3.

A NOTE ON SAFFRON: Saffron is considered the most expensive spice in the world. And it is difficult to find high-quality saffron. I recommend always buying the saffron threads, because that way you know what you are buying. I was surprised to learn that excellent saffron is grown in Ontario. It is called True Saffron.

MASHED POTATOES WITH CARAMELIZED ONIONS AND LEMON

Serves 4 to 6

When Acre-born, Arab-Israeli chef Osama Dalal and Jewish-Israeli chef Yossi Elad were in Toronto to cook together at fundraising events for Shalva, a rehabilitation hospital in Jerusalem, they did a warm-up demo for us at Anthony Rose's restaurant Rose and Sons. Yossi made an herb tabbouleh salad (page 63), and Osama made fantastic mashed potatoes, a dish he learned from his grandmother, who taught him to cook. I've loosely based this recipe on his original version.

2 lb Yukon Gold potatoes, cleaned

1 tsp + 1 tsp kosher salt

2 Tbsp butter + more to taste

2 Tbsp extra virgin olive oil + more to taste

3 onions, thinly sliced

Juice of ½ lemon (about 2 Tbsp) + more to taste

¼ tsp freshly ground black pepper

⅓ cup chopped fresh flat-leaf parsley or cilantro leaves

1. Cut the potatoes in halves or quarters, depending on their size. Cook in boiling water with 1 tsp salt for 20 to 25 minutes, or until tender when pierced with a knife. Drain and remove skins if preferred.

2. Meanwhile, heat the butter and olive oil in a large saucepan over medium heat. Add the onions and cook until caramelized, about 25 to 35 minutes.

3. Mash the potatoes coarsely and stir in half of the onions. Add the lemon juice, 1 tsp salt, and pepper. Stir in the parsley and additional olive oil or butter to taste. Adjust seasoning to taste. Spoon the remaining onions on top.

CRISPY PERSIAN TAHDIG RICE WITH SAFFRON

Serves 6

"Tahdig" refers to the layer of crispy rice that forms at the bottom of the pot the rice is cooked in, which becomes the top when you turn it out. There are many ways to make it, and you may never see the same method used twice. The first couple of times you make it, it may not be perfect—you have to get used to your pot, the heat of your stove, and the timing—but don't worry, it will still be delicious! The goal is to have the tahdig come out in one piece, but sometimes it shatters and other times it has to be scraped from the pot; it happens to everyone, so join the club. Know that the salt added in steps 1 and 2 is to season the rice and most of it is drained off.

2 cups basmati rice, rinsed until the water runs clear

Kosher salt

10 cups + ½ cup boiling water

¼ tsp saffron threads

2 Tbsp + 2 Tbsp butter

2 Tbsp extra virgin olive oil

1. Soak the rice in a large bowl of cold water with 1 Tbsp salt for 1 to 2 hours. Drain. Rinse a few more times and drain again.

2. Bring 10 cups of water to a boil in a large saucepan. Add 1 Tbsp salt and the rice. Cook for 5 to 6 minutes, or until almost tender. Drain well. Rinse with cold water.

3. Meanwhile, place the saffron in a glass measuring cup or small bowl and crush with the back of a spoon. Add the ½ cup of boiling water and 1 tsp salt, and let the saffron infuse for 5 minutes, or until using. Add 2 Tbsp butter, stir to melt, and set aside.

4. To make the tahdig, you'll need a deep nonstick skillet or pot, about 9 or 10 inches wide at the bottom, with a tight-fitting lid. Wrap the lid in a clean tea towel, tightly tying the ends around the lid handle so there is no chance of it burning by hanging over the sides (see page 100), then set aside.

5. Heat the olive oil and 2 Tbsp butter in the skillet set over medium-high heat until sizzling and just beginning to brown. Add about 2 cups cooked, drained rice, so that rice covers the bottom of the skillet about ½ inch thick. Pat the rice down to form a base, which will become the tahdig. Cook for 2 to 3 minutes to start browning the base. Add the remaining rice gently to cover but don't mix together. Mound the rice slightly in the middle. Using the handle of a wooden spoon, make about six holes in the rice but not through the tahdig.

continued . . .

6. Place the wrapped lid on the skillet. Reduce the heat to low and steam the rice for 20 minutes. Drizzle the saffron water over the rice and into the holes, and cook for 20 to 30 minutes longer, covered, or until a brown crust forms on the bottom (you can lift up a bit of the crust to peek). If you check after 30 minutes and no crust has formed, increase the heat to medium and cook for 5 more minutes. Cool off the heat for 5 minutes.

7. Loosen the rice around the edges of the skillet, place a large, flat, serving platter over the top, and carefully flip it onto the platter in one swift movement. If the crust hasn't come out with the rice, lift the crust out of the skillet, break it into chunks and place it on top of rice. And smile.

Fish & Vegetarian Mains

ROASTED CAULIFLOWER STEAKS WITH TAHINI AND Z'HUG

Serves 4 to 6

Vegetable steaks have become very popular and can be made with portobello mushroom caps, slices of large eggplants, rounds of butternut squash, sweet potato halves, and even cauliflower. Most of us think of cauliflower cut up into florets or roasted as a whole head. But if you slice a cauliflower top to bottom or crosswise, you end up with cauliflower steaks that look like fantastical trees. These cauliflower steaks can be served as a vegan main course, as a side dish or salad, or in a wrap or pita sandwich. They're delicious warm or at room temperature. Instead of tahini sauce, if the dish does not have to be vegan, you can use labneh or thick yogurt (see page 6).

1 medium cauliflower (about 1½ lb), trimmed at the base but left whole

2 Tbsp + 1 Tbsp extra virgin olive oil

1 Tbsp honey

1 tsp kosher salt

¼ tsp freshly ground black pepper

1½ cups cooked chickpeas (canned or freshly cooked, see page 24)

1 tsp harissa or other hot sauce

Basic Tahini Sauce (page 17)

Z'hug (page 13)

Suggested Toppings

2 Tbsp roasted pine nuts

2 Tbsp roasted pumpkin seeds

2 Tbsp roasted sunflower seeds

1. Preheat the oven to 425°F and line a baking sheet with parchment paper.

2. Carve the cauliflower by standing it up on a cutting board (the base should be trimmed so it can stand). Cut it vertically into ½-inch slices. The middle slices will be whole, others will be chunky, and the edges may crumble a bit, but don't worry, they all taste great once roasted. Arrange the slices and any broken pieces in a single layer on the lined baking sheet and drizzle with 2 Tbsp olive oil and the honey. Sprinkle with the salt and pepper. Roast for 20 minutes without flipping.

3. Combine the chickpeas with 1 Tbsp olive oil and harissa. Sprinkle over the cauliflower and continue roasting for 10 to 15 minutes, or until the cauliflower has browned nicely and is tender.

4. While cauliflower is roasting, making the tahini sauce and z'hug.

5. Arrange the cauliflower steaks and pieces, and chickpeas in a shallow serving dish. Drizzle liberally with the tahini sauce and as much z'hug as you wish. Sprinkle with the pine nuts and seeds, if using.

MOROCCAN-INSPIRED TAGINE WITH ROASTED VEGETABLES

Serves 4 to 6

I love this tomato sauce and the versatility of this recipe. I have been making versions of it for years, ever since first tasting something like it at a Moroccan restaurant in Jerusalem. The word "tagine" refers to both a specific cooking vessel from North Africa and a slow-cooked braised recipe, but don't feel you need a tagine (pot) to make a dish called a tagine. While I also serve this tomato sauce with chicken thighs or fish, typically there are specific tagine recipes for each of those foods. When a private class at my cooking school requested a vegetarian main course, I adapted this recipe and it turned out to be a fantastic vegetarian option. You can vary the vegetables to suit your taste.

Roasted Vegetables

2½ lb vegetables (all or a combination of butternut squash, carrots, parsnips, baby potatoes, fennel, cauliflower, shallots, or mushrooms), cut into 1½- to 2-inch chunks

3 Tbsp extra virgin olive oil

1 Tbsp honey or maple syrup

1 tsp smoked paprika

1 tsp kosher salt

1 tsp harissa or other hot sauce

1. For the roasted vegetables, preheat the oven to 425°F and line a large baking sheet with parchment paper. Place the vegetables on the lined baking sheet and drizzle with olive oil, honey, paprika, salt, and harissa. Toss well. Spread the vegetables in a single layer on the baking sheet, cut side down, and roast for 25 to 30 minutes, or until browned, turning once if browning too much on the bottom.

2. For the sauce, heat 2 Tbsp olive oil in a large, deep skillet set over medium heat. Add the onions and garlic and cook gently for 5 to 10 minutes, or until translucent but not browned. Add the cumin, cinnamon, and harissa and cook for 30 seconds, then reduce the heat to medium-low. Add the tomato paste and preserved lemon peel and cook for about 1 minute, stirring continuously.

3. Add the tomatoes, crushing them up with a wooden spoon, and bring to a boil. Cook gently for 10 to 15 minutes, uncovered, or until reduced and thickened.

4. Add the honey and then the chickpeas. Cook for 5 minutes and season well to taste.

5. Add the roasted vegetables and gently stir until coated well with the tomato sauce. Place a piece of parchment paper directly on the surface of the vegetable mixture. Cook over low heat for 15 to 20 minutes, or until the sauce and vegetables are married.

6. Serve with charmoula or tahini sauce and cilantro, if using.

Sauce

2 Tbsp extra virgin olive oil

1 large onion, coarsely chopped

2 garlic cloves, chopped

1 tsp ground cumin (preferably toasted)

¼ tsp cinnamon

1 to 2 tsp harissa or other hot sauce (depending on your heat tolerance)

2 Tbsp tomato paste

1 Tbsp finely chopped preserved lemon peel or grated fresh lemon peel

One 28 oz/796 mL can plum tomatoes

1 Tbsp honey

1 to 2 cups cooked chickpeas (canned or freshly cooked, see page 24)

Kosher salt

Suggested Toppings

Charmoula (page 15) **or Basic Tahini Sauce** (page 17)

Fresh cilantro leaves

Variations

VEGETABLE STEAKS: For the most elegant and flavorful version of this vegetable tagine, instead of cutting the vegetables into chunks, cut them into steaks and roast them following the instructions in the recipe for roasted cauliflower steaks on page 105 (step 2), serving the tomato sauce spooned overtop. However, if you are short on time, just add the vegetables raw in step 5 and cook them in the sauce for 20 to 25 minutes, or until tender.

CHICKEN TAGINE: Coat 2 to 3 lb chicken pieces (I like bone-in, skin-on thighs) with the vegetable seasonings. Cook right away or refrigerate up to overnight. Brown the chicken skin side down in a deep, heavy-bottomed, large skillet. Remove and reserve. Make the tomato sauce in the same pan and re-add the chicken at the end of step 4. Cook for 35 to 45 minutes, covered, or until the chicken is completely cooked and tender, then continue with the recipe.

FISH TAGINE: This is Anna's favorite version. Instead of using vegetables, generously season 4 to 6 portion-sized pieces of thick fish fillets (such as halibut, cod, or salmon) with salt and pepper. Make the tomato sauce and add the seasoned fish fillets to the sauce in a single layer at the end of step 4. Spoon some of the sauce on top and cook, covered, for 8 to 10 minutes or just until the fish is cooked through. Anna also loves to add shrimp and scallops, putting them in a few minutes after the fish, as they take less time to cook.

KOSHARY

Serves 6

Koshary is Egypt's unofficial national dish and one of the best vegan recipes around. Considered a street food, it is assembled in many layers, each of which is cooked separately. Here's my home version—I saved us a few steps and a few pots to clean. I recommend using the small black or green lentils, as they will keep their shape. Traditionally, the tomato sauce is spicy, but if you have a husband like mine, go easy on the heat and serve with hot sauce at the table.

Onions, Rice, and Lentils

⅓ cup **extra virgin olive oil** + more as needed

4 onions, thinly sliced

2 garlic cloves, finely chopped

¼ tsp **ground allspice**

¼ tsp **ground coriander seeds**

¼ tsp **ground cumin**

¼ tsp **ground turmeric**

½ cup **small black or green lentils,** picked through for stones and rinsed

1 cup basmati rice, rinsed until the water runs clear

2 cups cooked chickpeas (canned or freshly cooked, see page 24)

2½ cups **water**

1½ tsp **kosher salt** + more to taste

⅛ tsp **freshly ground black pepper** + more to taste

1. For the onions, rice, and lentils, heat ⅓ cup olive oil in a deep skillet or Dutch oven over medium-low heat. Add the onions and cook slowly. As the onions start to brown, remove and reserve about ¼ cup. Continue cooking the remaining onions for about 20 to 30 minutes, or until deeply browned but not burnt. Lift the onions out of the oil using a slotted spoon and spread on paper towel to drain and crisp up. Return the pan to the heat with any oil remaining in it. If necessary, add a few tablespoons of oil to the pan to make at least 3 Tbsp, and heat over medium heat.

2. Add the garlic, allspice, coriander, cumin, and turmeric. Cook, stirring, for about 30 seconds, then add the reserved ¼ cup onions, lentils, and rice. Cook, stirring, for about 1 to 2 minutes, then stir in the chickpeas. Add the water, salt, and pepper. Bring to a boil, then reduce the heat to simmer. Cover and cook very gently for 20 to 25 minutes, or until the rice and lentils are tender and liquid is absorbed. Stir in salt and pepper to taste. Keep covered until ready to serve.

3. Meanwhile, prepare the tomato sauce. Heat olive oil in a deep skillet or wide saucepan over medium-low heat. Add the garlic and cook gently for about 2 minutes without browning. Add the tomato paste, harissa, and paprika, and cook gently for 1 more minute. Add the tomatoes and cook over medium heat for about 10 minutes, crushing the tomatoes when they burst. If at any time the pan seems dry, add 2 Tbsp water or more to make sure the mixture doesn't burn. Season to taste with salt and pepper and more harissa if desired.

Tomato Sauce

2 Tbsp extra virgin olive oil

3 garlic cloves, finely chopped

1 Tbsp tomato paste

1 tsp harissa or other hot sauce + more to taste

½ tsp smoked paprika

4 cups cherry tomatoes or one 28 oz/796 mL can plum tomatoes

Kosher salt and freshly ground black pepper

Pasta

½ lb penne or rotini (or a combination)

Extra virgin olive oil

Kosher salt

Toppings

Lemon suprèmes or thin slices (see note)

Fresh cilantro leaves

4. Just before serving, cook the pasta in a large pot of boiling salted water. Drain. If you're cooking this ahead, rinse the pasta to avoid sticking. Drain well and season with a few tablespoons of olive oil and salt to taste.

5. Arrange the pasta on a big platter, spoon the rice mixture on top and the tomato sauce over the rice, and top with the reserved crispy onions, lemon suprèmes, and cilantro. Toss and serve.

NOTE: Little pieces of lemon add a bright taste to this delicious dish. To make suprèmes (the cheffy word to describe when the membrane of a citrus segment is removed), cut the top and bottom off a lemon (or other citrus fruit) and place the lemon standing up on a cutting board. Cut away the peel and pith with a sharp knife, starting at the top and working down to expose the sections. Cut out the suprèmes (sometimes called fillets) from between the membranes. Alternately, you can just use lemon segments or very thin slices of lemon.

NOVA SCOTIA HODGEPODGE

Serves 6 to 8

This traditional dish—a patchwork of vegetables—is much loved in Nova Scotia. I discovered it when visiting friends in Port Medway (see Port Medway Shellfish Stew on page 125). This recipe varies from region to region, season to season, and family to family, as all of these determine which vegetables are used and how they are cooked. Some people serve it as a main course, as I do, whereas others serve it as a side dish. And sometimes it's served with more liquid, like a soup. In some recipes the vegetables are added all together, but I like to add them according to the amount of cooking time they need. This is wonderful over roasted or grilled fish, making it fancier!

1 lb baby potatoes, scrubbed and halved if large

1 tsp kosher salt + more to taste

1 lb carrots, scrubbed or peeled and sliced on the diagonal

1 small fennel bulb, trimmed, halved and cut into wedges through the core

1 leek, white and light green part only, sliced into ¾-inch rounds and cleaned (see note)

½ lb green or yellow beans (or a combination), trimmed

½ lb broccoli, cut into 1-inch florets

2 cups cherry tomatoes

2 Tbsp butter

1 Tbsp fresh lemon juice

1 cup fresh or frozen peas

½ cup whipping cream

Freshly ground black pepper

1 Tbsp chopped fresh dill or tarragon leaves

Handful of fresh chives or 2 green onions cut into 2-inch lengths

1. Bring 4 cups of water to a boil in a large, deep skillet or saucepan. Add the potatoes and salt. Reduce the heat to medium. Cover and cook for 10 minutes.

2. Add the carrots, cover, and cook for 5 minutes. Add the fennel and leeks, cover, and cook for 3 minutes. Add the beans and broccoli, cover, and cook for 5 minutes. If the water in the pan evaporates while the vegetables are cooking, add more so that there is always about 1 cup or 1 inch of water in the pan. Add the cherry tomatoes and cook, uncovered, until most of the liquid has evaporated, about 3 minutes. If there is a lot of liquid left in the pan, remove it for later use as vegetable broth (it freezes well); by the end of the cooking time, there should only be a few tablespoons left in the pan.

3. Add the butter and lemon juice. Cook, uncovered, for 1 to 2 minutes, or until the butter melts. Add the peas and cream, and bring to a boil. Season with salt and pepper to taste. Sprinkle with dill and chives before serving.

A NOTE ON CLEANING LEEKS: Leeks often have a lot of sand between their layers. One of the many techniques Jacques Pépin shared with us when he taught at my cooking school, one that I still use today, is how to clean a leek. I think of him every time I do it. To start, cut off the darkest green leaves at the top (rinse them and save for broth). Slice the remaining leek as required by the recipe. Place in a large bowl of cold water. Swish the leeks around in the water to release the dirt. Let rest for a few minutes so that the dirt settles at the bottom of the bowl. The cleaned leeks will float to the top. Lift out the leeks, leaving the dirty water behind.

PASTA WITH OVEN-ROASTED TOMATO SAUCE

Serves 3 to 4

This recipe that I now make all the time happened by accident. One weekend, Ray, Anna, and I were on our way to my brother-in-law Wayne's cottage, and a good friend who was already there, Shelly Cohen, was making spaghetti for dinner. Shelly said it was his version of my recipe, which was my version of a Giuliano Bugialli recipe (that's how recipes get around!). I had always baked the tomatoes for about 30 minutes as per Giuliano, but Shelly cooks them longer. That night, because we were late arriving, they had been in the oven for even longer, and all the tomato juices had evaporated, leaving the tomatoes cooked down in the olive oil. The concentrated flavor was outstanding. When we added the cooked pasta to the tomatoes, I added some of the pasta cooking liquid to moisten the sauce and make it creamy. Shelly and I made a great team: I learned to cook down the tomatoes, and he loved the trick of adding pasta cooking liquid to the sauce (it's actually an old Italian trick that I am happy is catching on).

3 lb Roma or plum tomatoes, sliced about ½ inch thick

1½ oz anchovies, finely chopped

6 garlic cloves, peeled

¼ to ½ tsp chili flakes, depending on your heat tolerance

Kosher salt

½ cup extra virgin olive oil + more for serving

1 lb pasta (such as spaghetti, penne, or rigatoni)

¼ cup fresh flat-leaf parsley leaves

NOTE: If you or the people you are serving hate anchovies, use them anyway. They melt down, add amazing flavor, and no one knows they are there! (Of course, leaving them out because of allergies is a different thing and it will still taste amazing.)

1. Preheat the oven to 400°F.

2. Place the tomatoes in a large, deep, heavy-bottomed skillet or shallow Dutch oven that can be used on the stovetop and in the oven. Add the anchovies, garlic (halved if large), chili flakes, and 1 tsp salt, and drizzle everything with the olive oil. Roast uncovered for about 1 hour, or until almost all the liquid released from the tomatoes has evaporated and the tomatoes, anchovies, and garlic are melted into the olive oil. Stir every 15 minutes, and after 45 minutes stir more often, to make sure the tomatoes aren't burning—each oven and pan is a bit different. (You can make this ahead.)

3. Meanwhile, bring a large pot of water to a boil. When the tomatoes are ready, add 1 Tbsp salt to the boiling water, add the spaghetti, and stir. Cook the spaghetti until just tender (the best way to tell is by tasting it).

4. Transfer the pan of tomatoes to the stovetop and set over medium heat. When the pasta is just tender, lift it out of the water with tongs or a spider strainer, and transfer directly into the tomatoes, reserving 1 cup of the pasta cooking liquid. Stir the pasta and tomato sauce together in the pan and add about ½ cup of the reserved liquid. Cook gently and stir until the pasta and tomatoes come together in a creamy sauce from the starchy cooking liquid. Add more liquid if necessary, a little at a time or a few more tablespoons of olive oil to taste.

5. Season to taste and top with parsley.

SPAGHETTI WITH SHRIMP, GARLIC, AND OLIVE OIL

Serves 3 to 4

I learned so much about Italian cooking from Marcella Hazan. When she first started teaching cooking in Bologna in the late '70s, I took classes with her there. We followed her around the food markets, eating mascarpone out of her hand and tasting balsamic vinegar that couldn't be found in Toronto at the time. Some of the balsamic we tasted was 150 years old. What were considered the "cheaper" versions were still 30 years old and quite expensive. (At that time, balsamic vinegar was just starting to be commercially produced.) Marcella told us that balsamic was originally used for medicinal purposes only, and helped ease the pain of childbirth. (I remember thinking about that when I was giving birth to Mark a few years later, but went for the epidural instead.) Marcella used extra virgin olive oil with abandon, and it was the beginning of my dependency on that product for both its flavor and its health benefits—still unrivaled by any other oil, if you ask me. Marcella's recipes seemed simple, but sometimes the easiest recipes using wonderful ingredients turn out best. Take this one, for example.

2 Tbsp + 6 Tbsp extra virgin olive oil + more as needed

½ cup fresh homemade or panko breadcrumbs

3 garlic cloves, finely chopped

¼ tsp chili flakes

1 lb shrimp, shells removed and deveined, diced into ½-inch pieces

2 Tbsp + 2 Tbsp chopped fresh flat-leaf parsley

Kosher salt

¾ lb spaghetti

Freshly ground black pepper, to taste

1. Place 2 Tbsp olive oil in a large, deep skillet set over medium-high heat. Add the breadcrumbs and cook, stirring continuously for a few minutes, or until lightly browned. Remove the breadcrumbs to a bowl and wipe out the pan with paper towel.

2. Add 6 Tbsp olive oil to the pan, along with the garlic and chili flakes. Cook very gently over medium-low heat for a few minutes, or until the garlic is fragrant and tender but not browned. Add the shrimp, 2 Tbsp parsley, and 1 tsp salt. Cook for about 1 minute, just until the shrimp are opaque. Remove from the heat. (You can make this ahead.)

3. Just before serving, bring a large pot of water to a boil. Add 1 Tbsp salt and the spaghetti and stir. Cook until just tender (the best way to tell this is by tasting it).

4. Lift the spaghetti out of the cooking liquid using tongs or a spider strainer, and add to the shrimp in the pan, reserving 1 cup of the pasta cooking liquid. Toss the spaghetti and shrimp together well and cook over low heat until any liquid is absorbed. If the pasta seems at all dry, add some of the reserved cooking liquid, about ¼ cup at a time, and some extra olive oil. Add breadcrumbs, remaining 2 Tbsp parsley, and salt and pepper to taste.

LINGUINI WITH WHITE CLAM SAUCE

Serves 3 to 4

This is another one of those recipes that is so fast and easy, it's hard to believe how incredible it tastes. Not only that, but it has the power to transport you to your favorite little Italian restaurant—or maybe even to Italy. You can also use clams out of the shell (ask a fishmonger to do that). If you don't want to use pancetta or bacon, omit it and add 2 more tablespoons of extra virgin olive oil.

2 lb littleneck clams or other small clams (about 48 to 60)

3 Tbsp extra virgin olive oil

4 oz pancetta or bacon, cut into ½-inch pieces

3 garlic cloves, finely chopped

¼ tsp chili flakes

1 cup dry white wine or broth

1 Tbsp Kosher salt + more to taste

¾ lb linguine or spaghetti

½ cup chopped fresh flat-leaf parsley

2 Tbsp butter or additional olive oil

Freshly ground black pepper

TOMATO VARIATION:
Add 2 Tbsp tomato paste to the garlic and chili flakes after they have cooked for about 30 seconds. Cook for another 30 seconds. Add the wine and once it has reduced, add 2 cups cherry tomatoes. Cook for 4 to 5 minutes, or until the tomatoes start to split, then add the clams. Continue as per the recipe.

1. Look through the clams and discard any that are chipped or broken, any that do not open or close when tapped, along with clams that seem unnaturally heavy, as they could be filled with sand. Scrub (if gritty) and soak in clean water for about 30 minutes.

2. Heat the olive oil in a large, deep skillet set over medium heat. Add the pancetta, and cook for 5 minutes or until lightly browned and crisp. Remove from the pan, drain on paper towel, and set aside. Remove all but 2 or 3 Tbsp of oil from the pan.

3. Add the garlic and chili flakes to the pan and cook gently for 2 to 3 minutes, or until very fragrant but not browned. If the pan is too hot, add about ¼ cup water and reduce the heat. When the garlic is tender, pour in the wine and bring to a boil. Cook until the wine is reduced by about half, 5 to 8 minutes.

4. Meanwhile, bring a large pot of water to a boil. Add 1 Tbsp salt. Add the pasta and cook for 10 to 12 minutes, or until almost tender.

5. While the pasta boils, add the clams to the pan with the garlic mixture. Stir, then cover. Cook over medium-high heat for 5 to 7 minutes or just until most of the clams have opened. Discard any clams that haven't opened.

6. Once the pasta and the clams are cooked, lift the pasta from the cooking liquid, using tongs (or drain), reserving 1 cup of the pasta cooking liquid. Add the pasta to the clams. Add ½ cup reserved pasta cooking liquid. The pasta liquid will make your sauce creamy. Cook for a few minutes, until the pasta is the perfect texture and well coated with sauce. If the pasta seems dry, add more pasta cooking liquid.

7. Add the reserved pancetta, half of the parsley, and the butter to the pasta, and stir to combine. Season with salt and pepper to taste. Sprinkle with the remaining parsley.

LOBSTER RISOTTO

Serves 4 to 6

In our house, for special dinners, lobster risotto can't be beat. Years ago, we started what has become a tradition of having New Year's Eve dinner together as a family, and lobster risotto has become part of it. You can buy the lobsters and cook them yourself, but the easiest way to make this dish is to buy the lobsters pre-cooked at your fish store (ask that they be a bit under-cooked, as you'll be cooking them more). The shop will even remove the meat for you, if you ask. For extra flavor, ask for the shells too and make your own lobster broth, or cook the shells for 30 minutes in chicken or vegetable broth, then strain and use in the risotto. Risotto gets its creaminess from the Italian short-grain rice rubbing together while cooking and the slow addition of liquid while stirring. Your guests should be at your house before starting the risotto because it must be served as soon as it is ready. If you are serving this as a first course, make a main course that is ready to serve so you won't have to scramble at the last minute.

3 Tbsp extra virgin olive oil

2 shallots, chopped

2 garlic cloves, finely chopped

2 cups Italian short-grain rice (such as arborio, carnaroli, or vialone nano)

Kosher salt and freshly ground black pepper

½ cup dry white wine

6 to 8 cups lobster, chicken, or vegetable broth, hot

2 lobsters (at least 1 lb each), cooked and meat removed from shells and cut into 1- to 2-inch chunks

¼ cup butter

1 Tbsp truffle oil, optional

1 cup fresh or frozen peas

2 Tbsp chopped fresh flat-leaf parsley leaves, green onions, or chives

1. Heat the olive oil in a deep skillet or large Dutch oven set over medium heat. Add the shallots and garlic, and cook gently for about 5 minutes, or until tender and fragrant but not browned.

2. Add the rice and stir to coat well with the oil. Cook gently for a few minutes but do not brown. Add a pinch each of salt and pepper.

3. Add the wine and cook, stirring constantly, until the liquid evaporates. Start adding the hot broth, ½ cup to ¾ cup at a time, stirring almost constantly and not adding another batch of liquid until the pan is almost dry. Once you start adding liquid, it should take 15 to 20 minutes for the rice to become tender. Don't worry if you don't use all the liquid (freeze it for a later use). If you need more liquid and you've used all the broth, use boiling water.

4. When the rice is almost tender, stir in the lobster, and cook until the lobster is heated through and the rice is perfect. Stir in the butter, truffle oil, if using, and salt and pepper to taste. Add the peas and cook for about 2 minutes. Sprinkle with parsley, and serve immediately from the pan.

NOTE: Instead of lobster, you can use 2 lb cooked or uncooked shelled and deveined shrimp with the tails left on. The raw shrimp will take only a few extra minutes to cook. And, of course, you could also make this with three lobsters instead of two.

JEWELED ROASTED SALMON WITH HERBS

Serves 6 to 8

I was trying to plan something to cook for one of my first virtual classes when I stumbled upon a bright, colorful photo of salmon covered in "jewels," on Instagram @laineskitchen and I was inspired. The jewels I am using here are pomegranate seeds, orange suprèmes (see note on page 109), rose petals, and pistachios. Other fresh fruit such as cherries, grapes, apricots, or berries can be used along with dried cherries, and apricots (especially the sour ones). This dish is always a hit, whether I serve it hot with rice or at room temperature with salad. I like to cook a large piece of salmon whole because the fish stays juicier, but you can also make this using individual fillets, and you can substitute any thick fish, like halibut or cod, for the salmon.

2½ lb boneless, skinless salmon fillet, thick center cut if possible

3 Tbsp extra virgin olive oil

1 Tbsp honey

1 tsp kosher salt

Freshly ground black pepper

1 Tbsp grated lemon or lime peel

Sprigs of fresh thyme

⅔ cup Tahini Yogurt (page 18)

Jewel Topping

1 cup combination of coarsely chopped fresh cilantro, flat-leaf parsley, dill, and mint + whole sprigs

1 tsp kosher salt

Freshly ground black pepper

1 Tbsp grated orange peel

⅓ cup pomegranate seeds

¼ cup chopped pistachios or coarsely chopped roasted almonds (or a combination)

3 oranges peeled and cut into suprèmes (see note on page 109)

2 Tbsp extra virgin olive oil

1 tsp dried rose petals, optional

1. Place the salmon on a baking sheet lined with parchment paper. Combine the olive oil with the honey, salt, pepper to taste, and lemon peel. Rub into the salmon and let it rest at room temperature for up to 30 minutes, or longer in the refrigerator. Top with the sprigs of fresh thyme once it has marinated.

2. Preheat the oven to 425°F. Roast the salmon for 10 to 15 minutes, or until just cooked when pressed in the center with the back of a spoon or until an instant-read thermometer registers 140°F to 145°F when inserted into the thickest part. Remove the sprigs of fresh thyme and discard.

3. Coat the salmon with the yogurt tahini sauce.

4. For the jewel topping, sprinkle with the chopped fresh herbs, salt, pepper, and orange peel. Then top with the pomegranate seeds, nuts, orange suprèmes, and sprigs of fresh herbs. Drizzle with olive oil and sprinkle with dried rose petals, if using.

NOTE: If barbecuing the salmon, leave the skin on and coat both sides of the whole piece with a few tablespoons of mayonnaise to help prevent sticking.

ROASTED ARCTIC CHAR WITH LEMON AND HERBS

Serves 4 to 6

I like to say fish is the original fast food. (Not because it's addictive like French fries but because it cooks so fast!) I like to cook it in bigger pieces, as it looks more impressive that way and also stays juicier, but if you'd like to cook it in individual servings, that's completely fine too, and it's easier to serve. Arctic char is milder than salmon, but both work well in this recipe. Thick, white-fleshed fish like halibut or cod would work well too. This is delicious at room temperature, so it's a good choice for a lunch salad or even a picnic. Leftovers can be made into salads or fish cakes (page 163).

1½ to 2 lb boneless, skinless Arctic char or salmon, whole or in portioned pieces

2 Tbsp + 2 Tbsp extra virgin olive oil

Grated peel of ½ lemon

1 tsp kosher salt + more for tossing

⅛ tsp freshly ground black pepper

3 sprigs fresh rosemary + more to serve

3 sprigs fresh thyme + more to serve

1 lemon, sliced

2 cups cherry tomatoes

2 cups broccoli florets, cut into 1-inch pieces

1. Preheat the oven to 425°F and line a baking sheet with parchment paper.

2. Arrange the fish on the lined baking sheet with the skin side (or what was the skin side) down. Drizzle with 2 Tbsp olive oil and sprinkle with lemon peel, salt, and pepper. Turn the fish over a few times to coat well. Scatter the rosemary and thyme sprigs over the fish and arrange the lemon slices beside, around, or on top of it. Toss the cherry tomatoes and broccoli florets with 2 Tbsp olive oil and some salt. Arrange them around the fish.

3. Depending on the thickness of the fish, cook for 10 to 12 minutes or longer, or until the fish is just cooked through. Press the thickest part of the fish with the back of a spoon; if it flakes, it's cooked. Arctic char (usually about ¾ inch thick) will cook faster than salmon (usually about 1 inch thick), but both will cook quickly. The tomatoes and broccoli should be just cooked.

4. Replace the now dried sprigs of herbs with fresh sprigs. To serve, arrange the roasted lemon slices on top of the fish and the vegetables around.

FISH KEBABS WITH CHRAIME

Serves 6 to 8

Chraime is a spicy North African tomato sauce usually cooked with fish. In Israel, this dish is often served for Friday night dinner, and as an appetizer during the Jewish holidays. When I first tasted it at the King David Hotel in Jerusalem in 2005, on the very first culinary tour I led with Rabbi Elyse Goldstein and our guide, Judy Stacey Goldman, I loved it so much that I knew I wouldn't be making gefilte fish often anymore. Since I started making chraime after that trip, my version has continuously evolved and, for one thing, is much less spicy than that first one I tasted. Also, I started using cherry tomatoes but you can substitute canned tomatoes (preferably San Marzano), or 3 lb chopped fresh tomatoes when tomatoes are local, in season, and delicious. Instead of the Mediterranean fish typically used, I started using fish like halibut and Arctic char, but everything came together when I started making the dish with fish kebabs. In Israel, a kebab is usually a patty made with ground meat or fish and isn't necessarily something grilled on a skewer. This recipe, especially now that I use chopped fish, is even more appropriate as an alternative for gefilte fish. (No offense to gefilte fish lovers—I know there are a few of you out there.)

Fish Kebabs

1 large or 2 small shallots, or 1 small onion, chopped

2 Tbsp + 2 Tbsp extra virgin olive oil

2 lb white-fleshed fish (like cod, haddock, or halibut)

¾ cup chopped fresh dill, cilantro, or flat-leaf parsley (or a combination)

1 egg, lightly beaten

1½ tsp kosher salt

¼ tsp ground cardamom

¼ tsp ground coriander seeds

¼ tsp ground cumin

¼ tsp sweet paprika

¼ tsp ground sumac

¼ tsp ground turmeric

⅛ tsp freshly ground black pepper

1. For the fish kebabs, in a skillet set over medium heat, cook the shallots in 2 Tbsp olive oil for 5 to 10 minutes, or until tender but not browned. Set aside to cool.

2. Chop the fish with a big, sharp knife until some smallish pieces remain and some are finely minced. If you are doing this in a food processor, cut the fish into about 1-inch pieces and then pulse until the fish resembles hand-chopped fish—try not to overprocess it. Transfer the fish to a bowl, then add the cooled shallots, herbs, egg, salt, cardamom, cumin, sweet paprika, sumac, turmeric, and pepper. Mix well. Shape the mixture into 16 to 20 small patties, about 2 oz each.

3. Add 2 Tbsp olive oil to a large, deep, heavy-bottomed skillet set over medium-high heat. Cook the patties for 1 to 2 minutes per side, or until browned—you will probably have to do this in batches. Don't worry about cooking them through, as they will finish cooking in the sauce. Set the browned patties aside.

continued . . .

Sauce

3 Tbsp extra virgin olive oil

2 small onions, thinly sliced

3 garlic cloves, finely chopped

1 jalapeño, halved, seeded, and chopped

1 tsp ground cumin

1 tsp sweet paprika

1 tsp ground turmeric

½ tsp smoked paprika

½ tsp kosher salt

1 Tbsp tomato paste

1 tsp to 1 Tbsp harissa, depending on your heat tolerance (see page 5)

6 cups cherry tomatoes

¼ cup water + more as needed

¼ cup + ¼ cup coarsely chopped fresh cilantro

1 long red chili, thinly sliced into rounds

1 jalapeño, thinly sliced into rounds

For Serving (optional)

Basic Tahini sauce (page 17)

Z'hug (page 13)

Rice pilaf (page 95)**, couscous, mashed potatoes, or freekeh**

4. For the sauce, heat the olive oil (in the same pan that you used to brown the fish) over medium heat (just make sure to wipe out any burned bits). Add the onions and cook for 4 to 6 minutes, or just until tender and lightly browned. Add the garlic, chopped jalapeño, cumin, sweet paprika, turmeric, smoked paprika, and salt. Cook for about 1 minute. Add the tomato paste and harissa. Cook for another minute. (At any point if the pan seems dry, add a few tablespoons of water.) Add the tomatoes and water. Bring to a boil (increase the heat if necessary), then cook on medium heat until the tomatoes split and collapse. Add ¼ cup cilantro. Let the tomatoes cook for a few minutes into a sauce while retaining a little of their shape. Season well.

5. Add the patties to the tomato sauce and gently cook for 5 to 8 minutes, covered, or until just cooked through. Sprinkle with the remaining cilantro and chilies, and serve with tahini sauce, and z'hug, if using.

FISH FILLET ALTERNATIVE: To make this recipe with fish fillets instead, skip steps 1 and 2 and add 2 lb boneless, skinless fish fillets, seasoned with salt and pepper, to the sauce in a single layer in step 3. Cook just until the fish is cooked through, 7 to 10 minutes, depending on the thickness. When I am making this for more than 6 people, and the fish will not fit in the pan in a single layer, I usually make the sauce first and roast the fish separately on a large baking sheet, then spoon the sauce over the roasted fish to serve.

NUT- AND SEED-CRUSTED FISH WITH BROWN BUTTER

Serves 4 to 6

I have always said that when someone doesn't like a certain food, they just haven't had it in the way that's right for them yet. Case in point: I had forgotten about this wonderful recipe that I adapted from a dish I tasted at Jean-Georges Vongerichten's restaurant in Vancouver, but Anna reminded me of it—and that when our close friend, Rob Dittmer, who had always disliked fish, tasted it, he was converted. Brown butter (page 88), as you now know, is a secret sauce. Its unique flavor of roasted nuts is incredibly delicious and makes everything taste fancy. For a simpler alternative, I will sometimes just drizzle the cooked fish with the brown butter and sprinkle toasted hazelnuts or ½ cup dukkah (page 11) overtop. But the recipe as written adds another layer of flavor that is very special.

¼ cup roasted almonds

¼ cup roasted hazelnuts

2 Tbsp roasted sunflower seeds

1 tsp ground coriander seeds (see note)

1 tsp kosher salt

¼ tsp freshly ground black pepper

2 egg whites

1½ to 2 lb boneless, skinless thick fish fillets (such as cod, halibut, salmon, or Arctic char), about ¾ inch thick, cut into 4 to 6 pieces

¼ cup butter

Grated peel of ½ lemon

2 Tbsp chopped fresh flat-leaf parsley or cilantro, optional

NOTE: In this recipe, because the nuts and seeds are in a crust that will be roasted, it isn't entirely necessary for the nuts to be roasted if they aren't already or if you want to save time.

1. Preheat the oven to 425°F and line a baking sheet with parchment paper.

2. Chop or gently crush the almonds, hazelnuts, and sunflower seeds (I use a meat pounder to crush the nuts, but you could use the bottom of a heavy-bottomed skillet or side of a heavy knife). Combine with the ground coriander, salt, and pepper. Spread out in a wide, shallow bowl.

3. Place the egg whites in another wide, shallow bowl, and beat lightly with a fork to loosen.

4. Pat the fish dry with paper towel. Dip the top side of the fish in the egg white, then press into the nut mixture. Place on the lined baking sheet, crusted side up. (You can do this a few hours ahead.) Keep the fish refrigerated until 30 minutes before roasting. If the fish is cold, it may just take an additional 1 or 2 minutes in the oven.

5. Roast in the preheated oven for 10 to 14 minutes, or until the fish just separates when the thickest part is gently pressed with the back of a spoon (that's your piece). The cooking time will depend on your oven, the thickness and type of fish, and the temperature of the fish going into the oven.

continued . . .

6. While the fish cooks, prepare the brown butter. Place the butter in a small, heavy-bottomed pan and melt over medium-low heat. The butter will sizzle a bit, and when it stops, it will start to brown and smell like roasted nuts. Keep stirring or swirling the pan, and remove from the heat when the butter is medium brown. Be careful—it can burn easily. Stir in the grated lemon peel.

7. To serve, spoon about 1 Tbsp brown butter over each piece of fish and sprinkle with herbs, if using.

NOTE: When Madhur Jaffrey taught at my school, she always toasted and ground her spices *just* before using. I have to admit (please don't tell Madhur) that I usually toast and then grind a batch each of coriander seeds and cumin seeds and then freeze them, to have on hand. I also usually have roasted almonds, hazelnuts, pecans, and walnuts in the freezer, ready for cooking, baking, or as a snack.

PORT MEDWAY SHELLFISH STEW

Serves 6 to 8

My friends Cynthia Wine and Philip Slayton moved to Port Medway, on the south shore of Nova Scotia, about 20 years ago. To raise money to restore the town's historic Meeting House, they started the Port Medway Readers' Festival, which is celebrating its 20th anniversary in 2022. Visiting authors have included Margaret Atwood, Calvin Trillin, Michael Crummey, Ami McKay, and Michael Ondaatje. I was honored to be their first cookbook author, and Cynthia and Philip, authors themselves, were the perfect hosts, showing us the area and introducing us to the community. Cynthia is a wonderful cook and her food, including this recipe, seemed extra delicious when eaten while sitting on the veranda overlooking the ocean. But here at home, even without the ocean view, this stew is amazing. I like to serve roasted garlic aioli with each portion, along with some focaccia croutons browned in olive oil.

¼ tsp saffron threads

¼ cup boiling water

2 Tbsp extra virgin olive oil

1 onion, chopped

1 long mild red chili, halved, seeded, and chopped, or pinch of chili flakes

1 leek, white and light green part only, cleaned and chopped (see note on page 110)

1 bulb fennel, trimmed and chopped (fronds reserved for garnish, if there are any)

2 garlic cloves, finely chopped

2 Tbsp tomato paste

1 cup dry white wine or additional broth

2 cups fish, chicken, or vegetable broth, or water

One 28 oz/796 mL can plum tomatoes (preferably San Marzano), with juices, crushed

1 bay leaf

Kosher salt and freshly ground black pepper

1. Place the saffron in a glass measuring cup or small bowl and crush with the back of a spoon. Add the boiling water and let the saffron infuse for at least 5 minutes, or until using.

2. Heat the olive oil in a wide, deep skillet or Dutch oven over medium heat. Add the onions, chili, leek, fennel, and garlic. Cook gently for 5 to 10 minutes, or until very fragrant and tender. Add the tomato paste and cook for about 1 minute, stirring. Add the wine, bring to a boil, and cook for 5 minutes or until reduced by about half. Add the broth and the saffron water, canned tomatoes, and bay leaf. Bring to a boil, reduce the heat to medium-low, add a pinch each of salt and pepper and cook, stirring often, for about 30 to 35 minutes, or until slightly thickened. Discard the bay leaf and season well to taste.

continued . . .

1½ lb halibut, cod, haddock, or salmon, cut into large chunks

1 lb shrimp, shells removed and deveined

1 lb scallops

1 lb mussels

2 Tbsp chopped fresh flat-leaf parsley, optional

Toppings

Garlic aioli (see sidebar)

Focaccia croutons (see sidebar)

3. Just before serving, add the fish, cover the pan, and cook for 5 minutes. Add the shrimp, scallops, and mussels and cook, covered, for 3 to 5 minutes longer, or until the mussels open (discard any that remain closed) and the fish and shellfish are just cooked.

4. Serve in large bowls sprinkled with parsley or fennel fronds (the tops of the fennel), garlic aioli, and focaccia croutons.

TO MAKE THE ROASTED GARLIC AIOLI: Cut off the top quarter of one head of garlic. Drizzle the cut surface of the bulb with olive oil and wrap in aluminum foil. Bake in a preheated 400°F oven for 45 to 60 minutes, or until the garlic is very soft. Cool. Squeeze the garlic into a bowl and mash with a fork, then stir in ½ cup mayonnaise, 1 Tbsp fresh lemon juice, ¼ tsp smoked paprika, and ½ tsp chipotle puree or Tabasco Chipotle Sauce.

FOR THE FOCACCIA CROUTONS: If you've made the focaccia recipe on page 201, you can use about one-quarter of the finished focaccia to make croutons here or you can use a store-bought focaccia. Break up the focaccia into 1-inch chunks (about 3 cups) and lightly brown in 3 Tbsp extra virgin olive oil, in batches, in a skillet set over medium heat, adding more oil if necessary. Sprinkle with a little flaky sea salt. This will likely give you more than you need so freeze any extra croutons.

Poultry &
Meat Mains

SHEET PAN CHICKEN WITH LEMON AND OLIVES

Serves 6

Sheet pan dinners have become extremely popular and I think they're great. The idea for this recipe came from one of my favorite dishes, Moroccan chicken tagine with lemon and olives. I started making this dish on a baking sheet because my tagine (the cooking pot) only has enough room for 3 or 4 servings but also because I love the way it looks when I serve it right on the sheet pan. I like to make it with chicken legs (thighs, or thighs and drumsticks), which have always been a chef favorite, as they have more flavor than chicken breasts and stay juicy and delicious even if overcooked. If you do use chicken breasts, use bone-in and skin-on to help them stay juicy, and be careful not to overcook them (use an instant-read thermometer and cook to 165°F). Serve with rice, couscous, or freekeh.

3 lb chicken pieces (12 chicken thighs or 6 whole legs)

2 onions, quartered

1 head garlic, halved horizontally

1 bulb fennel, trimmed, halved, and cut into thick wedges

1 lemon, thinly sliced (or 2 if you don't have preserved lemons)

1 cup coarsely chopped fresh cilantro or flat-leaf parsley + more for serving

½ cup large green olives, pitted by gently smashing or tearing apart

¼ cup sliced preserved lemon peel (see page 16)

¼ cup extra virgin olive oil

1 Tbsp honey

1 Tbsp kosher salt

1 tsp ground coriander

1 tsp ground cumin

1 tsp sweet paprika

1 tsp ground turmeric

1. Place the chicken pieces in a large bowl, along with the onions, garlic, fennel, lemons, cilantro, olives, preserved lemon peel, olive oil, honey, salt, coriander, cumin, paprika, and turmeric. Toss well to mix. Marinate in the refrigerator for a few hours if you have time, or cook right away.

2. Preheat the oven to 400°F. Arrange the chicken pieces in a single layer on a baking sheet lined with parchment paper or in a large baking dish or shallow Dutch oven, skin side up. Spoon the fennel-lemon mixture over and around the chicken. Cover with aluminum foil and roast for 20 minutes.

3. Uncover and roast for another 30 minutes. If the chicken hasn't browned yet, increase the oven temperature to 425°F and cook for 10 minutes longer or until the chicken and vegetables are nicely browned.

4. Serve topped with the cooked lemon slices and olives, and the fresh cilantro.

DELICIOUS CHICKEN PATTIES
(DESERVING OF A BETTER NAME)

Serves 4

Anna and I were talking one day and decided I should test a new recipe for chicken burgers. But it was raining out, and cold, and I didn't feel like barbecuing or asking Ray to barbecue. So instead, I cooked them in a skillet on the stove (though they would still be great on the grill!), and rather than toasting buns, I roasted tomatoes for a topping and served the patties as is over mashed potatoes (though you could always put them in a bun). Moral of the story is, I did not make chicken burgers but came up with a really delicious weeknight dinner. Leftovers make great sandwiches or you can reheat and serve with an egg on top for brunch.

2 Tbsp + 2 Tbsp extra virgin olive oil

1 small onion, chopped

1 garlic clove, finely chopped

1 Tbsp tomato paste

1 egg

1 Tbsp grated lemon peel

1½ tsp kosher salt

1 tsp hot sauce (such as harissa, chipotle, or sriracha)

¼ tsp baharat (page 10), optional

½ cup combination of chopped fresh cilantro, dill, and flat-leaf parsley

1 lb ground chicken

½ cup breadcrumbs (preferably panko)

Suggested Toppings

Roasted cherry tomatoes (page 87), **tomato sauce, or salsa**

Charmoula (page 15)

1. Line a baking sheet with plastic wrap.

2. Heat 2 Tbsp olive oil in a small skillet set over medium heat. Add the onions and garlic and cook until tender but not browned, about 5 minutes. Stir in the tomato paste and cook for 1 more minute. Spread the mixture on a plate to cool quickly.

3. In a mixing bowl, mix the egg with the lemon peel, salt, hot sauce, and baharat, if using, then stir in the chopped herbs. Add the cooled onion mixture and chicken and mix to combine. Mix in the breadcrumbs. The mixture will be a little sticky.

4. Shape the chicken mixture into 8 to 10 patties, about ¼ cup each, about ¾ inch thick and 3 inches in diameter. Place in a single layer on the lined baking sheet. If not cooking right away, cover with plastic wrap and refrigerate.

5. To cook, heat 2 Tbsp olive oil in a large skillet on medium-high heat and add the chicken patties in a single layer—you will probably have to do this in batches. Lower the heat to medium if the patties are browning too quickly. Cook for 5 to 7 minutes per side, or until browned and cooked through (cut one open to be sure—that one is yours).

6. Serve with roasted cherry tomatoes (page 87) or any tomato sauce or salsa you have on hand, and/or charmoula (page 15).

NOTE: To stop ground meat mixtures (chicken or fish) from sticking to your hands when shaping patties, meatballs or fish kebabs, try wetting your hands with water, coating them with oil or wearing disposable plastic gloves (I had never done that but during the pandemic I used disposable plastic gloves and it worked so well!).

THREE-CUP CHICKEN

Serves 4

Martin Yan was the first guest to ever teach at my cooking school, before he became the famous television chef he is today. Incredibly, he's hosted his television show, *Yan Can Cook*, for over four decades. He was so kind and so knowledgeable that his three-hour class ran for over five hours, and everyone was glued to their seats the entire time. I've been making various versions of his Three-Cup Chicken ever since. It is a dish that is so delicious and easy, it has become one of my favorite quick dinners. I've been told it gets its name from using 1 cup each of sesame oil, soy sauce, and rice wine, but I have never seen a recipe for it with those proportions. For quick cooking, I make it with boneless, skinless chicken thighs, which are juicier than chicken breasts and do not overcook as easily. But, of course, you can use chicken breasts if you prefer. I also usually add vegetables. Try adding up to 2 cups of diced carrots, squash, or broccoli stems to the chicken when you add the liquid in step 3. You could also add 1 cup of frozen peas about 2 minutes before it's ready.

Sauce

¼ cup mirin

⅓ cup soy sauce

2 Tbsp water

1 Tbsp granulated sugar

1 tsp sriracha

1 Tbsp toasted sesame oil

2 Tbsp vegetable oil or extra virgin olive oil + more as needed

1-inch piece fresh ginger, peeled and thinly sliced

6 large garlic cloves, peeled and halved

6 green onions, cut into 2-inch pieces

1½ lb boneless, skinless chicken thighs, cut into 1- to 2-inch pieces

2 large handfuls of baby spinach

1 cup fresh Thai basil or cilantro (or a combination)

Steamed rice or noodles, for serving

1. In a small bowl, combine the mirin, soy sauce, water, sugar, sriracha, and sesame oil. Set aside.

2. Heat the vegetable oil in a wok or large skillet set over medium-high heat. Add the ginger, garlic, and green onions. Cook, stirring constantly, for 1 minute or until fragrant. Remove from the pan and set aside.

3. Add a little more oil to the pan if necessary and increase the heat to high. When hot, add the chicken pieces to the pan and brown well on all sides. This will probably have to be done in batches.

4. Return all the chicken to the pan, along with the green onion mixture and the reserved sauce. Bring to a boil, reduce the heat, and simmer, uncovered, 10 to 12 minutes, or until the chicken is cooked through and the sauce is thicker but still syrupy enough to spoon over rice. Add the spinach and cook for about 1 minute, or until the spinach is barely wilted. Remove from the heat and stir in the basil. Serve over the steamed rice or noodles.

SICILIAN CHICKEN "SCHNITZEL" WITH LEMON DRESSING

Serves 6 to 8

This is one of my favorite main courses that I have been so excited to share with you. It's loosely based on a dish that Giuliano Bugialli, the famous Italian scholar, cooking teacher, and cookbook author, made when he taught at my school. There are lots of wonderful recipes for schnitzel and many countries claim to have invented it. The technique is usually the same: dip very thin slices of veal, chicken, turkey, or eggplant first into flour to dry them, then into egg to make the breadcrumbs stick, and then into breadcrumbs before frying in oil in a deep skillet (for the ultimate discussion on schnitzel, and for a million other reasons you need to visit the Alps, see Meredith Erickson's incredible travel-guide-meets-cookbook, *Alpine Cooking*). My version is a little different. I wanted to bake the chicken in the oven to avoid frying, which has to be done at the last minute for best results, but the thin slices never browned enough in the oven or became crispy without being overcooked. So I started using thicker pieces of chicken. I bread them as usual, but spoon dressing on them before baking and then halfway through. This way they are always juicy and crisp. I hope you love this recipe as much as we do. It's a great recipe to make up to 1 day ahead. Serve with olive and fennel salad (see page 62).

2½ lb boneless, skinless chicken breasts or thighs (or a combination)

1 tsp + 2 tsp kosher salt

Pinch + ¼ tsp freshly ground black pepper

1 cup all-purpose flour

3 eggs, beaten

2 cups panko breadcrumbs

¼ cup chopped fresh flat-leaf parsley

1 garlic clove, finely chopped

1 Tbsp dried oregano

1. Line a baking sheet with parchment paper. If you're making this ahead (see recipe intro), place a wire rack on another baking sheet and set aside.

2. Pat the chicken dry with paper towel, then pound the meat into even pieces about ½ inch to ¾ inch thick. Season with 1 tsp salt and a pinch of pepper. Arrange separate shallow bowls of flour, eggs, and breadcrumbs. Add the parsley, garlic, oregano, 2 tsp salt, and ¼ tsp pepper to the bowl with the breadcrumbs and mix well. Dip a piece of chicken into the flour, shaking off the excess. Place the chicken in the eggs, letting any excess egg drip back into the bowl before transferring the chicken to the breadcrumbs. Press the chicken firmly into the breadcrumbs on both sides. If you're making ahead, place in a single layer on the prepared rack and repeat the process with the remaining pieces of chicken; cover loosely with plastic wrap and refrigerate up to overnight. If you're cooking the chicken right away, place it directly on the baking sheet lined with parchment paper (no rack needed).

3. For the lemon dressing, combine the garlic with the lemon juice, olive oil, dried oregano, salt, and pepper. If not cooking right away, be sure to whisk the dressing well before spooning onto the chicken.

Lemon Dressing

2 garlic cloves, minced or grated

⅔ **cup fresh lemon juice**

⅔ **cup extra virgin olive oil**

2 tsp dried oregano

1½ tsp kosher salt

⅛ **tsp freshly ground black pepper**

8 sprigs fresh oregano or flat-leaf parsley

8 lemon slices or wedges

4. When you're ready to cook, preheat the oven to 400°F. If you haven't done so already, arrange the chicken on the lined baking sheet in a single layer. Use two baking sheets if necessary. Whisk the dressing well to emulsify it, then spoon about half of it over the chicken just before baking. Bake for 20 minutes. Turn the chicken over and, after whisking the remaining dressing well, spoon it over the chicken. Bake for another 15 to 20 minutes, or until the chicken is browned and crisp.

5. Serve with sprigs of fresh oregano and lemon slices.

ALSATIAN PAN PIZZA

Makes one 10-inch pizza

I first had this pizza-like tart in Berlin at Restaurant Renger-Patzsch. They offered many versions but the one I loved was this one, with goat cheese, crème fraîche, and bacon. Their crust was very thin, but now when I make it, I use this easy pan pizza crust recipe I adapted from Jim Lahey, the baker who made no-knead bread so popular years ago. Honestly, we eat this pizza for dinner, and then eat more instead of having dessert. And you know how much I love dessert.

Crust

2 cups all-purpose flour

1½ tsp instant yeast

1 tsp kosher salt

½ tsp granulated sugar

¾ cup water

2 Tbsp extra virgin olive oil

Toppings

6 oz bacon, cut into 1-inch pieces

3 onions, thinly sliced

6 oz goat cheese, ricotta, or grated cheddar or Swiss

½ cup crème fraîche, thick yogurt, or lightly whipped cream

1 tsp kosher salt

¼ tsp freshly ground black pepper

⅛ tsp freshly ground nutmeg + more to taste

1. For the crust, place the flour in a large bowl with the yeast, salt, and sugar. Whisk to combine. Stir in the water—it should make a sticky but firm dough. Mix or knead for about 30 seconds. (Only add more water if the dough is very dry and hasn't come together.) Cover the bowl and let the dough rise for 2 hours at room temperature, or until it has almost doubled in size.

2. Oil a 10-inch cast iron pan, braiser, or heavy-bottomed deep skillet with olive oil all the way up the sides. (You could also use a 9 × 13-inch baking pan, but the crust will be crisper in cast iron). Place the dough in the pan and spread it to fit in the bottom as best as you can by pushing it out with your fingers. Turn the dough over so both sides are oiled and press again to cover the bottom of the pan. If the dough shrinks back as you push, cover it and leave it for 10 minutes, then try again. It will work eventually, I promise. Cover loosely with plastic wrap and let rise for about 1 hour, or until almost doubled.

3. While the dough is rising, cook the bacon in a skillet set over medium heat until it is about three-quarters cooked. Remove from the pan to a paper towel–lined plate and set aside. Remove all but 2 Tbsp of the bacon fat from the pan and add the onions. Cook for 15 to 20 minutes, or until onions are starting to brown well and are caramelized. Set aside.

4. In a small bowl, combine the goat cheese with the crème fraîche. Add the salt, pepper, and nutmeg.

5. Preheat the oven to 450°F and place an oven rack at the bottom of the oven. Spread the cheese mixture over the dough, right to the edges. Top as evenly as possible with the bacon and onions. Bake for 20 to 25 minutes or longer, or until the bottom of the crust is crispy (lift a corner to check). If it isn't brown enough on top, run it under the broiler for a minute or two, but watch it closely to make sure it doesn't burn!

NOTE: If you want this pizza to be vegetarian, for the topping, omit the bacon and cook the onions in 3 Tbsp extra virgin olive oil. Remove the onions from the pan. Add a bit more oil to the pan if it's dry, then add ¾ lb sliced cremini mushrooms and 2 chopped garlic cloves. Cook for about 15 minutes, or until the mushrooms are browned and any liquid has evaporated. Combine the mushrooms and onions and season with salt and pepper. Or simply omit the bacon and add 1 cup grated smoked cheddar or smoked mozzarella cheese.

TAHCHEEN WITH SAFFRON RICE AND BRAISED CHICKEN

Serves 8 to 10

Tahcheen is an upside-down Persian chicken and rice dish with a crispy top that forms on the bottom as it cooks. The first time I saw someone make something similar was at a wonderful family-style cooking class where Anat Sourani made tbit, an Iraqi Jewish dish usually made for Shabbat. There are many versions of tbit, including one where the chicken is cooked whole buried in rice, but the one Anat made at this class was similar to this tahcheen (although it was kosher style, without any dairy). I was hooked on the deliciousness and started researching similar dishes. A recipe in the award-winning Persian cookbook *Bottom of the Pot*, by Naz Deravian, was my next inspiration. This is Anna's favorite of all the upside-down dishes we make. She says that although it may seem like a bit of an undertaking, her first time making it was a huge success: it tasted incredibly delicious and got rave reviews.

3 cups basmati rice, rinsed until the water runs clear

Kosher salt

¼ tsp saffron threads

½ cup boiling water

2 Tbsp + 2 Tbsp extra virgin olive oil

2 medium onions, sliced or chopped

2 garlic cloves, finely chopped

1-inch piece fresh ginger, peeled and finely chopped

3 lb boneless, skinless chicken thighs, cut into 1-inch chunks

Freshly ground black pepper

2 Tbsp fresh lemon juice

6 cardamom pods, gently crushed

1 cinnamon stick, halved

2½ Tbsp + 2½ Tbsp butter

1 cup thick yogurt or Greek yogurt

1 egg + 1 yolk

1. Soak the rice in a large bowl of cold water with 1 Tbsp salt for 30 minutes or for up to 2 hours. Drain well.

2. Bring a large pot of water to a boil. Add 1 Tbsp salt. Add the rice and cook for 4 to 6 minutes, or until not quite tender (the timing depends on the type and age of rice, so be careful not to overcook it). Drain the rice, rinse with cold water, and drain again well. Set aside.

3. Place the saffron threads in a 1-cup glass measuring cup, crush lightly with the back of a spoon, and add the boiling water. Let infuse for at least 5 minutes, or until using.

4. Heat 2 Tbsp olive oil in a large skillet set over medium heat. Add the onions and cook for 10 to 15 minutes or longer, or until golden. Add the garlic and ginger and cook for a few minutes, or until fragrant. Remove to a bowl and return the pan to the heat. Add 2 Tbsp olive oil.

continued . . .

SHEET PAN ROAST TURKEY BREAST WITH LOTS OF VEGETABLES

Serves 6

Turkey is most often thought of as the main course for Thanksgiving or Christmas, typically two epic meals that feed an army. Part of why Ray and I love Thanksgiving so much is because our eldest daughter Fara, her husband, Mark Moors, and their dog, Hattie May, come to visit from Ottawa. But what about turkey for mid-week? I hadn't thought much about it, but Leonie Eidinger, whom I've worked with for many years, often told me about cooking just a turkey breast and I thought it was a great idea. Although most people say it's the stuffing and gravy that they like best, I challenge you to make this recipe on a regular night without a crowd, to give turkey a real chance. Plus, the leftovers are handy and delicious in sandwiches, wraps, or salads for lunch. The secret to roasting the turkey breast so it's moist and juicy is to buy a good one and use an instant-read thermometer so you don't overcook it. I like to serve this with just the pan juices—I don't need the cranberry sauce and/or gravy because it isn't that kind of big-occasion turkey dinner. (Meaning you are off the hook.) However, for those of you who are cooking for family members who disagree with this (e.g., Ray and Mark), I have included quick recipes for cranberry sauce and gravy below. And a great substitute for the stuffing (as required by Anna and Fara) would be the cornbread on page 200 with the gravy.

3 lb single, boneless, skin-on turkey breast

2 Tbsp extra virgin olive oil

2 Tbsp honey

1 Tbsp Dijon mustard

1 tsp kosher salt

⅛ tsp freshly ground black pepper

1 Tbsp chopped fresh rosemary

Vegetables

4 garlic cloves, sliced

2 carrots, scrubbed or peeled, cut into chunks

1 red onion, cut into wedges

1 lb butternut squash, cut into chunks

1 lb red potatoes or sweet potatoes, scrubbed or peeled, cut into wedges

1. Place the turkey breast in a baking dish. Combine the olive oil, honey, mustard, salt, pepper, and chopped rosemary and rub onto the turkey. Marinate at room temperature for up to 30 minutes while prepping the vegetables, or refrigerate up to overnight.

2. Preheat the oven to 375°F and line a large baking sheet with parchment paper.

3. For the vegetables, combine the garlic, carrots, onions, squash, potatoes, and lemon slices in a large bowl. Combine the olive oil, salt, pepper, and harissa, and toss with vegetables. Spread on the lined baking sheet. Nestle the turkey breast, skin side up, in the center of the vegetables, making sure that it's touching the baking sheet as much as possible. Scatter the herbs overtop. Cover loosely with aluminum foil and roast for 30 minutes.

4. Uncover, and roast for 30 minutes more, or until nicely browned and an instant-read thermometer registers 165°F to 175°F in the thickest part. If the turkey breast is browning too much, cover the turkey (but not the vegetables) lightly with aluminum foil. Cooking time will vary, depending on the thickness of the turkey and your oven.

1 lemon, sliced

¼ cup extra virgin olive oil

1 tsp kosher salt

⅛ tsp freshly ground black pepper

1 tsp harissa or other hot sauce, optional

3 sprigs fresh rosemary + more for serving

3 sprigs fresh thyme + more for serving

3 sprigs fresh flat-leaf parsley + more for serving

3 sprigs fresh sage + more for serving

5. Remove and discard the herbs that have dried. Slice the turkey breast, dip the slices into the pan juices, and arrange on or with the vegetables. Spoon any remaining pan juices overtop. Top with fresh herbs for serving.

CRANBERRY SAUCE: It is very easy and fun to make cranberry sauce. When the cranberries pop, it's like they are talking to you and saying "Almost ready." Place 3 cups fresh or frozen cranberries in a medium saucepan. Add ¾ cup granulated sugar and 1 cup water (or orange, cranberry, or pomegranate juice). Bring to a boil, reduce the heat, and simmer until the cranberries pop and deflate. The sauce will thicken when cool.

GRAVY: Heat 3 Tbsp butter, schmaltz (chicken fat) or extra virgin olive oil in a saucepan. (If you have mushrooms, slice about ¼ lb and cook in the butter for a few minutes. They will add a deep color and flavor.) Add 3 Tbsp all-purpose (or gluten-free) flour and cook for a few minutes, stirring, until lightly browned. Stir or whisk in 3 cups chicken broth and 1 Tbsp each soy sauce or tamari, Worcestershire sauce, and fresh lemon juice. Bring to a boil. Add salt and Tabasco sauce to taste. Cook, uncovered, for about 10 minutes. When the turkey is ready to serve, add any pan juices to the gravy. Re-season to taste.

MIDDLE EASTERN COMFORT MEATLOAF

Serves 4 to 6, depending on how much you love meatloaf

For many people, including Ray, meatloaf is the ultimate comfort food. Over the years, I've made so many versions. This one was inspired by the kebaburgers in Adeena Sussman's incredible Israeli cookbook *Sababa*. Coincidentally, Adeena's husband, Jay Shofet, loves meatloaf just as much as Ray does. The same mixture works as meatballs or as burgers. You can also make this with ground chicken or turkey instead of beef. Serve with mash and peas—I love it with rice too. Top with tahini, z'hug (page 13), spicy tomato sauce, or roasted cherry tomatoes (page 87)—or all of them. Use leftovers in pita sandwiches or crumble for use in tacos, spaghetti sauces, or rice/grain bowls. Leftovers keep for about 1 week in the refrigerator or in the freezer for 2 to 3 months.

1 onion, chopped

2 garlic cloves, chopped

2 Tbsp extra virgin olive oil

2 eggs

½ cup chopped fresh cilantro

½ cup chopped fresh dill

½ cup chopped fresh flat-leaf parsley

1 Tbsp tomato paste

2 tsp harissa (or ¾ tsp ground cumin + ½ tsp hot sauce)

2 tsp kosher salt

¾ cup panko breadcrumbs

2 lb ground beef (or half beef and half lamb)

1. Preheat the oven to 350°F. Line a 5 × 9-inch loaf pan with parchment paper, allowing some to hang over on the two long sides for easy removal.

2. Heat a skillet over medium heat, then cook the onions and garlic in the olive oil until tender. Spread on a plate to cool quickly.

3. Beat the eggs with the cilantro, dill, parsley, tomato paste, harissa, and salt. Stir in the cooled onions and breadcrumbs.

4. Mix the egg mixture with the meat until well combined.

5. Pat the meat firmly into the lined pan. Cover with a piece of parchment paper. Bake for 45 minutes. Uncover and bake for another 20 to 25 minutes, or until the top is well browned. Cool for 10 minutes. Carefully pour off any juices in the pan. Remove from the pan and serve with any of the toppings or pairings suggested in the recipe intro.

NOTE: Make a gluten-free version using quick-cooking oats instead of breadcrumbs. And if you, like Ray, love a more traditional meatloaf, omit the cilantro and harissa and serve it with barbecue sauce.

KOREAN MARINATED FLANK STEAK

Serves 6 to 8

This easy marinade is perfect for steak, Miami ribs, lamb chops, and tofu steaks. Flank steak is quite lean, but if it is grilled rare and then thinly sliced across the grain, it is very tender. When deciding how big of a steak to cook, it's helpful to keep in mind how much waste (bone, fat, or gristle) is typical for the type of steak you are using. Because a flank steak is boneless and has very little fat, 2 lb might be plenty for six people or maybe even more, depending on how much other food you are serving. Flank steaks come in different sizes, so you may need one or two.

½ **cup soy sauce**

¼ **cup granulated sugar or light brown sugar**

2 **garlic cloves, grated**

1-inch **piece fresh ginger,** peeled and grated

1 **Tbsp toasted sesame oil**

2 **lb flank steak**

3 **green onions,** sliced on the diagonal

1 **Tbsp toasted sesame seeds,** optional

1. In a bowl, mix the soy sauce with the sugar, garlic, ginger, and sesame oil until the sugar dissolves. Transfer to a baking dish or heavy-duty resealable plastic bag, along with the steak. Turn the steak a few times to coat. Marinate for 1 hour at room temperature, or up to overnight in the refrigerator.

2. If you remember, remove steak from the refrigerator 30 minutes before grilling (if you forget, don't worry, it just may take a few extra minutes to cook). Heat the barbecue on high. Grill the steak for 4 to 5 minutes per side, or until an instant-read thermometer reaches 125°F to 130°F when inserted into the thickest part. Keep a close eye, because flank steak can become tough and chewy when overcooked.

3. Slice thinly against the grain (it may be a bit tough if sliced too thick). Sprinkle with green onions and sesame seeds, if using. This is delicious served hot or at room temperature, and leftovers make for hearty salads or sandwiches.

CARVING NOTE: A flank steak looks a little like your hand with the grain running lengthwise like your fingers. If you're horrified by this analogy, stop reading now. If you're still with me, carry on. When carving, slice on the diagonal across your fingers (so to speak).

GRILLED MIAMI RIBS WITH STICKY POMEGRANATE MARINADE

Serves 5 to 6

I love short ribs, whether they are sliced thin like these ones and cooked quickly, or in chunks and braised. Miami ribs (sometimes called Korean ribs) used to be much harder to find than they are now. They are beef ribs cut very thin (¼ inch to ⅓ inch thick) and across the bone. Although beef short ribs are thought of as a tough cut of meat that you generally braise or stew, when they are cut this thin, they cook very quickly. I can easily eat a few Miami ribs myself, so it's hard to know how many people this recipe will serve. But any leftovers are great in rice bowls, tacos, and in fried rice, so I never worry about making too much.

Marinade

½ cup pomegranate molasses

2 Tbsp honey, maple syrup, or brown sugar

2 Tbsp soy sauce

2 Tbsp sherry vinegar

2 Tbsp extra virgin olive oil

1 Tbsp fresh lemon juice

1 large garlic clove, minced or grated

1-inch piece fresh ginger, peeled and minced or grated

Ribs

4 lb Miami ribs (about 12 to 16 strips), about ¼ inch to ⅓ inch thick

3 green onions, thinly sliced on the diagonal, or chives

⅓ cup pomegranate seeds, optional

1. For the marinade, combine the pomegranate molasses, honey, soy sauce, vinegar, olive oil, lemon juice, garlic, and ginger. Spread over the Miami ribs in a large pan, making sure they are all coated with the marinade. Refrigerate for a few hours or up to overnight. Remove from the refrigerator 1 hour before cooking.

2. Heat the barbecue on high. The ribs can also be cooked under the broiler (watch carefully) or in a very hot cast iron skillet or grill pan.

3. Remove the ribs from the marinade. Transfer the marinade to a saucepan, bring to a boil and cook for 3 minutes, then reduce the heat to medium and cook until the mixture is syrupy.

4. Cook the ribs in a single layer on the hot barbecue for about 3 to 4 minutes per side or until browned—we like them charred in a few spots. You may have to do this in batches.

5. Drizzle the reduced marinade (you will probably only have about ⅓ cup) over the ribs and sprinkle with green onions and pomegranate seeds, if using.

BRAISED BEEF ITALIAN STYLE

Serves 6 to 8

In 2015, the World Expo was in Milan and the theme, "Feeding the Planet, Energy for Life," was food and diet. One part of the United States' Expo program was to bring chefs from all over the U.S. to Milan to host special dinners showcasing the diversity and creativity of American food. We attended a dinner, prepared by Andrew Carmellini, an award-winning American chef and restaurateur. He made a braised beef dish we loved so much that we recreated it and have been making this homestyle version ever since. Serve with polenta (see right), risotto, or mashed potatoes.

4 lb boneless beef shoulder (blade, chuck, or boneless short ribs), cut into 2-inch chunks

Kosher salt and freshly ground black pepper

2 Tbsp all-purpose flour

2 Tbsp extra virgin olive oil

2 large onions, coarsely chopped or sliced

3 large garlic cloves, halved

1 Tbsp dried oregano

¼ tsp chili flakes

1 Tbsp tomato paste

1½ cups dry red wine or beef broth (or a combination)

One 28 oz/796 mL can plum tomatoes with juices, crushed (preferably San Marzano)

Coarsely chopped fresh flat-leaf parsley leaves

1. Preheat the oven to 350°F. Season the meat generously with salt and pepper, and dust lightly with flour. Heat the olive oil in a large Dutch oven set over medium-high heat. Brown the meat well on all sides. You'll need to do this in batches—do not overcrowd the pot or the meat will not brown properly. Set aside. Discard all but 2 to 3 Tbsp of oil from the pot or add more oil if necessary.

2. Reduce the heat to medium, add the onions, and cook gently for 5 to 10 minutes, or until tender, then add the garlic, oregano, and chili flakes. Cook for a few minutes longer, until fragrant. Stir in the tomato paste and cook for 30 seconds. Add the wine to the pot and bring to a boil, scraping off any bits from the bottom. Cook until the wine has reduced by about half. Add the tomatoes, break them up with the spoon, and bring to a boil.

3. Return the meat to the pot, along with any accumulated juices, and stir to combine. Bring to a boil. Remove from heat. Cover the surface directly with a piece of parchment paper and then cover tightly with a lid or aluminum foil. Cook in the oven for 2½ to 3 hours, or until the meat is very tender when pierced with a fork. Check every 30 minutes, and add water or beef broth if the pot seems dry.

4. Remove the meat to a serving dish. Skim any fat off the surface of the sauce. If the sauce is too thin, cook on medium-high heat, uncovered, until reduced. If it is too thick, thin with water or broth. Season to taste and spoon over the meat. Sprinkle with parsley.

NOTE: Braising usually involves cooking tougher cuts of meat in a flavorful liquid until tender. I don't recommend buying anything labeled "stewing beef," as it usually is too lean and cooks up tough. Cuts with a little fat will cook up juicy and delicious. Braised dishes taste great the next day, so you can cook this one ahead, make more than you need, and save for future meals and/or freeze some too.

HERE'S A QUICK POLENTA RECIPE: Bring 4 cups of water and 2 tsp kosher salt to a boil in a large saucepan. Stirring constantly, slowly whisk 1 cup of quick-cooking polenta into the water. Cook on medium-low heat, stirring, for 5 minutes or until creamy and coming away from the sides of the saucepan. Add 2 Tbsp butter. Optionally, stir in ½ cup whipping cream or ½ cup grated Parmigiano-Reggiano, or both. Season to taste. Serves 4 to 6.

BONNIE'S BRISKET WITH HOMEMADE BARBECUE SAUCE

Serves 10 to 14

To me, brisket is the epitome of family dinner. My mother used to make it at least once or twice a month for Friday night dinner, and so it holds a special place in my heart. This recipe has become a regular at our Friday night dinners and so has my nephew Chuck. Every single time I make it, he tells me, "Bonnie, this is the best brisket you have ever made." (I love it when he comes for dinner.) I used to make a recipe like this using a store-bought barbecue sauce and adding additional ingredients. But when a guest was coming to dinner who was allergic to all chilies and peppers and I couldn't confidently identify what was in the store-bought sauce, I started making my own. Chuck confirmed that it was, in fact, the best brisket I had ever made. I always buy a whole brisket, because it includes the single end, which is quite lean, and also the double end (the part I like), which has more fat and is juicier. This way, everyone can have the part they want. I also like making a whole brisket, as the leftovers are so delicious—hot or cold in sandwiches; in tacos with guacamole; added to ramen, beef, or barley soup; on pasta; and lots more. It also freezes well.

Brisket

2 Tbsp light brown sugar

1 Tbsp kosher salt

1 Tbsp garlic powder

1 Tbsp smoked paprika

½ tsp freshly ground black pepper

8 to 10 lb whole brisket

2 Tbsp extra virgin olive oil

6 large onions, thickly sliced

6 large garlic cloves, halved lengthwise

2 cups boiling water

2 lb carrots, scrubbed or peeled

2 Tbsp chopped fresh flat-leaf parsley

1. For the brisket, combine the sugar, salt, garlic powder, paprika, and pepper, and rub into both sides of the meat. Marinate for 30 minutes at room temperature or up to overnight in the refrigerator.

2. For the barbecue sauce, in a food processor or blender, puree the tomatoes, sugar, maple syrup, Worcestershire sauce, soy sauce, vinegar, molasses, mustard, ginger, paprika, salt, cumin, allspice, cloves, chipotles, and pepper, if using.

3. Preheat the oven to 325°F. Spread 2 Tbsp of olive oil over the bottom of a large Dutch oven or roasting pan that will hold the brisket. Spread the onions and garlic over the bottom of the pan. Place the brisket on top of the onions and garlic, and spoon the barbecue sauce over and around the brisket. Pour 2 cups of boiling water around the brisket. Cover the surface of the meat directly with a piece of parchment paper, then cover the pot tightly with a lid or aluminum foil. Roast in the preheated oven for 4 to 5 hours, or until the meat is very tender when pierced with a fork. Check every hour and add an additional 1 cup of boiling water if the pan seems dry. Every brisket and every oven is different, so don't worry—just cook until tender. (Another reason it's good to make ahead.) After 3 hours of cooking, add the carrots (whole or cut into large chunks if you prefer), then cover the pot tightly and return to the oven to finish cooking.

Barbecue Sauce

One 28 oz/796 mL can plum tomatoes, with juices, mashed or pureed

¼ cup light brown sugar

¼ cup maple syrup

¼ cup Worcestershire sauce

¼ cup soy sauce

¼ cup apple cider vinegar or rice vinegar

2 Tbsp molasses

2 Tbsp Dijon mustard

1 tsp ground ginger

1 tsp smoked paprika

1 tsp kosher salt

¾ tsp ground cumin

½ tsp ground allspice

½ tsp ground cloves

1 tsp pureed canned chipotle chilies (see page 5) **or Tabasco Chipotle,** optional

¼ tsp freshly ground black pepper, optional

NOTE: To make the sauce on its own, for example for chicken or ribs, cook 2 chopped onions and 2 finely chopped garlic cloves in 2 Tbsp extra virgin olive oil until tender, but not browned, and then add the remaining sauce ingredients. Cook for about 30 minutes, uncovered, or until the sauce becomes a bit thicker.

4. Once the meat is tender, remove the cover and parchment paper, increase the oven temperature to 400°F, and cook for 15 to 20 minutes longer, or until the top is nicely browned. (If the top has already browned skip this step.)

5. Transfer the brisket to a carving board. Remove the carrots and set aside. If you have made the brisket ahead, see the Make Ahead note, and refrigerate the brisket overnight, as it is easier to slice when cold. Spoon off and discard any fat on the surface of the sauce. If there is a lot of cooking liquid, cook uncovered on medium-high heat until the sauce thickens and is reduced to about 2 cups. Carve the meat across the grain and arrange overlapping slices in a large baking dish. Add the cooked carrots and spread the sauce overtop. If you are reheating the brisket from cold, see the note for directions. If you are reheating the brisket from warm, cover tightly with aluminum foil and place in a preheated 350°F oven for 30 minutes or until very hot before serving. Sprinkle with parsley just before serving.

MAKE-AHEAD: Brisket is a great make-ahead dish, as it reheats perfectly and is easier to carve when cold. Plus, any fat will rise to the surface of the sauce and can be removed before reheating. If making ahead, refrigerate the brisket and sauce (reduced if necessary) separately. Slice the meat when cold. Place in overlapping slices in one or two pans for reheating. Discard any fat solidified on the sauce and spread the sauce over the meat. To reheat, cover with parchment paper and then cover tightly with aluminum foil and reheat in a preheated 350°F oven 40 to 45 minutes, or until very hot. (If you want to freeze the brisket, slice it first and freeze with the sauce. Defrost overnight in the refrigerator and reheat at 350°F until hot.)

COOKING NOTE: When I was in chef training, I learned that when tougher cuts of meat are pot-roasted, braised, or stewed, they should be browned first for extra flavor. But brisket is big and a little unwieldy to brown first, so I do what my mother used to do: once it is cooked, I remove the cover, increase the oven temperature a bit, and cook until the top browns. Now this method is known as reverse browning and is becoming quite popular (because it makes sense!). My mom died 22 years ago (may her memory be a blessing), but she had a great sense of humor and I know she would laugh about this now being a "technique."

BEEF KEBABS WITH EGGPLANT, CHICKPEAS, SWISS CHARD, AND TAHINI

Serves 8

This dish, served to me the first time I went to dinner at my good friend Janna Gur's house, accompanied by green rice (page 94) is all you need to make a show-stopping dinner. If you want to break it down into parts, you can make the tahini sauce, the tomato sauce, and even the meatballs a day ahead. If you are using greens with thick stems, like Swiss chard, separate the stems from the leaves, dice the stems, and add them after the onions have cooked a bit. Or you can save the stems for soup. Coarsely chop the leaves and add them near the end, since they cook so quickly.

Kebabs

2 lb ground beef or lamb (or a combination)

1 onion, grated or finely chopped

2 garlic cloves, minced or grated

2 eggs

½ cup panko breadcrumbs or quick-cooking oats

2 Tbsp finely chopped fresh cilantro or flat-leaf parsley

2 tsp kosher salt

1 tsp baharat (page 10)

Eggplant

1½ lb oval eggplants, sliced about ½ inch thick

¼ cup extra virgin olive oil

1 tsp kosher salt

1. Preheat the oven to 425°F and line two large baking sheets with parchment paper.

2. For the kebabs, combine the beef with the onions, garlic, eggs, breadcrumbs, cilantro, salt, and baharat. Shape into about 40 balls, about 2 Tbsp per kebab. Arrange the kebabs on one of the lined baking sheets and bake for 20 to 25 minutes, shaking the baking sheet a few times during cooking, until browned and cooked through. You can also do this on the stovetop, with about 2 Tbsp olive oil, browning the kebabs in batches.

3. For the eggplant, arrange the eggplant slices in a single layer on the second lined baking sheet. Drizzle with olive oil and sprinkle with salt. Roast for 30 to 40 minutes, or until browned and tender, turning once.

continued . . .

Tomato Sauce

2 Tbsp extra virgin olive oil

1 onion, chopped

2 garlic cloves, finely chopped

1 Tbsp tomato paste

1 tsp baharat (page 10)

1 tsp kosher salt + more to taste

¼ tsp freshly ground black pepper

¼ tsp chili flakes

One 28 oz/796 mL can plum tomatoes, crushed or pureed

1 cup water

2 cups cooked chickpeas (canned or freshly cooked, see page 24)

1 bunch Swiss chard or black kale (see recipe intro)

Suggested Toppings

1 cup basic tahini sauce (page 17)

Roasted pine nuts

Chopped fresh cilantro or flat-leaf parsley

4. For the tomato sauce, heat the olive oil in a large, deep skillet or Dutch oven. Add the onions and garlic to the pan. Cook for a few minutes. (Add Swiss chard stems if using and cook about 5 minutes longer.) Add the tomato paste, baharat, salt, pepper, chili flakes, and cook for about 30 seconds. Add the tomatoes and their juices. Pour the water into the empty tomato can, swish it around, then add to the sauce. Bring to a boil. Add the kebabs and cook over medium heat for 15 to 20 minutes, or until tender and the sauce has thickened. Add the chickpeas, roasted eggplant, and Swiss chard leaves. Cook for 5 to 10 minutes until the chard wilts. Season to taste.

5. Drizzle with tahini sauce, and sprinkle with pine nuts and cilantro.

BRAISED LAMB SHANKS WITH DRIED PERSIAN LIMES

Serves 8

Ray and I have always loved lamb, but my kids? Not so much. However, after cooking this recipe for a family meal upon returning home from Israel, where I had three similar versions, I can confidently say that my kids now love lamb too. You can substitute 4 lb of boneless lamb shoulder (cut into 2-inch chunks), beef short ribs or boneless shoulder, or even chicken thighs (cook only 1 hour). This is even better if you make it the day before, and it freezes perfectly.

2 Tbsp extra virgin olive oil

8 lamb shanks, 10 to 12 oz each (see note)

Kosher salt and freshly ground black pepper

2 onions, halved and sliced

1 bunch Swiss chard (about 1 lb), leaves and stems chopped separately

6 garlic cloves, gently smashed

2 tsp dried fenugreek leaves

1 tsp ground cumin

½ tsp ground allspice

½ tsp ground turmeric

1 bunch fresh cilantro, chopped

1 bunch fresh dill, chopped

1 bunch fresh flat-leaf parsley, chopped

4 Persian limes, gently cracked or carefully pierced with a knife

2 Tbsp pomegranate molasses

3 cups chicken or beef broth or water

2 cups cooked chickpeas (canned or freshly cooked, see page 24)

2 Tbsp pomegranate seeds

Additional chopped fresh cilantro, dill and/or parsley

1. Preheat the oven to 350°F.

2. Heat the olive oil in a large Dutch oven set over medium-high heat. Sprinkle the meat generously with salt and pepper. In batches, brown the shanks well on all sides (do not overcrowd the pan). Repeat until all the lamb is browned. Set aside.

3. Add the onions to the pot and cook for a few minutes until wilted. Add the chopped Swiss chard stems and cook for a few minutes longer with the onions. Add the garlic, fenugreek leaves, cumin, allspice, and turmeric. Cook for 1 minute, stirring, or until fragrant.

4. Add the Swiss chard leaves, cilantro, dill, and parsley, and cook for about 5 minutes, or until the leaves turn dark. Add the dried limes, pomegranate molasses, broth, 2 tsp salt, and the lamb, and bring to a boil. Remove from heat. Cover the surface with parchment paper and then cover tightly with a lid or aluminum foil (I use both because my lid doesn't fit perfectly). Transfer the pot to the oven and cook for 1 hour. Then add the cooked chickpeas and cook for 1 to 1½ hours longer, or until the lamb is very tender and falling off the bones. The herbs and greens will be dark green and a little mushy—perfect.

5. Sprinkle with pomegranate seeds and chopped fresh herbs. Serve with rice or mashed potatoes.

NOTE: If your lamb shanks are too large for a single serving, once they are tender, remove the meat in chunks from the bone and serve it boneless. Persian limes are available at any Middle Eastern market or spice shop. In Toronto I buy them at Ararat. They can also be ground up and used as a seasoning, which I haven't done yet but will keep you posted.

Leftovers

Before moving to the United States, Jacques Pépin used to cook for the presidents of France. When asked whether he served them leftovers, he would say, "Yes, I served them leftovers all the time. But I never called them leftovers."

Who doesn't like leftovers? I know these people exist, but maybe it's because they don't realize all the things you can do to transform them! Or maybe they haven't had them the right way yet. So let me tell you about some of our favorites.

Challah

If you have leftover challah here are three things to do with it. You could make breadcrumbs by putting chunks of stale or dried bread into your food processor and pulsing on and off until fine or chunky, the way you like them, then keep them in the freezer in a resealable plastic bag for a few months. Or you could make challah chips (like bagels chips). Slice the bread into ¼-inch-thick pieces, arrange in a single layer on a baking sheet, brush with extra virgin olive oil and sprinkle with kosher salt. Bake at 300°F for 20 to 30 minutes or until crisp. Keep in a sealed container on the counter for snacking. The third option is our gold standard—French toast. Cut the challah into ½-inch-thick slices. For 4 slices of challah, crack 2 eggs into a baking dish, add a splash of milk, 1 tsp vanilla, a pinch of cinnamon and a pinch of kosher salt. Soak the bread in the egg mixture until the mixture is soaked into the bread. Melt 1 Tbsp butter in a non-stick pan over medium heat and cook until browned on both sides.

Risotto

Everyone knows risotto is best served right away. But not everyone knows about using leftover risotto to make risotto cakes. Mix the leftover risotto with a beaten egg, and form into patties. Heat a pan with olive oil and pan-fry the risotto cakes. You could make them like arancini (shaped into balls with a piece of cheese or a piece of brisket in the middle) and roll them in breadcrumbs, then fry them. Delicious!

Brisket

What can't you do with leftover brisket? First of all, it freezes very well. So make a brisket larger than you need, so that you can use leftovers the next day, and from frozen in a few weeks or months. I often use it to make braised beef pasta. For this, I break the brisket up into chunks and partially shred it. Put the brisket into a pan along with some of the sauce and cooked onions and thin with pasta water. If you like, add cherry tomatoes. Toss with your favorite cooked pasta. Another amazing thing to make with leftover brisket is homemade braised beef poutine. Roast fingerling or other small potatoes in the oven (see page 78, step 4). Warm up the brisket, and when the potatoes are just about done, top with the warm, saucy brisket and some grated cheese or cheese curds. Also try leftover brisket in tacos and quesadillas.

Rice

Cooked, cold rice makes for great fried rice. Sauté chopped onions, garlic, and carrots in vegetable oil in a large skillet set over medium heat until tender. Add any chopped cooked vegetables you have on hand (clean out the refrigerator!). Add the leftover rice and cook a bit longer until it is hot. Beat an egg, and move the rice so there's an empty spot in the pan to add it. Add the egg and let it cook a little, then start scrambling/mixing through the rice. The final step is to add soy sauce, hoisin, sriracha, or a combination of them all.

Roasted Vegetables

Anna loves to use leftover roasted vegetables to make a pashtida (page 169) which is similar to a crustless quiche. Another great option is hash or soup. For hash, cut the vegetables into chunks, add extra virgin olive oil to a skillet, and heat/crisp up the vegetables until caramelized. If you have leftover meat, you can add that too, and top it with a fried egg. For soup, cook about 2 cups leftover vegetables with 3 cups broth or water, puree, and add more liquid and seasoning if necessary.

Fish

Someone once told me that "roast turkey is only a roast turkey once." This is how I feel about fish. Instead of reheating it as is, I either serve it cold in a salad or use it in fish cakes. To make fish cakes, break the leftover fish up into chunks and combine with the same amount of leftover mashed potatoes (or freshly cooked and cooled mashed potatoes) and chopped fresh herbs (like green onions or flat-leaf parsley). Form into cakes and pan-fry in extra virgin olive oil or vegetable oil until browned.

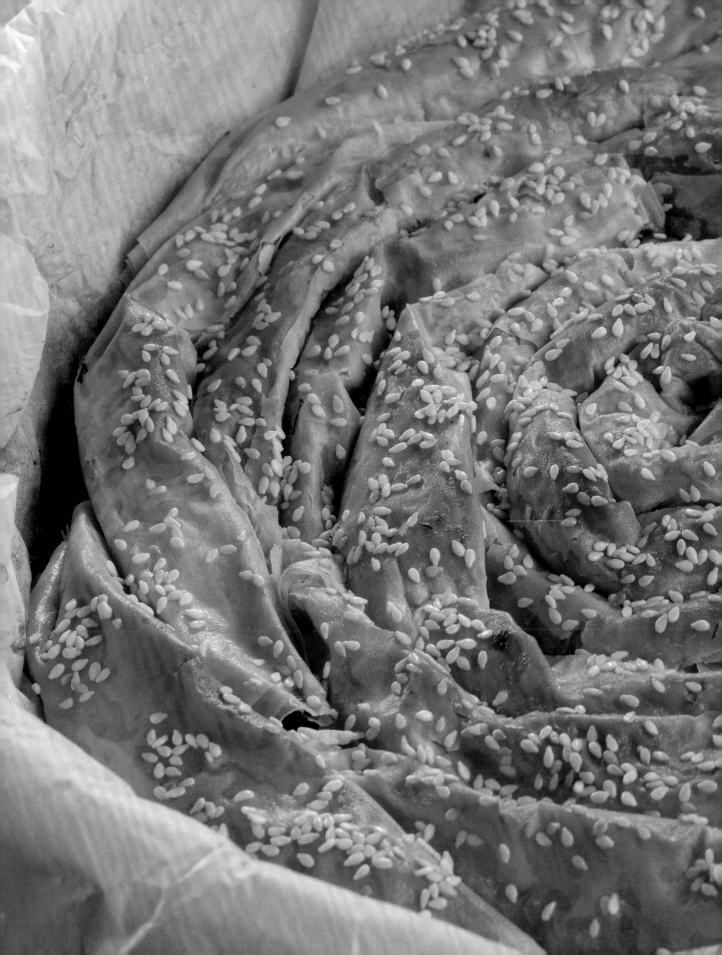

All-Day Breakfast

BOUREKA TART WITH TAHINI, EGGS, TOMATOES, AND MICROGREENS

Serves 4 to 8

Bourekas are one of the most popular Middle Eastern foods. Every country has a version, and there are so many different fillings, pastries, shapes, sizes, names, and spellings for them. This version, adapted from Israeli chef Benny Cohen, looks and tastes fantastic. It can be an appetizer, vegetarian main course, or a perfect brunch dish. When you open a package of phyllo, it should come apart in whole thin sheets. If the paper-thin pieces fall apart a little bit, don't worry—when you patch them up with melted butter, no one will know the difference and it will taste amazing.

2 Tbsp extra virgin olive oil

1 large leek, white and light green part only, cleaned and chopped (see note on page 110)

8 oz baby spinach, baby kale, beet greens, Swiss chard, or rapini, coarsely chopped

6 oz ricotta cheese, drained if necessary

4 oz feta cheese, crumbled

Kosher salt and freshly ground black pepper

Grated nutmeg

Phyllo

6 sheets phyllo pastry (about 12 × 18 inches each)

½ cup butter, melted

½ cup panko breadcrumbs

1 tsp sesame seeds or za'atar

Toppings

Basic tahini sauce (page 17)

2 hard-cooked eggs, coarsely chopped or crushed (see note on page 73)

½ cup cherry tomatoes, quartered, seeds removed if very juicy

Handful of microgreens or pea shoots

1. Preheat the oven to 350°F and line a baking sheet with parchment paper.

2. Heat the olive oil in a large skillet set over medium-low heat. Cook the leeks gently for 5 to 10 minutes, or until tender. Add the spinach and cook just until wilted. (If using baby kale, beet greens, Swiss chard leaves, or rapini, adjust the cooking time accordingly, until they are wilted and tender.) Cool the spinach, squeeze out the excess liquid as much as possible, and chop again if there are still large pieces.

3. Gently mix the ricotta and feta into the cooled spinach. Season well with salt, pepper, and nutmeg to taste.

4. Remove the phyllo from its packaging and cover the sheets you are not using with plastic wrap or an extra-large, heavy-duty resealable plastic bag. Arrange 1 phyllo sheet on your work surface, with the longer side horizontal in front of you. Brush with the melted butter and sprinkle with panko. Top with 2 more phyllo sheets, brushing each with butter and sprinkling with panko. Cut the stack of phyllo in half horizontally so that you now have two long horizontal stacks in front of you.

5. Spoon or pipe one-quarter of the filling along the bottom horizontal edge of each stack. Gently roll up the phyllo over the filling so that you now have two filled ropes approximately 18 inches long (the length of the phyllo sheet).

continued . . .

Wind one into a coil and transfer to the lined baking sheet. Wind the second rope around the outside edge of the first one, continuing it to make the coil bigger. Brush with melted butter and sprinkle with sesame seeds. Repeat these steps with the remaining 3 sheets of phyllo to make another coil of the same size. (Alternately, you could add onto the first complete coil you made, making it even bigger. Or you could make 4 individual small ones.)

6. Bake for 25 to 30 minutes, or until browned. Serve warm or at room temperature, drizzled with tahini sauce, and top with eggs, cherry tomatoes, and microgreens.

NOTE: I love the way Benny prepares the hard-cooked eggs for the topping, and I have found that many Israeli chefs also use this technique—just squish the cooked eggs in your hand! I do this all the time now, even just for my egg salad.

FROM THE GARDEN PASHTIDA

Serves 8 to 10

Pashtida is an Israeli dish that's somewhere between a quiche and a frittata, and it's so incredibly versatile. Really, you can make a pashtida with any cooked vegetable. If using leftover vegetables, omit steps 1 and 2. You need anywhere from 4 to 6 cups—the more vegetables you use, the thicker it will be. Instead of cheddar you could use crumbled feta or spoonfuls of drained ricotta—or clean out your cheese drawer. Use leftover pashtida to make sandwiches (regular or open-faced), appetizer bites, or even sushi rolls. You can halve the recipe easily and bake it in an 8- or 9-inch pan.

2 lb sweet potatoes, scrubbed or peeled and cut into 1-inch chunks

2 lb broccoli or cauliflower, cut into 1-inch pieces (or a combination)

1 red onion, sliced

2 Tbsp extra virgin olive oil

Kosher salt

2 cups cherry tomatoes

2 Tbsp chopped fresh cilantro or flat-leaf parsley

2 Tbsp chopped fresh dill

1½ cups grated smoked cheddar, aged cheddar, or smoked mozzarella

4 oz goat or feta cheese, crumbled

2 cups chopped spinach

12 eggs

⅓ cup all-purpose flour

1 tsp baking powder

⅛ tsp freshly ground black pepper

⅛ tsp grated nutmeg + more if freshly grated

1½ cups cream or milk (or a combination)

1 tsp pureed chipotle chilies (see page 5) **or your favorite hot sauce,** optional

¼ cup roasted pumpkin seeds

1. Preheat the oven to 425°F and line two baking sheets with parchment paper.

2. Toss the sweet potatoes, broccoli, and onions with olive oil and 1 tsp salt. Spread in a single layer on the lined baking sheets and roast for 30 to 35 minutes, or until tender and lightly browned. After 25 minutes, add the tomatoes. Let the vegetables cool and reduce the oven temperature to 350°F. (If you are using previously cooked vegetables, you will need to preheat the oven to 350°F.)

3. Line a 9 × 13-inch baking dish with parchment paper. Transfer two-thirds of the vegetables to the dish, and sprinkle with half the cilantro, half the dill, and half the cheese. Top with the remaining vegetables and chopped spinach.

4. In a large bowl, whisk the eggs. In a small, separate bowl, combine the flour with the baking powder, 1 tsp salt, pepper, and nutmeg. Whisk the flour mixture into the eggs, then add the cream and chipotles. Pour the mixture over the vegetables. Top with the remaining herbs and cheese, and sprinkle with pumpkin seeds.

5. Bake for 40 to 50 minutes, or until browned and puffed and just set in the center. If the top is browning too much, cover loosely with aluminum foil. Rest the pashtida at least 10 minutes before serving.

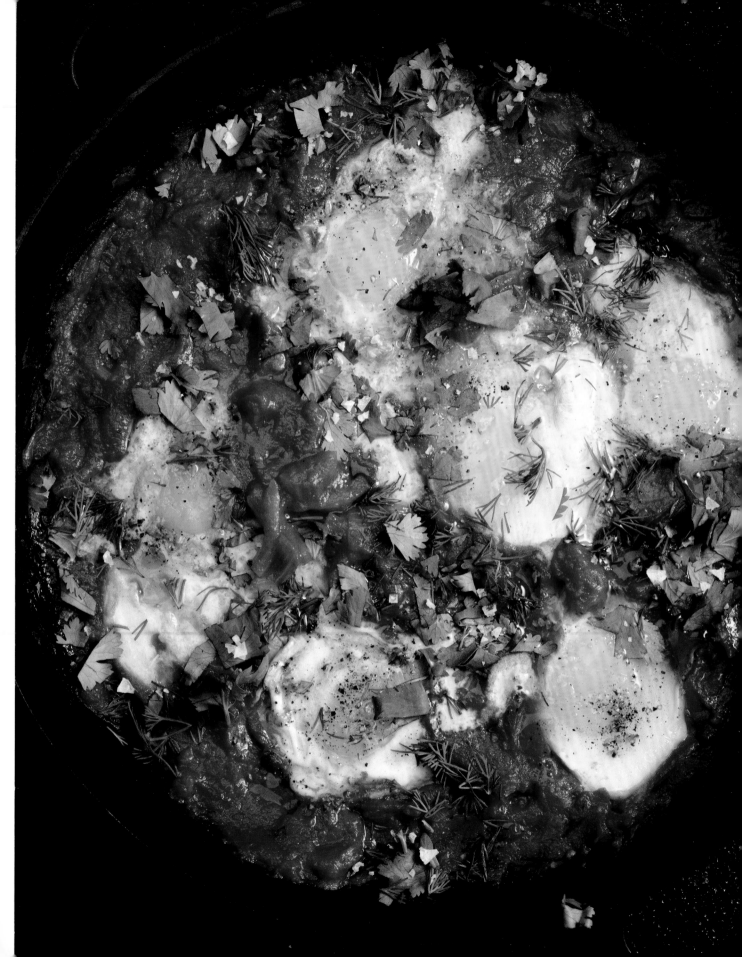

TOMATO-SEASON SHAKSHUKA

Serves 4 to 6

Shakshuka has become a mainstay on brunch menus around the world. Originally, "shakshuka" referred to eggs cooked in tomato sauce with peppers, but now you can find versions that include eggplant, spinach, Swiss chard, red and yellow bell peppers, cheese, spicy lamb sausages, and many more. But this shakshuka, which I made at my sister's cottage, with ingredients from local farmers, was so simple and very special.

2 Tbsp extra virgin olive oil

2 large onions, sliced

1 to 2 tsp harissa, depending on your heat tolerance, optional

3 lb tomatoes, any size or color, coarsely chopped (see note)

1 tsp kosher salt + more as needed

Handful of fresh cilantro, coarsely chopped

Handful of fresh dill, coarsely chopped

6 to 8 eggs

Challah, pita, or tortillas, to mop up the sauce

1. Heat the olive oil in a large, deep skillet set over medium heat. Add the onions and cook for 5 to 10 minutes, or until lightly browned and getting tender. Add the harissa and cook, stirring, for about 30 seconds. Add tomatoes and bring to a boil. Stir in the salt. Reduce the heat to medium and continue cooking, uncovered, for about 20 to 30 minutes, or until much of the liquid has evaporated and the sauce is thick.

2. Reserve about 2 Tbsp each of the cilantro and dill for serving, and add the remainder to the sauce. Season well to taste as after you add the eggs it is difficult to adjust the seasoning. Make little wells in the sauce for the eggs and break an egg into each one. Cook gently until the egg whites firm up (ideally, the yolks stay liquid). Some people put a lid on at this point for a few minutes, others put the pan under the broiler for a minute, but I prefer to let the sauce bubble up around the eggs—after 5 to 7 minutes, it's ready.

3. Sprinkle with the reserved cilantro and dill. Serve in the pan with your favorite bread alongside.

When tomatoes aren't in season, you should definitely still make shakshuka (that's most of the year in Canada). Substitute one 28 oz/796 mL can of plum tomatoes with juices (pureed or broken up) and 2 Tbsp tomato paste for the fresh tomatoes in step 1 and cook until thick. Add 2 cups cherry tomatoes in step 2 with the herbs. Cook for about 8 to 10 minutes, or until starting to soften when pressed with a wooden spoon. Season well to taste. Continue with step 2, adding the eggs.

TO POACH EGGS: While the eggs in this recipe are poached in tomato sauce, if you're looking for tips on how to poach eggs in water, here's my mother's method, which I still use: Bring a skillet of water to a boil, add 1 Tbsp white vinegar, and then gently break the eggs, one at a time, into the water. Cook at a simmer for 5 to 6 minutes or until the whites are firm but yolks are still runny, or however you prefer them. The fresher the eggs, the less the whites will scatter over the water. Lift the eggs out of the water using a spatula (preferably slotted) to a paper towel–lined tray and trim off the superfluous whites. More recently, I learned the simple trick of breaking each egg carefully in a strainer, letting the excess egg white drain away, and then gently turning the egg out into the water. I like to poach 4 or fewer eggs at a time so that they can all have my attention.

VANILLA BUTTERMILK PANCAKES WITH TONS OF FRUIT ON TOP

Serves 4

At brunch a few years ago, at an Australian restaurant in Toronto called Baddies, I ordered the pancake and received a big, beautiful pancake covered in fruit. I have been making them that way ever since. This recipe makes 4 large single serving pancakes but of course you can make smaller ones. A few things to keep in mind: If you want to use local fruit but are making these pancakes in the winter, use frozen berries and cook them down with sugar or a little jam. Other great toppings are caramelized apples or pears, or fruit compote. For a savory version, top each pancake with a fried egg and bacon. When I cook bacon, I arrange the strips on a wire rack set over a baking sheet, drizzle the bacon with maple syrup and sriracha, and bake at 400°F until crisp—a trick I learned from Chef Anthony Rose.

2 cups all-purpose flour (or half whole grain)

2 Tbsp granulated sugar

2 tsp baking powder

½ tsp baking soda

½ tsp kosher salt

2 eggs

3½ cups buttermilk + more as needed

1 Tbsp vanilla paste or pure vanilla extract

3 Tbsp butter, melted + more for the pans

Maple syrup

Toppings

Seasonal fruits or other options mentioned in the recipe intro

NOTE: If you don't have buttermilk, you can make your own by putting 2½ Tbsp white vinegar or fresh lemon juice in a 4-cup glass measuring cup and then adding enough milk to reach the 2½-cup mark. Or you can use half yogurt and half milk.

1. In a large bowl, whisk together the flour, sugar, baking powder, baking soda, and salt.

2. In another bowl, whisk the eggs with the buttermilk, vanilla, and melted butter.

3. Add the egg mixture to the flour mixture and stir until just combined—the batter should be thick and lumpy. Add a bit more buttermilk if it's too thick, but do not overmix.

4. Brush two 9- or 10-inch nonstick skillets with melted butter and heat over medium-high heat until melted. Add 1 cup of the batter to each pan, spreading it slightly if necessary so the pancakes aren't too thick. Cook each for a few minutes on the first side, or until the top loses its sheen, small bubbles appear in the surface, and the bottom is browned. Reduce the heat if the pancake is browning too much. Flip and cook the second side until browned and the pancake is cooked through (be sure to check, especially if your husband also comments that he doesn't love "rare" pancakes). This should take about 10 minutes in total. Repeat with the remaining batter.

5. Drizzle with maple syrup, and top with the fruit of your choice.

NOTE: Instead of drizzling the pancakes with maple syrup, you can sweeten some thick yogurt or sour cream with a little maple syrup and spread over the pancakes, then top with fruit. Or use my Maple Tahini Sauce (page 18).

Breads &
Quick Breads

Challah

Although challah has become trendy and popular in recent years, for most Jewish people, it's steeped in tradition. I came by my love of challah honestly. My mother's mother, Jenny Soltz, lived in Grand Valley, Ontario, with my grandfather and their 11 children. The family was very poor. But every year, my grandmother entered her beautiful challah into the county fair and won enough flour to make challah for her family all year. For me, there's also something about the fact that Jewish people all over the world are taking part in a similar custom on Friday night, that is really meaningful.

I have so many memorable stories about challah, but here's one of my favorites. I went to a wonderful Jewish summer camp in the Maritimes called Camp Kadimah, and it was a life-changing experience for me. A few years ago, I was invited back to teach a challah class for the kids on Shabbat. When I arrived at camp, the kids had made signs that said "Welcome Home, Bonnie." I cried my eyes out. (In fact, I'm crying right now, telling Anna the story—for the millionth time.) About 25 campers were chosen to participate to make enough challah for the evening meal, for 250 people. The kids did an amazing job. And there was extra dough, which I was taking back to my friend's house, where I was having Shabbat dinner. The drive there was about an hour and a half, and it was a very hot day. The car was sweltering, and by the time I got to the house, I had punched down the dough, which had continuously risen, at least 10 times (don't worry, I was in the passenger seat). Guests other than myself were also coming for dinner, and I was beside myself thinking that the challah would be terrible. Now, I'm not telling you to do this, but it was one of the best challahs I've ever made. The moral of the story is: do not worry when you make challah.

Making challah isn't the same as making bread. Challah is about building and continuing a tradition. Someone who attended one of my virtual cooking events for City Shul emailed me afterward to say how much she enjoyed the class, and also told me that my challah recipe helped her through the pandemic. She said she was isolated all year because she was taking care of her mother, and although she baked a lot, she had never made challah before. She started baking it every Friday, and as well as sharing one with her mother, she gave away one each week as a gift to someone she knew. When we spoke, she explained that it connected her to people in a personal way that she would never have expected. She also said that she felt part of a worldwide tradition of people making challah (or similar significant breads). Wow.

My method and ingredients have changed a bit over time, after baking with challah experts here in Toronto and in Israel, but this is my favorite way to make it now. Thanks to Uri Scheft of Lehamim Bakery in Tel Aviv and author of *Breaking Breads* for being everyone's challah inspiration, and to Erez Komarovsky, who brought exceptional artisanal bread to Israel in the '90s with his Lehem Erez bakeries.

Don't worry if your challah isn't perfect the first time you make it. And don't worry if it isn't perfect the 100th time you make it. Perfection isn't the point.

As I mention in the yield, this amount of dough will make several challahs—I like to make the full recipe, and if I have extra, it is a blessing to give a challah away. (Otherwise, you can freeze a baked or unbaked challah, or the unshaped dough.)

CHALLAH

Makes 1 huge, 2 large, or 3 medium challahs

7 cups all-purpose flour, or half whole wheat flour + more as needed, preferably sifted and then measured

½ cup granulated sugar

1 Tbsp kosher salt

1½ Tbsp instant yeast (or 1½ individual packages)

2 eggs

1½ cups water, room temperature

½ cup + 1 Tbsp extra virgin olive oil or vegetable oil (or a combination)

Egg Wash and Toppings

1 egg, lightly beaten

1 tsp water

Pinch kosher salt

Sesame, poppy, or nigella seeds, or flaky sea salt, optional

NOTE: I started sifting my flour for challah after taking lessons with Uri Scheft (see intro). If you do not sift the flour (and you do not have to) you may need less flour to make the dough.

NOTE: For a great gluten-free challah recipe that you can braid, we recommend *Canelle et Vanille Bakes Simple* by Aran Goyoaga.

1. If you are doing this by hand, start with 5 cups of sifted flour in your work bowl. If you are doing this in a stand mixer, start with 5½ cups flour. Either way, whisk the flour with the sugar, salt, and yeast for 30 seconds to combine evenly.

2. In another bowl, whisk the eggs. Whisk in the water and oil.

3. If doing this by hand, stir the liquid ingredients into the dry ingredients with a wooden spoon. The dough will be a little sticky. Stir in more flour, about ¼ cup at a time, until it is less sticky and hard to stir. Stir in just enough additional flour that the dough is too stiff to continue stirring by hand. Sprinkle ¼ cup flour on your work surface. Turn the dough out onto the floured area. With the heels of your hands, knead in enough flour (adding more if needed) so that the dough doesn't stick to your hands but is still moist, about 10 minutes. If doing this in a stand mixer, use the dough hook attachment. Begin by adding the liquid ingredients to the dry on low speed. As the dough comes together, add enough flour so that the dough does not stick to the sides of the bowl (it's okay if it is a little sticky on the bottom). On medium-low speed, knead for about 4 minutes, or until the texture is a little soft and silky. The dough will still be a bit sticky but shouldn't stick to your hands. I think it is always better to have a slightly soft, moist dough than a dry one, as it is more difficult to add liquid to a dry dough than it is to add flour to a moist one. I usually use 6½ to 7 cups sifted flour (less if unsifted) in total (or more), but this varies, depending on the weather, the season, the eggs, and a million other things.

4. Oil a large bowl with 1 Tbsp oil. Place the dough in the bowl and turn it over so it's oiled on all sides. Cover the bowl with plastic wrap and then a clean tea towel. Let rise at room temperature until almost doubled in size, usually 1½ to 2 hours, depending on the temperature in the kitchen. Gently push (not punch) the dough down to release the air, and knead it again to form a ball.

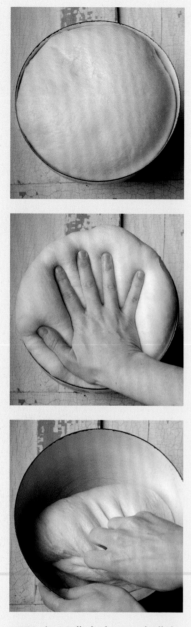

5. Only on special occasions do I use this amount of dough (about 3½ lb) to make 1 really large challah. Usually, I cut the ball in half for 2 large challahs, or in thirds for 3 medium challahs (or 2 medium challahs and a tray of buns—you get the idea). Take the dough you will be using for 1 challah, and set aside the remainder, covered with plastic wrap. Divide the dough into 3 or 4 equally sized pieces (depending on whether you're making a three- or four-braid challah). Cover with plastic wrap the pieces you're not working with and, one at a time, press the piece of dough into an approximate rectangle shape using your fingertips. Then roll the rectangle up tightly into a small cylinder or log, and press the lengthwise edge to seal it. Next, taking both hands, roll the dough from the center to the outside edge into a rope. If at any point the dough does not want to extend, just set it aside for a few minutes and then try again. Repeat for the other pieces and cover the ropes while they wait to be braided. This rolling technique is another technique I learned from Uri. If you're used to shaping the dough into small balls and rolling it into ropes, do it that way.

6. Braid as you like with either three or four strands. (The easiest way to learn to do this is to see it in action. I've created videos on my Instagram page and website for just this purpose!) Place the challahs on parchment paper–lined baking sheets, with enough space for them to rise and bake. Cover loosely with plastic wrap and let rise for 30 to 60 minutes, or until almost doubled in size. Small challahs or buns will rise faster.

7. Halfway through the second rise, preheat the oven to 350°F. For the egg wash, mix the egg with the water and salt. Brush the challah gently with the egg wash just before baking. If you want a darker glaze, wait 10 minutes and glaze a second time. Sprinkle with seeds or salt or nothing. Bake for 25 to 30 minutes or longer. (Small breads or buns will bake faster. Big breads will take longer.) Check the bread after 20 minutes, and if it is browning too much, reduce the oven temperature to 325°F and cover the bread lightly with aluminum foil. Bake until an instant-read thermometer registers between 185°F and 195°F when inserted into the center of the bread. Transfer the bread to a wire rack to cool.

NOTE: I usually bake my challah free-form on a baking sheet. They also come out beautifully (and rise higher) if braided and then baked in a loaf pan, or shaped into a circle and baked in a round cake pan. In that case, place in the loaf or cake pan (lined with parchment paper or sprayed with non-stick cooking spray) after braiding so that the second rise takes place in the pan.

NOTE: It is hard to tell when bread is ready without a thermometer. One method is to turn the loaf upside down (taking it out of the pan if necessary) and tap on the bottom—if it sounds hollow, it's ready. The more you bake bread, the easier it will be to recognize this hollow sound and tell when it's ready. But to be honest, I have never heard this hollow sound so I always use an instant-read thermometer.

ROSEMARY GARLIC PULL-APART CHALLAH KNOTS

Makes 12 to 16 buns

This has become the most requested variation of my challah at Friday night dinner. Because I can make two or three breads out of one challah recipe, if I want to make these knots, I'll make one less bread and use that dough for knots instead. They're a perfect little appetizer, especially if people come over early, if kids need a snack after school, or if you just need a bite of challah because the smell of freshly baked bread is so overpowering but you don't want to cut into the big challah yet. They will be gone in a flash. Serve them on their own or with dips like hummus (page 24) or chirshi (page 26).

⅓ batch challah dough on page 183 (about 1 to 1¼ lb)

½ cup extra virgin olive oil

1 garlic clove, minced or grated

2 tsp chopped fresh rosemary + a few sprigs

¾ tsp kosher salt

1 egg

Flaky sea salt

1. Let the dough rise at least once.

2. While it's rising, combine the olive oil, garlic, chopped rosemary, and salt in a shallow bowl or 8-inch baking dish.

3. Line a baking sheet with parchment paper or you can use a lined round or square pan.

4. Push the dough down gently and divide the dough into pieces about 1½ oz each—about 12 to 16 pieces for this amount of dough. (Don't worry if they aren't all the same size. In fact, I like when they're not.) Roll each piece into a rope about 6 inches long, then twist into a knot—make a loop and tuck one end through. When all the knots are formed, dip each bun into the olive oil mixture to coat on both sides and arrange on the lined baking sheet in rows or circles, side by side. I like when they are just barely touching each other so that they bake into pull-apart buns. Cover loosely with plastic wrap and let rise at room temperature for 25 to 30 minutes, or until almost doubled in size.

5. Preheat the oven to 350°F while the buns are rising. Beat the egg in a small bowl. Brush the tops of the buns with the egg and sprinkle lightly with flaky sea salt. Scatter or surround with sprigs of fresh rosemary.

6. Bake for 15 to 20 minutes, or until lightly browned and an instant-read thermometer registers 185°F to 195°F when inserted into the thickest bun.

SAVORY BABKA-CHALLAH WITH ROSEMARY AND GARLIC

Makes one large or two smaller babkas

Babkas have become so popular that I decided to convert my rosemary garlic buns into savory babka loaf. My favorite babkas are from Lehamim in Tel Aviv, where the brilliant baker Uri Scheft uses a croissant-style dough (laminated with multiple layers of butter), which changed the babka game. You can make babkas the traditional way, using a rich, sweet, challah-type dough without rolling in extra layers of butter, or you can meet these methods in the middle by adding one layer of butter as I do here. You also have these options for my cinnamon buns (page 193), either as buns or babka style.

½ **batch challah dough on page 183 (about 1½ lb),** cold

½ **cup + ⅓ cup butter,** room temperature

1 **large garlic clove,** minced or grated

2 **Tbsp chopped fresh rosemary + a few small sprigs**

2 **Tbsp chopped fresh flat-leaf parsley**

1 **tsp kosher salt**

1½ **cups grated cheese (such as cheddar, Swiss, or Lappi),** optional

Topping

1 **egg,** beaten

2 **tsp flaky sea salt**

1 **Tbsp coarse sugar,** optional

Extra virgin olive oil

1. Line two 5 × 9-inch loaf pans with parchment paper and set aside. Or use one 8- or 9-inch square pan, with the two babkas side by side.

2. Roll the dough out to a rectangle approximately 12 × 18 inches or larger. If the dough is hard to roll, let it rest, covered, for 5 to 10 minutes, then try again.

3. With the shorter side of the rectangle parallel to the edge of the countertop in front you, spread ½ cup room temperature butter over two-thirds of the dough—across the top and down toward you—leaving the third section of dough closest to you unbuttered. Fold the dough into thirds like a letter—bring the unbuttered third up over the middle third, and the buttered top third down over that. The dough should now be about 12 inches in length and 6 inches high. Turn the dough so that the lengthwise opening is perpendicular to the edge of the countertop in front of you, on the right. Pat the dough down. Wrap in plastic wrap and refrigerate for 30 minutes or up to a few hours.

4. Roll the dough out again with the lengthwise open end to the right (as it was before) and roll it out to approximately the same size, 12 × 18 inches. If the top or bottom of the dough is sticking at any time, or if any pieces of butter are exposed, flour lightly. Combine the garlic, rosemary, parsley, and salt with ⅓ cup room-temperature butter and spread over the dough. Sprinkle with cheese, if using. Roll up tightly lengthwise so that you have one long 18-inch roll.

continued . . .

5. Cut the roll in half crosswise so you have two 9-inch-long ropes. Then cut each rope in half lengthwise so you can see the garlic-rosemary filling peeking out. Working with one part at a time, crisscross the two halves in the middle, cut sides up, and wind them together from the middle cross out. Place, cut side up, in the lined pan. Repeat with the second rope. Cover loosely with plastic wrap and let rise at room temperature for 30 to 45 minutes, or until almost doubled in size.

6. Halfway through the rise, preheat the oven to 350°F.

7. Brush the tops of the babkas with beaten egg and sprinkle with flaky sea salt, coarse sugar, and little sprigs of rosemary. Drizzle with olive oil.

8. Bake for 30 to 35 minutes, or longer, until an instant-read thermometer registers between 185°F and 195°F when inserted into a bready part of the babka. If it isn't ready or if it is browning too much after 30 minutes, reduce the oven temperature to 325°F and cover loosely with aluminum foil. Cool for about 20 minutes in the pan, then continue cooling on a wire rack if you haven't torn it apart and eaten it all by then.

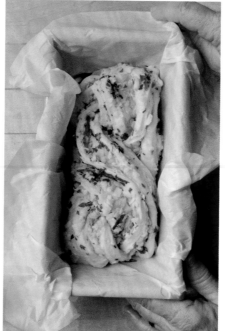

CHALLAH CINNAMON BUNS WITH BROWN SUGAR GLAZE

Makes 12 to 15 buns

According to Mark, Ray, Fara, my sister Jane (okay, all of us!), there is nothing better than cinnamon buns, but then I get in trouble for making them because we all eat too many. I even made a giant cinnamon bun birthday cake for Mark one year. When you make challah, if you know you'll be using part of the dough for cinnamon buns, you can use soft butter instead of oil, and milk instead of water for a richer dough, as long as the challah doesn't need to be dairy-free. I particularly like this glaze from Tasting Table.

½ **batch challah dough on page 183 (about 1½ lb)**

½ **cup butter,** softened

1½ **cups packed light brown sugar**

1½ **tsp cinnamon**

Brown Sugar Glaze

⅔ **cup granulated sugar**

2 **Tbsp light brown sugar**

⅓ **cup whipping cream**

¼ **cup butter**

1 **tsp pure vanilla extract**

¼ **tsp kosher salt**

1. Roll out the dough into a 12 × 18-inch rectangle (or larger, for more spirals). Spread the softened butter to cover the dough, leaving about ½ inch of dough unbuttered along one of the long edges. In a small bowl, combine the brown sugar and cinnamon, and sprinkle over the buttered dough as evenly as possible. Pat the sugar mixture into the butter. Roll the dough up lengthwise, starting at the side that has the butter and cinnamon sugar spread all the way to the edge.

2. Preheat the oven to 350°F. Generously butter a 9 × 13-inch baking pan (or line it with parchment paper and butter the paper).

3. Cut the roll crosswise into 12 to 15 pieces, each approximately 1½ inches thick, and arrange, cut side up, in the pan. Cover loosely with plastic wrap. Let rise at room temperature for about 30 minutes, or until almost doubled in size.

4. If you're worried about spills, place the baking dish on a baking sheet lined with aluminum foil. Bake for 22 to 25 minutes, or until puffy and gooey and browned. Cool in the pan on a wire rack.

5. While the buns are baking, make the glaze. (Or, if using, make the cream cheese icing; see note on next page.) Place the granulated sugar, brown sugar, cream, and butter in a saucepan and bring to a boil, stirring constantly. Cook gently for a few minutes, until the sugar dissolves. Add the vanilla and salt. When the buns are cool, drizzle the glaze on top (or spread with icing).

CINNAMON BUN BIRTHDAY CAKE: You can bake cinnamon buns in a round pan, and once they're out of the oven, dress them up as a birthday cake. But when I made a cake for Mark, I did it a bit differently: I made one huge cinnamon bun. Line a 12-inch round baking pan or deep pizza pan with parchment paper and butter the bottom. Follow step 1 but stop when it is a rectangle covered with butter, brown sugar, and cinnamon and do not roll up the dough. Instead, pat the sugar down into the butter to help prevent it from falling out. Cut the dough lengthwise into approximately 10 long strips. Roll the first strip into a coil and place in the middle of the pan. (Don't roll too tightly, as the dough will need room to rise, but not too loosely either.) Gently pick up the second strip and continue coiling from where the first one left off. Continue until all the strips are used. You should now have one giant cinnamon roll. If your pan isn't large enough to accommodate all the strips, bake the remaining ones separately for the chef to eat! Cover the giant roll lightly with plastic wrap and let rise at room temperature for about 30 minutes, or until almost doubled in size. While it is rising, preheat the oven to 350°F. Bake for 20 to 25 minutes, or until browned. Once the "cake" has cooled for about 15 to 20 minutes, drizzle or spread with the glaze. Or make Mark's favorite **cream cheese icing** (4 oz full-fat brick-style cream cheese beaten with ¼ cup soft butter, 1 cup sifted icing sugar, and 1 tsp pure vanilla extract) which also tastes great here. Write "Happy Birthday Mark!" on top of the cake or on the serving platter. (Oops—put in the name of *your* birthday person.)

SWEDISH CRACKED RYE BREAD

Makes one 5 × 9-inch loaf

This is a quicker version of the delicious, dense, moist, and healthful Scandinavian breads I fell in love with on my trips to Denmark, Sweden, and Norway. It uses yeast rather than sourdough, and don't be surprised when the dough is very sticky. This recipe is with thanks to Chef Cole Baker at the Swedish Embassy in Ottawa for his inspiration and encouragement, and to my Danish colleague Tina Scheftelowitz for her expertise.

¼ **cup flax seeds**

¼ **cup roasted sunflower seeds**

¼ **cup roasted pumpkin seeds**

1 **cup cracked rye**

1 **cup water,** room temperature

1½ **cups buttermilk**

2 **Tbsp molasses**

1 **cup dark rye flour**

1 **cup spelt flour**

1 **cup whole wheat flour or all-purpose flour**

1 **Tbsp kosher salt**

1 **Tbsp instant yeast**

1. Combine the flax seeds, sunflower seeds, and pumpkin seeds in a mixing bowl. Add the cracked rye and water. Soak for at least 1 hour, or until the water is absorbed.

2. In another bowl, whisk the buttermilk with the molasses until well mixed.

3. In a large bowl (or bowl of a stand mixer), whisk together the rye flour, spelt flour, whole wheat flour, salt, and yeast to combine. Stir in the buttermilk mixture. The dough should be very sticky—add a bit more water if it seems dry. Add the seed mixture (drain first if necessary). The dough will look like a heavy coffee cake batter rather than a traditional bread dough.

4. Oil and then line a 5 × 9-inch loaf pan with parchment paper or use non-stick cooking spray. Place the dough in the prepared pan—it should fill the pan about two-thirds to three-quarters full. Cover loosely with oiled plastic wrap and let rise at room temperature for 3 to 4 hours or for 8 hours (overnight) in the refrigerator. The dough will rise to about the top of the pan, but it won't double in size, so don't worry. If letting the bread rise in the refrigerator, leave it at room temperature for 1 hour before baking.

5. Preheat the oven to 350°F. Bake the bread for 50 to 60 minutes, or until an instant-read thermometer registers 195°F when inserted into the center. Remove from the pan and cool on a wire rack. Wrap in aluminum foil while warm and slice the next day.

ANNA'S GLUTEN-FREE BREAD

Makes one 5 × 9-inch loaf

This is the best gluten-free bread I have made to date. A cookbook author and friend, Carrie Davis, recommended a challah book that I tried to purchase, but I ordered a completely different book by accident. (Now you know I'm not very good at buying things online.) Luckily, what I accidentally ordered was great, *Rising: The Book of Challah*, by Rochie Pinson. I have adapted her recipe for a gluten-free challah and changed it quite a bit, but it gave me a strong starting point. This dough is more like a batter bread and cannot be braided, but you could buy a challah-shaped baking pan if you want it to look more challah-like (for a challah you can braid, see note on page 183). Once it cools, Anna slices what she isn't eating right away and keeps it in the freezer. I am so happy that I get to make her bread on Fridays even though she can't eat my traditional challah.

1 Tbsp + 2 Tbsp granulated sugar

½ cup + 1½ cups warm water

4 tsp instant yeast

2 cups gluten-free oat flour

2 cups gluten-free flour (such as Cup4Cup)

2 tsp kosher salt

1½ tsp xanthan gum

2 eggs

¼ cup extra virgin olive oil, vegetable oil, or very soft butter

Egg Wash and Topping

1 egg

1 Tbsp water

Pinch of kosher salt

1 Tbsp coarse sugar

1 Tbsp flaky sea salt

1 Tbsp chopped fresh rosemary

OR

Seeds like sesame, poppy, nigella, pumpkin, sunflower, or flax

1. Dissolve 1 Tbsp sugar in ½ cup warm water and sprinkle with the yeast. Stir and let stand for 8 minutes, or until bubbly.

2. In a large bowl or the bowl of a stand mixer fitted with the paddle attachment, combine the oat flour with the gluten-free flour, 2 Tbsp granulated sugar, salt, and xanthan gum.

3. In another bowl, combine the eggs, olive oil, and 1½ cups warm water. Stir down the yeast mixture and add to the egg mixture.

4. Mix the liquid ingredients with the dry ingredients with a wooden spoon or in the stand mixer for about 2 minutes on low speed to thoroughly combine. It will look like a thick batter. (You do not knead this bread.) Cover the bowl with plastic wrap and place in a warmish spot to rise for 20 to 35 minutes or longer, or until almost doubled in size.

5. Stir the batter down. Butter or spray all sides of a 5 × 9-inch loaf pan or line with parchment paper. Spoon the batter into the pan.

6. For the egg wash, beat the egg with water and salt.

7. In a small bowl, combine the sugar, flaky salt, and rosemary. Brush the top of the bread with the egg wash and sprinkle with the rosemary mixture or with any of the seeds. Cover loosely with plastic wrap and let rise at room temperature for about 20 to 30 minutes, or until almost doubled in size.

8. While the bread rises, preheat the oven to 350°F. Bake for 45 to 55 minutes, or until an instant-read thermometer registers 195°F when inserted into the center. Cool on a wire rack.

BUTTERMILK CORNBREAD WITH PUMPKIN, CHEESE, AND JALAPEÑO

Makes 12 pieces or muffins

One thing that is so wonderful about cornbread is that it's a quick and easy way to serve homemade bread, and it feels like a real treat. Cornbread works well in turkey stuffing or used for breadcrumbs in meatloaf (page 148)—or toast leftovers for croutons to add to salads. But our absolute favorite way to eat cornbread was introduced to us by our wonderful friend Chef Anthony Rose. At Rose and Sons, one of Anthony's Toronto restaurants, his cornbread is served in a big wedge, topped with brisket, a fried egg, maple syrup, and hot sauce. Delish! You could do that with this recipe too.

1 cup yellow cornmeal

1 cup all-purpose flour or whole wheat flour

¼ cup granulated sugar

1½ tsp baking powder

¾ tsp baking soda

½ tsp kosher salt

1 tsp smoked paprika, optional

2 eggs

1½ cups buttermilk (see note on page 178)

⅓ cup butter, melted, **or extra virgin olive oil**

1 jalapeño, halved, with ribs and seeds removed, finely chopped, **or ½ to 1 tsp hot sauce**

1 cup grated aged or smoked cheddar or any other semi-firm cheese

1 cup grated butternut squash, carrots, or sweet potatoes

¼ cup roasted pumpkin seeds

1. Preheat the oven to 400°F. Butter or spray a 9-inch square baking dish or a 12-cup muffin pan.

2. In a large bowl, whisk together the cornmeal, flour, sugar, baking powder, baking soda, salt, and paprika for at least 30 seconds. In another bowl, whisk the eggs with the buttermilk and melted butter. Stir into the cornmeal mixture just until combined. Add the jalapeño, cheese, and squash.

3. Spoon the batter into the prepared pan. Top with pumpkin seeds.

4. Bake for 25 to 30 minutes (or 20 minutes for muffins), or until the top is lightly browned and springs back when touched gently in the center, or an instant-read thermometer registers between 185°F and 195°F when inserted into the center. Cool on a wire rack for 10 minutes before serving. Cut into 12 pieces.

NOTE: Even though it's easy to substitute gluten-free flour in any cornbread recipe, if you want a pure cornmeal cornbread, we recommend Mitchell Davis' recipe in his cookbook *Kitchen Sense*.

GIULIANO BUGIALLI'S FOCACCIA WITH TOMATOES AND OREGANO

Makes 1 large focaccia

Giuliano Bugialli, cookbook author and culinary historian, was one of the most memorable and knowledgeable teachers who taught at my cooking school. Incredibly, he taught for us every November for 20 years. He was always very serious about his classes, but he was also a show-man, and his classes were fun and entertaining. His recipe for focaccia has proven time and time again to impress and please everyone. By the way, whenever Giuliano said add "a little" olive oil or "a little" salt, he was lying about the "little" part. I have adapted his recipe slightly.

Sponge

1 cup warm water

1 tsp granulated sugar

2 Tbsp instant yeast

1 cup + 1 Tbsp all-purpose flour

¼ cup semolina flour

¼ tsp kosher salt

Dough

3½ cups all-purpose flour + more as needed

¼ cup semolina flour

1 cup warm water

2 Tbsp extra virgin olive oil

2 tsp kosher salt

Tomatoes

1 lb ripe fresh tomatoes, seeded and chopped, drained (I like to use plum or cherry tomatoes)

2 Tbsp extra virgin olive oil

1 tsp dried oregano

1 tsp kosher salt

⅛ tsp freshly ground black pepper

1. For the sponge, combine the water and sugar in a 2-cup glass measuring cup. Sprinkle with yeast and stir together. In a medium or large bowl, whisk together 1 cup all-purpose flour, semolina flour, and salt. When the yeast is frothy (about 5 to 6 minutes), stir it down and then combine with the flour mixture. Sprinkle the top with 1 Tbsp flour and cover with oiled plastic wrap. Let rise at room temperature for 30 to 40 minutes, or until almost doubled in size. It will be sticky.

2. Meanwhile, in the bowl of a stand mixer, make the dough. Whisk together the all-purpose and semolina flours, or if you are doing this by hand, use a large mixing bowl. Set aside. In another bowl or measuring cup, combine the water, olive oil, and salt. Set aside.

3. For the tomatoes, in a medium mixing bowl, combine the drained tomatoes with the olive oil, oregano, salt, and pepper. Set aside.

4. For the garlic, in a small bowl, combine the garlic with the salt, oregano, and olive oil. Set aside.

5. When the sponge has risen, stir it down and add to the flour mixture, along with the water–olive oil mixture. Combine on low speed (or with a wooden spoon) until a dough forms, then knead in the stand mixer for 5 minutes (or for 5 to 10 minutes by hand). The dough should be sticky but not stick to your hands too much. Add a little more all-purpose flour if necessary. Place the dough in an oiled bowl, turn over in the bowl to coat with oil, cover with plastic wrap, and let rise for 1 to 1½ hours at room temperature, or until almost doubled in size.

continued . . .

Garlic

6 large garlic cloves, cut into slivers

½ tsp kosher salt

1½ tsp dried oregano

2 Tbsp extra virgin olive oil

To Bake and Serve

¼ cup + ¼ cup extra virgin olive oil

1 Tbsp flaky sea salt

1 Tbsp dried oregano

Sprigs of fresh oregano, optional

6. Brush a 15-inch round or 12 × 18-inch baking sheet (with sides) with ¼ cup olive oil. Push down the dough and, on a lightly floured work surface, roll it out to approximately fit the pan. Place the dough in the pan and push and pull the dough until it covers the bottom. If the dough shrinks back, wait 5 to 10 minutes, then press to fit the pan again—eventually it will relax and fit. Cover loosely with plastic wrap and let rise for about 30 minutes at room temperature.

7. With your thumb, make about 10 deep indentations all over the surface of the dough. Put some of the tomatoes and juices in each indentation. Make 8 to 10 more indentations and put some of the garlic with the olive oil in those. Cover loosely with plastic wrap and let rise again for 30 minutes. Preheat the oven to 400°F.

8. Drizzle the dough with ¼ cup olive oil, and sprinkle with salt and oregano. Bake for 25 to 30 minutes, or until the bread is nicely browned, and an instant-read thermometer registers 195°F when inserted into the thickest part. Drizzle with "a little" more olive oil and scatter with sprigs of fresh oregano, if using. Cool on a wire rack. Cut into strips and then across on an angle into diamonds.

LESLIE'S SOUR CREAM AND CHIVE ALMOND CRACKERS

Makes about 50 crackers

Our friend Leslie Davis always comes up with new and delicious recipes that work well for people on special diets. Here's a gluten-free and egg-free cracker that I cannot stop eating. Neither can Anna. They are too delicious. And they are perfect for Passover.

2 cups almond flour (see page 6)

⅓ cup full-fat sour cream, thick yogurt, or coconut yogurt

2 Tbsp chopped fresh chives or 1 tsp chopped fresh rosemary

1 tsp sea salt or kosher salt

½ tsp garlic powder, optional

1. Preheat the oven to 250°F.

2. In a large bowl, mix together by hand the almond flour, sour cream, chives, salt, and garlic powder, if using. Knead for 30 seconds or until smooth.

3. Place the dough on a 12 × 18-inch piece of parchment paper and place another piece of parchment paper on top. With a rolling pin, roll the dough between the two sheets of parchment, as thin as possible, about ⅛ inch thick.

4. Remove the top sheet of parchment and transfer the bottom sheet, with the dough, to a large baking sheet. Score the dough into about 1½-inch squares with a pizza cutter, pastry cutter, or knife—you're not cutting all the way through.

5. Bake for 50 to 60 minutes, or longer, until the crackers are lightly browned. Check the oven often in case they get too dark.

6. Cool completely and break into the prescored squares.

ROYAL WEDDING BUTTERMILK SCONES

Makes 8 or 9 large scones

I have always been somewhat neutral when it comes to the royal family, but when William and Kate got married, for some reason I was up at 5:30 a.m. baking scones. Everyone who makes scones has their own secrets. The biggest secret, for me, is to make them fresh. Even a few hours can turn them dry and hard, so be sure to warm them when serving if making ahead. When serving them with jam and cream, I like plain scones, but you can flavor them in many ways. For savory scones, add 1 Tbsp chopped fresh herbs and ½ tsp freshly ground black pepper, 1 cup grated cheese, and sprinkle with flaky sea salt. For afternoon tea scones, increase the sugar to 3 or 4 Tbsp and add ½ tsp ground cardamom, ½ cup chopped dried fruit, and 1 Tbsp grated lemon peel, and sprinkle with coarse sugar.

½ **cup butter,** diced and very cold (see note)

2 cups all-purpose flour

2 Tbsp granulated sugar

4 tsp baking powder

½ **tsp kosher salt**

1 egg

¾ **cup buttermilk** (see note on page 178)

Suggested Toppings

Lemon curd (page 223)

Berries or berry sauce (page 222)

Mascarpone or whipped cream

NOTE: A new technique is to grate cold butter for scones, pastry, and cakes instead of cutting butter into small pieces, leaving the pieces more or less uniform. After grating, freeze it for at least 15 minutes before using, as it softens quickly. Use the same grating blade as for cheddar cheese, and watch your fingers. Try it and see if you like it!

1. Preheat the oven to 425°F and line a baking sheet with parchment paper.

2. In a large bowl, whisk together the flour, sugar, baking powder, and salt for about 1 minute. In another bowl, beat the egg with the buttermilk.

3. Add the cold butter to the flour and cut it in with a pastry blender or your fingertips until it's in very small pieces. Make a well in the center of the flour mixture and add all but 2 tablespoons of the egg mixture. Gently and quickly gather the ingredients together to form a rough, soft dough. (Add the extra egg mixture by the teaspoon if needed to form the dough and use buttermilk for the topping.) Flour your work surface lightly, and pat or flatten the dough out with your hands to a rough 7- or 8-inch square about ¾ inch thick. (Scones seem to rise more when you pat with your hands rather than use a rolling pin.) Fold the square in half, dusting off any flour that's on top. Gently flatten the dough once more into a square about ¾ inch to 1 inch thick. Cut the dough with a very sharp knife into quarters, then cut in half on the diagonal to make 8 fairly large scones, or you can cut the dough into 9 squares, or cut out circles. (If making circles, lightly push the scraps together to form a large substandard looking scone to eat yourself.)

4. Place the scones on the lined baking sheet. Brush the tops with the remaining egg mixture, or with buttermilk if you've used all the mixture. Bake for 12 to 14 minutes, or until browned and puffed, turning the baking sheet around after about 8 minutes. Serve with your choice of toppings.

WILD BLUEBERRY AND ORANGE MUFFINS

Makes 24 mini-muffins (or 12 regular-sized muffins)

These have become our very favorite muffins. They aren't big and glamorous, but they *are* irresistible! I first had them at Sugar Hill Inn in Gros Morne, when traveling up the west coast of Newfoundland with friends from my Camp Kadimah days. The muffins were originally made with partridge berries (also known as lingonberries outside of Newfoundland), but I also love them with wild blueberries. If using frozen berries, use them from frozen or their color will bleed too much into the muffins. Sometimes I use whole wheat flour or half whole wheat and half all-purpose. These muffins freeze well and are extremely easy to eat—especially the mini ones—and I prefer to make them mini because I feel less guilty when I can't stop at one.

1 medium orange (about 8 oz), ends trimmed off, cut into 1-inch chunks with the peel and pith (remove all seeds)

1 egg

½ cup milk

⅓ cup extra virgin olive oil or vegetable oil

1½ cups all-purpose flour

½ cup granulated sugar

2 tsp baking powder

1 tsp baking soda

½ tsp kosher salt

1 cup fresh or frozen wild blueberries or partridge berries or 1½ cups regular blueberries

1 Tbsp coarse sugar, optional

1. Preheat the oven to 375°F. Butter or spray a 24-cup mini-muffin pan (or 12-cup regular-sized muffin pan). Or line with paper muffin cups.

2. Put the orange pieces, egg, milk, and olive oil in a food processor and pulse until the orange is in tiny bits (about 30 pulses). You can also do this in a blender.

3. In a large bowl, whisk the flour with the sugar, baking powder, baking soda, and salt until well combined. Stir the orange mixture into the flour mixture just until combined. Stir in the blueberries.

4. Spoon about 2 Tbsp of the batter into each mini-muffin cup (about ¼ cup batter for regular-sized muffins). If you have leftover batter, you can bake it in a ramekin. If all the cups are not used, add a little water to each empty one to prevent them from burning. Sprinkle the muffin tops with coarse sugar, if using.

5. Bake for 15 to 20 minutes (regular-sized muffins may need 25 minutes) or until the muffins have risen and are browned, and an instant-read thermometer registers 195°F when inserted into the center. Cool for 10 to 15 minutes in the pan and then remove. If you don't eat them all immediately, they'll keep for 1 to 2 days covered at room temperature.

MORNING GLORY MUFFINS

Makes 12 muffins

I recently started craving these morning glory muffins, which I used to make all the time. They are full of wonderful add-ins—which you can add in or not—and you can substitute similar ingredients (though I like to think that the bran helps make your morning glorious!). You don't need any special equipment to make these, and if you don't have a muffin pan, you can bake the batter in a 9-inch square pan and call them muffin squares (it may take a bit longer to bake).

1½ cups all-purpose flour (or half whole wheat)

1 cup bran cereal (I use All-Bran Buds)

1 Tbsp baking powder

½ tsp baking soda

¼ tsp kosher salt

1 tsp cinnamon

1 egg

¾ cup buttermilk (see note on page 178)

½ cup extra virgin olive oil or vegetable oil

½ cup light brown sugar

2 Tbsp molasses

1 apple or pear, peel on or off, grated

1 large carrot or parsnip, scrubbed or peeled, grated

½ cup chopped pitted dates (see note) **or other dried fruit you like**

½ cup chopped roasted walnuts or other nuts

2 Tbsp toasted sesame seeds

2 Tbsp roasted pumpkin seeds

1. Preheat the oven to 350°F. Butter or spray a 12-cup muffin pan. Or line with paper muffin cups.

2. In a medium mixing bowl, whisk the flour with the bran cereal, baking powder, baking soda, salt, and cinnamon until well combined.

3. In another, larger bowl, whisk the egg with the buttermilk, olive oil, sugar, and molasses.

4. Stir the dry ingredients into the egg mixture, and mix only until combined. Add the apples, carrots, dates, nuts, and sesame seeds. Stir well.

5. Scoop the batter into the muffin cups. Sprinkle with the pumpkin seeds. Bake for 20 to 25 minutes, or until the muffins have risen and are browned, and an instant-read thermometer registers at least 185°F when inserted into the center. Cool for 10 to 15 minutes in the pan, then remove. The muffins will keep for a few days, covered, at room temperature, and they freeze well.

NOTE: It's easier to "chop" or slice dates or most other dried fruit by cutting them up with scissors.

For a gluten-free version of these muffins, substitute gluten-free flour, and use rolled oats, oat bran, or any gluten-free cereal instead of bran cereal.

Desserts & Cookies

ALMOND CAKE WITH CARAMELIZED PEARS

Serves 8 to 10

It's hard to imagine my kitchen without a food processor, but it wasn't until the '70s that Ed Weil, founder of Weil Company, brought Cuisinart products to Canada. I worked with the company to develop recipes, taught classes on how to use a food processor, and wrote two food processor cookbooks. This was a wonderful recipe for a food processor because being able to process the almond paste with butter so easily was a game changer. I first started making this cake in those classes and it is still one of my favorite cakes today. Over the years, I have redeveloped this recipe many times as good almond paste became hard to find and very expensive, while almond flour became more readily available, eventually incorporating all the ingredients for the almond paste directly into the recipe and making it easier all around. Anna refers to this as THE almond cake. Not only is it her favorite, but she says it's a sleeper—easy and unassuming, and will impress everyone. I've always told her that classics are timeless. The cake and pears are also delicious on their own.

1 cup butter, cubed

1¼ cups granulated sugar

1 cup icing sugar, sifted

6 eggs

2 tsp pure vanilla extract or paste

1½ tsp pure almond extract

2 cups almond flour

1 cup all-purpose flour

1 tsp baking powder

½ tsp kosher salt

Caramelized Pears

4 pears (preferably Bosc or Bartlett), firm but ripe

½ lemon, thinly sliced

¾ cup granulated sugar

1 vanilla bean, cut in half

3 cardamom pods, gently crushed

¼ cup dry white wine or water

¼ cup water

½ cup whipping cream, cold, optional

1. Preheat the oven to 350°F. Butter and line a deep 9-inch or 10-inch springform pan with parchment paper.

2. For the cake, in a stand mixer fitted with the paddle attachment, cream the butter and granulated sugar together on medium-low speed for 3 to 4 minutes, or until very light and pale. You can also cream it in a food processor, until smooth and just blended. Mix in the icing sugar. Add the eggs one at a time, mixing after each addition. Add the vanilla and almond extracts.

3. In a medium bowl, whisk together the almond flour, all-purpose flour, baking powder, and salt. Add the mixture to the batter and mix just until combined. Scrape the batter into the prepared pan. Bake for 35 to 45 minutes, depending on the thickness of the cake, or until the center of the cake feels firm when pressed, and a cake tester inserted into the center comes out clean, or when an instant-read thermometer registers at least 185°F when inserted into the center. Cool in the pan on a wire rack.

4. For the caramelized pears, peel the pears, cut them in half lengthwise, cut away the ends, and remove the cores (a melon baller works well for this). Set aside in a bowl of cold water with the lemon slices to prevent browning.

continued . . .

5. Sprinkle the sugar over the bottom of a deep 10-inch or 11-inch skillet. Cook for 4 to 5 minutes over medium-high heat, or until the sugar melts and starts to brown, shaking the pan (but not stirring) if the sugar is melting and browning unevenly. Do not leave the pan, as once it starts to brown, it burns quickly. (If it burns, DO NOT add the pears to see what happens next—discard and start again. At this point you are only wasting sugar and time. The vanilla bean, cardamom, lemon, and pears are still safe.) Once you've successfully made your caramel, add the vanilla bean, cardamom pods, and pears, cut side down, along with the lemon slices. The mixture may sputter a bit. Cook for 1 or 2 minutes. Turn off the heat and, standing back, pour in the wine and water. The mixture may bubble up, but don't worry.

6. Cook over medium-low heat, covered, for about 8 to 10 minutes, or until the pears are just tender. When the pears are ready, transfer them to a shallow serving dish along with the lemon slices. If there is lots of liquid in the pan, reduce it to about ⅓ cup. Pour over the pears. Discard the cardamom pods, but rinse off the vanilla beans, dry them, and keep them in your sugar canister.

7. Whip the cream, if using. Serve the pears with the sauce and lemon slices, warm or at room temperature, on or with the cake and cream.

NOTE: I think this cake is best eaten cold or at room temperature. It can be made 1 to 2 days in advance, or weeks in advance and frozen. This cake is perfect just plain (the way Anna likes it), but topping it with whipped cream and caramelized pears is pretty incredible too.

LOTS OF BLUEBERRIES CRUMB CAKE

Serves 8 to 10

There are so many wonderful recipes for blueberry cakes and muffins. I get so excited when it is blueberry season in Ontario, I start working my way through the recipes, and when I get to this one, I just stick with it until the season is over. (Maybe one year I will remember to start here.) It's delicious as is, or serve it with ice cream or unsweetened whipped cream.

2 cups all-purpose flour (or half whole wheat)

½ cup granulated sugar

½ cup light brown sugar

2 tsp baking powder

½ tsp kosher salt

¾ cup butter, cold and cut into bits (or grated and then frozen; see note on page 205)

½ tsp cinnamon

1 egg

½ cup milk

2 tsp pure vanilla extract or paste

3 to 3½ cups fresh or frozen blueberries (see note)

2 Tbsp coarse sugar, optional

1. Preheat the oven to 350°F. Butter or spray an 8- or 9-inch round springform pan and line with parchment paper.

2. In a large bowl, whisk together the flour, granulated sugar, brown sugar, baking powder, and salt. Use a pastry blender or your fingers to rub the butter bits into the flour mixture until it is in tiny bits. If you grated the butter, stir the frozen butter in with a fork. Remove 1½ cups of this crumb-like mixture to a small bowl and stir in the cinnamon. Set aside.

3. In another bowl, beat the egg, milk, and vanilla together. Add the egg mixture to the flour mixture (the one in the larger bowl without the cinnamon) and, using a hand mixer or wooden spoon, stir until combined. It doesn't have to be smooth.

4. Spread the batter evenly over the bottom of the prepared pan. Sprinkle with blueberries and then with the reserved crumb mixture. Sprinkle (I know—a lot of sprinkling) with the coarse sugar, if using.

5. Bake for 45 to 50 minutes, or until the top has browned and the center is firm, and an instant-read thermometer registers at least 185°F when inserted into the center of the cake layer (not the blueberry layer).

NOTE: If making this out of season and using frozen blueberries, use 3 cups and use them from frozen.

LEMON PISTACHIO LOAF

Serves 8 to 10

The last time we were in Tel Aviv, we were staying around the corner from Eats Cafeteria on Shenkin Street. Their food was very casual but also beautiful and delicious, with many vegan choices and truly wonderful gluten-free desserts, of which their lemon pistachio loaf was our favorite. Anna and I enjoyed it on far too many occasions. When we got home, we came up with this recipe, which based on our collective memory we believe is close.

¾ cup all-purpose flour

1 tsp baking powder

½ tsp kosher salt

1 cup finely ground pistachios (see page 6)

½ cup + 2 Tbsp butter, room temperature

1 cup granulated sugar

3 eggs

1 Tbsp finely grated lemon peel

1 Tbsp fresh lemon juice

1 tsp pure vanilla extract

½ tsp pure almond extract

Glaze and Topping

1 cup icing sugar, sifted

2 to 3 Tbsp fresh lemon juice

2 Tbsp pistachios, ground, chopped, or slivered

1. Preheat the oven to 350°F and line a 5 × 9-inch loaf pan with parchment paper.

2. In a medium mixing bowl, whisk the flour with the baking powder and salt. Stir in the ground pistachios. In another bowl, using a handheld mixer or in the bowl of a stand mixer fitted with the paddle attachment, beat the butter and granulated sugar together until light, 2 to 3 minutes. Add the eggs one at a time, beating after each addition just until combined. Add the lemon peel, lemon juice, and vanilla and almond extracts. Stir in the flour mixture just until combined.

3. Transfer the batter to the prepared pan and bake for 40 to 50 minutes, or until a cake tester inserted into the center comes out clean or an instant-read thermometer registers between 185°F and 195°F when inserted into the center. Let the cake cool completely or partially glaze when warm as described below.

4. To glaze the cake, combine the icing sugar with 2 Tbsp lemon juice. If it's not a drizzling consistency, add a little more lemon juice. Brush some over the warm cake when it comes out of the oven and drizzle some overtop of the loaf when it has cooled. Or drizzle when cool with as much as you like. Sprinkle with pistachios.

CARDAMOM VARIATION: I tried to sneak an ingredient into this cake. The problem is, ever since Anna was little, she could detect any slight change I made to any recipe. When she tasted my first try at recreating this loaf, she said, "This is delicious but it isn't the cake—you added cardamom." I gave in and made her a version closer to the original without cardamom. If you love cardamom, add ½ tsp ground cardamom in step 2 with the lemon peel and don't tell Anna.

UPSIDE-DOWN RHUBARB CAKE

Serves 8 to 10

Although I love the drama of rhubarb cakes with long strips of rhubarb in beautiful, perfect designs, I always find them hard to cut nicely when serving. So instead, I use 1-inch pieces in imperfectly executed patterns that are easy to serve in squares and still beautiful (albeit imperfectly). You can also just put the pieces in the pan and let them fall as if from heaven. Glenn, a child who went to the elementary school near my cooking school, once told me that it's all the same anyway when it's in your tummy. He used to help me after school when I first opened my cooking school and worked alone. He was always a great help and wonderful company. That's when I truly realized the wisdom of children.

Upside-Down Topping

¼ **cup butter,** melted

½ **cup packed light brown sugar**

1½ **lb rhubarb,** trimmed and cut into 1-inch pieces

Cake

1½ **cups all-purpose flour**

1½ **tsp baking powder**

½ **tsp baking soda**

¼ **tsp kosher salt**

½ **cup butter,** room temperature, cut into cubes

¾ **cup granulated sugar**

2 **eggs**

1 **tsp pure vanilla extract or paste**

¾ **cup buttermilk** (see note on page 178)

NOTE: This is the perfect cake to take you through the seasons—use whatever fruit you have: blueberries, raspberries, peaches, pears, plums, apricots, etc.

1. Preheat the oven to 350°F.

2. For the upside-down topping, pour the melted butter in an 8- or 9-inch square baking pan, and brush the butter up the sides of the pan. Sprinkle the bottom of the pan with brown sugar. Gently arrange the rhubarb, rounded side down, in a pattern (or not), pressing into the brown sugar. If there is rhubarb left over, just sprinkle it over the pattern.

3. For the cake, whisk the flour with the baking powder, baking soda, and salt until well combined. In another bowl, beat the butter and granulated sugar together until light, using a hand mixer, or mix by hand with a wooden spoon. Mix in the eggs one at a time, beating well after each addition. Add the vanilla.

4. Stir the flour mixture into the butter mixture in three or four additions, alternating with buttermilk, and beginning and ending with the flour mixture.

5. Carefully spread the batter evenly over the rhubarb in the pan and bake for 30 to 35 minutes, or until a cake tester inserted into the center of the cake layer (not the rhubarb layer) comes out clean, and an instant-read thermometer registers 185°F when inserted into the center of the cake layer. (An 8-inch cake may take a bit longer to bake, as the cake will be deeper.)

6. Cool the cake for 10 minutes, run a knife around the edge, and turn out onto a flat serving plate.

Fresh, marinated, or roasted fruit (raspberries, blackberries, strawberries, blueberries, red currants, figs, kumquats, kiwi, persimmons, mangoes, passion fruit, cherries, etc.)

Sauces: caramel (see page 236), **or raspberry sauce**

Crunchy Things: chopped roasted nuts, praline (page 241), **or tiny meringues**

Sprigs of fresh mint

Icing sugar

NOTE: Instant dissolving sugar has many names and uses. The main difference between it and granulated sugar is that it dissolves quickly without heat. It also goes by the names of fruit sugar, bar sugar (popular in cocktails), and caster sugar. You can buy it or make your own by processing regular granulated sugar in a food processor for about 30 seconds.

4. For the lemon curd, bring the sugar, lemon peel, and lemon juice to a boil in a medium saucepan. Cook gently for a few minutes, until the sugar dissolves. Mix the egg yolks in a small mixing bowl and slowly whisk in the lemon mixture. Return the mixture to the saucepan and cook gently, stirring, until it just comes to a boil and has thickened. Off the heat, whisk in the pieces of butter, a little at a time, and stir until the butter is melted into the curd. Strain into a clean bowl, cool, cover the surface directly with plastic wrap, and refrigerate until cold. This can also be done ahead of time—it will keep for up to 1 week in the refrigerator, or can be frozen for up to 4 months.

5. Whip the cream just before assembling.

6. To assemble, spread the pavlova with the lemon curd and then spread with cream, or partially fold the lemon curd into the whipped cream until streaky. Sprinkle with fruit to cover completely. Sometimes I like to coordinate the colors of the fruit (e.g., blueberries, blackberries, and figs; or mangoes, passion fruit, and cape gooseberries), and sometimes I just mix it all up. Drizzle with sauce or sprinkle with nuts, if using. Place mint sprigs over and around the pavlova and dust with icing sugar.

NOTE: Usually the bottom of the pavlova is too sticky for me to easily remove the parchment paper. I don't mind serving it on the paper, but if it bothers you, trim away the part that is showing with scissors or a sharp knife. When you serve the pavlova, be sure to lift each serving off the paper.

RUTHIE'S CHEESECAKE WITH PISTACHIOS

Makes about 25 squares

Have you ever had to make a difficult decision involving cheesecake? Like deciding whether to make your new favorite cheesecake recipe or your classic all-time favorite recipe? I found myself in this predicament and decided to combine them, for all our benefit. The cheesecake part is the one my mom always used to make. I find that little cheesecake squares are so versatile—always perfect for tea, snacks, parties, dessert, and even breakfast. The idea for the pistachio topping came from a big, luscious Israeli-style special occasion cheesecake from my friends Janna Gur and Einat Admony in their cookbook *Shuk*.

Crumb Crust

1½ cups shortbread cookie crumbs (page 250) **or graham wafer crumbs**

¼ cup butter, melted

Filling

1 lb full-fat brick-style cream cheese, cut into 2-inch pieces

½ cup granulated sugar

2 eggs

1 tsp pure vanilla extract or paste

Toppings

1¼ cups sour cream

1 Tbsp + 1 Tbsp icing sugar, sifted

1 cup lightly roasted shelled pistachios, chopped

¼ tsp ground cardamom

NOTE: My mom always used graham wafer crumbs for the crust, but this crust is a great way to use up leftover homemade cookies. You can even mix and match if you don't have enough of one or the other.

1. Preheat the oven to 350°F. Butter or spray an 8-inch square baking pan, then line with parchment paper, allowing some to hang over a little on two sides for easy removal. (If you are cutting the cake into small squares, it is easier to cut once the cake is removed from the pan.)

2. For the crumb crust, combine the cookie crumbs with the butter and press into the pan.

3. For the filling, in the bowl of a stand mixer fitted with the paddle attachment, or using a hand mixer, beat the cream cheese with the granulated sugar for about 2 minutes until light. Add the eggs and vanilla and beat for 2 minutes, or until smooth. Pour the filling evenly over the crust. Bake for 30 to 35 minutes or until set in the middle.

4. For the toppings, combine the sour cream with 1 Tbsp icing sugar. When the cake is baked, smooth the sour cream over the hot cake and return to the oven for 5 minutes to set. In a small bowl, mix 1 Tbsp icing sugar with the pistachios and cardamom together well. When the cake comes out of the oven, sprinkle the pistachio mixture evenly over the top. Cool the cake on a wire rack, and then refrigerate at least 4 hours or up to overnight.

5. To remove the cheesecake from the pan, run a knife around the two sides not lined with parchment paper and gently lift the cake out of the pan using the parchment paper ends to help. Trim the edges of the cake and eat those when no one is looking. Cut the cheesecake into small squares using a knife dipped into very hot water and wiped clean between cuts.

END OF SUMMER RUSTIC FRUIT TART

Serves 8 to 12

This tart, also called a galette, is another thing I first learned from Jacques Pépin. He taught at my school for 1 week each year for 10 years. This was pre-television days for him, and now when I watch his shows, I know how lucky my students, staff, and I were to receive this personal education. When Anna and Mark were little, I loved having them cook with me. On the next page, in the photo of the three of us making these rustic tarts together, mine looks relatively normal, whereas Mark and Anna each have a little pie in front of them that consists of an open circle of pastry with a whole intact plum, pit and all, sitting in the center. They both look so proud of themselves. It's so cute I can't stand it. I sent the photo to Jacques, and he loved it too. I change the fruit to use whatever is in season and it's always delicious, whether you are mixing fruits or using just one. I don't feel it is necessary to peel plums, peaches, apricots, or nectarines, but I do usually peel apples and pears. Even if you have never made pastry before, no matter what the tart looks like it will always be beautiful if you top it with fresh mint, berries, and icing sugar.

Pastry

2 cups all-purpose flour

1 Tbsp granulated sugar

¼ tsp kosher salt

1 cup butter, cold and cut into small evenly sized pieces

½ cup ice water + more as needed

Filling

2½ lb apples, purple plums, peaches, or blueberries (or a combination), peeled if necessary (see recipe intro), halved, pitted, and sliced or cut into chunks (about 6 to 8 cups)

½ cup light brown sugar

¼ cup all-purpose flour

1 tsp cinnamon

1. Preheat the oven to 425°F if you're going to bake this right away. If prepping the dough the day before, be sure to preheat your oven 30 minutes before baking.

2. For the pastry, combine the flour, granulated sugar, and salt in a large bowl. Reserve 2 Tbsp butter for the filling and cut the remaining ⅞ cup into the flour with a pastry blender or your fingertips until it is in very small pieces. Drizzle the ice water over the flour and toss with a large fork or your fingers until the flour is moistened. Add enough extra ice water, a little at a time, until you can gather the dough together lightly into a ball (add additional water 1 Tbsp at a time, but don't worry even if you need as much as 6 Tbsp more). Gently flatten the dough and if not using right away, wrap and refrigerate it for 30 minutes to overnight. If the dough has been in the refrigerator for longer than 1 hour, remove it 15 minutes before rolling it out. To make the dough in a food processor, place the flour, sugar and salt in the work bowl fitted with the steel knife. Pulse a few times to combine. Add the cold butter in small, evenly sized pieces and pulse 6 to 8 times or until the butter is in tiny bits. Sprinkle with ⅓ cup ice water and pulse just until the flour is moistened. The mixture will be crumbly. Turn the mixture onto a lightly floured work surface and gather together into a ball, adding additional ice water by the tablespoon if needed. You will not need as much liquid making pastry in a food processor as you will need making it by hand.

continued . . .

Toppings

1 egg, lightly beaten

¼ cup coarse sugar

Sifted icing sugar, optional

Berries, sprigs of fresh mint, edible flowers, optional

Ice cream or whipped cream, optional

NOTE: to make a smaller tart, halve the ingredients for the pastry and filling and bake the tart on a quarter-sheet pan at 425°F for 15 minutes, and then reduce the heat to 375°F and continue baking for 25 to 30 minutes.

3. Roll out the dough into a large circle on a lightly floured large piece of parchment paper to about 14 to 16 inches in diameter. Remember, this is rustic, so it does not have to be a perfect circle! Carefully transfer the dough and parchment paper to a large baking sheet. Don't worry if the pastry is hanging over the edges.

4. For the filling, toss the fruit in a large bowl with the brown sugar, flour, and cinnamon.

5. Spoon the fruit into the center of the pastry, flattening it out, and leaving a border of about 3 inches around the edge of the fruit. Dot with the reserved 2 Tbsp butter. Fold the dough over the fruit (it may have to be pleated in some spots), leaving the center open. Patch any holes in the pastry with extra bits of dough (sticking them on with the beaten egg used for the topping).

6. Brush the top of the pastry with the beaten egg and sprinkle with coarse sugar. Bake the tart for 20 minutes. Reduce the oven temperature to 375°F and bake for 30 to 40 minutes longer, or until the fruit is tender and the pastry is browned on the bottom as well as the top. Cover loosely with aluminum foil if the top is browning too much. Cool on a wire rack, then transfer to a flat serving plate. You can leave it on the parchment paper or slide the parchment out from underneath once transferred. This tart is beautiful as is, but you can dust with icing sugar and/or scatter berries, mint sprigs, and/or edible flowers overtop. Serve topped with ice cream or whipped cream.

PEANUT BRITTLE: Place 1 cup granulated sugar, ½ cup cold water, and ¼ cup corn syrup in a medium or large heavy-bottomed saucepan. Bring to a boil. Cook over medium or medium-high heat or until the mixture turns a caramel color, about 10 to 12 minutes. Watch closely to prevent burning. Stir in 1 Tbsp butter and ½ tsp baking soda. The mixture will bubble up. That's why you didn't use a small saucepan. Add 1½ cups salted, roasted peanuts, stir, and quickly spread on a buttered baking sheet. Sprinkle with ½ tsp flaky sea salt. Cool completely and chop on a wooden board. Keep in the freezer for emergencies. Makes about 2 cups.

BUTTERSCOTCH PUDDING

Serves 8 to 10

Butterscotch pie with whipped cream and sprinkles of instant coffee was my mother's signature dessert. She served it for company and special dinners, and we all loved it so much. She unapologetically used boxed pudding for the pie filling (never the instant kind, though), and when I started cooking professionally, I wanted to recreate her pie using homemade pudding. Although mine was always good, it never tasted quite like Ruthie's. It wasn't until I started caramelizing the dark brown sugar that the butterscotch started tasting strong enough (credit goes to award-winning Chef Nancy Silverton for that trick). Instead of trying to recreate a perfect memory, I started serving this dish as a pudding topped with caramel or chocolate sauce, whipped cream, and/or chopped peanut brittle. But when I thought to add a little coffee to the pudding itself, it took me right back to my mother's pies.

1¼ cups dark brown sugar, packed

¼ cup water

¼ cup butter

1½ cups whipping cream

1½ tsp kosher salt

1½ cups + ½ cup milk

1 Tbsp instant espresso powder or 3 Tbsp prepared extra-strong espresso coffee (decaf is fine)

4 Tbsp cornstarch

2 egg yolks, beaten

1 tsp pure vanilla extract or paste

Suggested Toppings

Chocolate sauce or caramel sauce (page 236)

Peanut brittle (see left) **or praline** (page 241)

Unsweetened whipped cream

1. Place the brown sugar and water in a large saucepan over medium heat. Stir until the sugar is dissolved. Increase the heat to medium-high and cook, stirring, until the sugar darkens, smells caramelized, and just starts to smoke, 5 to 8 minutes. Don't worry if the sugar foams up, but don't allow it to burn. (If you smell that it has burned, discard it and start again—you have only wasted the sugar and 5 to 10 minutes at that point.) Add the butter, cream, and salt, and bring to a boil. Don't worry if the sugar clumps up, just cook at a gentle simmer for about 3 minutes, or until smooth.

2. Add 1½ cups milk and the espresso powder, and heat thoroughly. In a small bowl, combine ½ cup milk with the cornstarch and whisk until smooth. Add to the sugar mixture. Cook, on medium heat, stirring, until the mixture thickens. Mix about 1 cup of the pudding into the egg yolks to warm them up and introduce them to each other, and then stir the egg mixture back into the pudding. Cook gently, stirring, for another 2 minutes.

3. Remove the pudding from the heat and stir in the vanilla. Strain into a bowl either for serving, or to spoon into individual dessert glasses. Cover the surface directly with plastic wrap or parchment paper to stop a skin from forming. Cool to room temperature and then refrigerate. Top with chocolate or caramel sauce, peanut brittle, or praline and/or whipped cream to serve.

NOTE: if you do want to use this for a pie filling, use 3 egg yolks instead of 2, and 5 Tbsp cornstarch instead of 4.

CHOCOLATE BUDINO

Serves 6 to 8

Okay, you caught us. We used a fancy word, but this is chocolate pudding. It's great as is but also can be dressed up with a variety of toppings. I love piling meringues on top. Anna will always pick praline, Mark loves whipped cream and salted nuts, and Ray loves a scoop of vanilla ice cream. And truthfully, we would all take a layer of caramel sauce (page 236) before putting anything else on. Please note that I am not suggesting you make various toppings for each member of your family/party—unless you want to make a chocolate pudding bar, which isn't the worst idea.

2 cups + 1 cup milk

½ cup s granulated ugar

3 Tbsp cocoa (unsweetened)

2½ Tbsp cornstarch

½ tsp kosher salt

2 egg yolks

8 oz semisweet or bittersweet chocolate, chopped

2 Tbsp butter, optional

1½ tsp pure vanilla extract or paste

½ tsp flaky sea salt

Suggested Toppings

¾ cup whipping cream

Grated chocolate, mini meringues, chopped praline (page 241)**, chopped peanut brittle** (page 230)**, or caramel sauce** (page 236)

1. Heat 2 cups milk in a small saucepan set over low heat, or in the microwave. Set aside.

2. Off the heat, in a large saucepan, whisk the sugar with the cocoa, cornstarch, and salt. Whisk in 1 cup cold milk until smooth. Whisk in the reserved hot milk.

3. Bring the mixture to a boil, whisking often (milk and chocolate both burn easily) then reduce the heat to medium-low and cook for a few minutes, until thickened.

4. Beat the egg yolks in a bowl and whisk in about 1 cup of the hot pudding to gently introduce heat to the egg yolks. Off the heat, mix the egg yolk mixture back into the pudding. Cook for another 1 to 2 minutes on medium-low heat, stirring, then strain into a bowl.

5. Add the chopped chocolate and the butter, if using. Stir to melt the chocolate until very smooth. Stir in the vanilla. Spoon into dessert glasses. Cover with plastic wrap or parchment paper directly on the surface and chill for at least 2 hours.

6. Just before serving, sprinkle the pudding with a little flaky sea salt (optional, but not really). Slowly whip the cream, if using, just until thick and soft peaks form. Place a spoonful of whipped cream on each pudding and sprinkle with whatever toppings you like— grated chocolate, praline, peanut brittle, caramel sauce, or everything.

A TIRAMISU CAKE

Serves 8

When Giuliano Bugialli taught at my school in 1980 and introduced us to tiramisu, it was the first time any of us had tried it. It was a taste of heaven. The word means "pick-me-up" in Italian, and he told us it was the favorite snack of nonnas, who liked to have some in the afternoon when their energy was low (as it was maybe more appropriate than an espresso and a shot). This version has evolved since that time, but it is still the one I like best. Instead of using marsala and brandy, you can experiment using rum, Grand Marnier, coffee liqueur, or, if you do not want to use any alcohol, coffee-flavored syrup. And yes, you can use decaf coffee, but it may not "tiramisu" you. It's best made at least 1 day ahead but can be made up to 3 days ahead or frozen. This can also be made in a trifle bowl or in individual preserving jars for different presentations.

3 egg yolks

¼ cup granulated sugar

2 Tbsp + 2 Tbsp brandy

2 Tbsp + 2 Tbsp marsala

1 cup whipping cream

½ lb mascarpone cheese

⅓ cup prepared espresso or strong coffee

20 to 25 dry Italian ladyfingers

6 oz semisweet or bittersweet chocolate, shaved

NOTE: Freeze leftover egg whites for your next pavlova (page 223).

1. In a heatproof bowl, using a hand mixer or whisk, beat the egg yolks with the sugar until pale yellow. Beat in 2 Tbsp each of the brandy and marsala. Set the bowl over a pot of gently simmering water (the bottom of the bowl should not touch the simmering water) and cook, stirring, just until thick. Pass the custard through a strainer into another bowl and cool.

2. Whip the cream until light and thick. Set aside.

3. In a large bowl, whisk the mascarpone until smooth. Whisk in the cooled custard, then fold in the whipping cream.

4. Combine the remaining 2 Tbsp each of the brandy and marsala with the espresso in a shallow baking dish.

5. To assemble, quickly dip the ladyfingers into the coffee mixture, one at a time, and place side by side in an 8- or 9-inch baking dish (line it with parchment paper if you want to remove it from the pan to serve). Spread half of the filling overtop, and sprinkle with half of the chopped chocolate. Repeat the layers—ladyfingers dipped in the coffee mixture, then the filling, and ending with chocolate. Cover and refrigerate overnight.

NOTE: For a gluten-free version you can use store-bought gluten-free ladyfingers, or do as I do, and make the shortcake recipe (page 222) with gluten-free flour. Bake it in the same size of pan you'll use to make your tiramisu, and cut it in half horizontally to form two layers. I like it just as much as the ladyfingers, and will happily use this method whether it needs to be gluten-free or not.

SALTED CARAMEL POPCORN WITH A SIDE OF BIRTHDAY CAKE

Makes 1 birthday cake

I am a very serious popcorn person. One person who has always understood this is Anna's best friend, Julia, who is also a very serious popcorn person. When they were little, even though microwave popcorn was the way to go, I always made popcorn the same way my mother did, in a big heavy pot on top of the stove. It made me so happy that something so simple made them so happy too. One year for Mark's birthday, I took popcorn to the next level. I made an ice cream cake with a homemade cookie crumb crust, topped with layers of hazelnut, coffee, and vanilla ice cream. I put caramel sauce in between the layers of ice cream and, to top it off, covered the whole thing with this caramel corn. It was a surprise for Mark, and I have to say, it was outstanding.

Caramel Corn

1 cup light brown sugar, packed

½ **cup butter**

¼ **cup corn syrup**

½ **tsp baking soda**

1 tsp flaky sea salt

1 Tbsp pure vanilla extract

8 cups popped popcorn (from about ⅓ cup unpopped popcorn)

½ **cup roasted almonds, cashews, pecans, or peanuts** (or a combination), optional

Cake Crumb Crust

1½ cups cookie crumbs (I like to use my shortbread, on page 250, oat cookies, on page 256, or Sbrisolona, on page 246)

¼ **cup butter,** melted

Filling

3 qts ice cream, any flavor or combination (I like coffee, hazelnut, and vanilla)

1 cup caramel sauce, room temperature (page 236)

1 cup chocolate sauce, room temperature (page 236)

1. Preheat the oven to 275°F. Butter or spray a large baking sheet.

2. For the caramel corn, bring the sugar, butter, and corn syrup to a boil in a large saucepan. Boil for 2 minutes, stirring continuously. Remove from the heat. Add the baking soda, salt, and vanilla. The mixture will bubble up. Stir in the popcorn, and the nuts if using, and mix to coat well. Spread on the prepared baking sheet.

3. Bake for 40 minutes, stirring every 10 minutes. Cool. Store in an airtight container until ready to use (or eat).

4. For the cake, line an 8-inch springform pan with parchment paper. For the crust, combine the cookie crumbs with melted butter and press firmly into the bottom of the pan. Place in the freezer for at least 30 minutes, or up to overnight.

5. Remove the ice cream from the freezer 15 minutes before assembling. For the filling, spread one flavor of ice cream over the cookie-crumb cake bottom and drizzle with about one-third of the caramel and/or chocolate sauces. Spread with another flavor of ice cream (or you can marble them) and drizzle with another third of the sauces. If the ice cream melts too much as you're assembling this, put the cake in the freezer for 30 minutes, then continue. When you're finished, freeze for at least 2 hours or up to overnight.

continued . . .

6. When the cake is frozen solid, remove it from the pan and spread the remaining third of the sauces around the sides and on top. Press the caramel corn into the sides and top. Store the cake in the freezer if not serving right away.

NOTE: It's hard to write "Happy Birthday" on a cake like this, so I usually write it on the serving platter with some of the sauce. Put the sauce in a ziploc bag and snip the corner for a quick and easy piping bag!

CARAMEL SAUCE: In a large saucepan set over medium-high heat, stir 1½ cups granulated sugar and ¼ cup water until the sugar is moistened, and then cook until the mixture comes to a boil. Brush down any sugar crystals from the sides of the pan with a pastry brush dipped in cold water. Cook, without stirring, for 8 to 10 minutes, or until the caramel turns deep golden. Remove from the heat and, standing back, add 1 cup whipping cream and ¼ cup diced butter. Return the pan to medium heat for 1 to 2 minutes, stirring until smooth. Remove from the heat and add 2 tsp pure vanilla extract or paste and ½ tsp flaky sea salt, or more to taste. It will thicken when cold, so be sure to warm it to your desired temperature before serving. Keep in the refrigerator for up to 1 month.

CHOCOLATE SAUCE: Place 8 oz chopped bittersweet or semisweet chocolate (or a combination) in a medium bowl. Bring 1 cup whipping cream to a boil over medium heat, and pour over the chocolate. Cover the bowl and let stand for 3 or 4 minutes, or until the chocolate melts when you stir the mixture. Add 2 tsp pure vanilla extract or paste and ½ tsp flaky sea salt, or more to taste. It will thicken when cold, so be sure to warm it to your desired temperature before serving. This also makes a wonderful glaze. Keep in the refrigerator for up to 1 month.

Rice Pudding

Not everyone knows this, but rice pudding launched my career. A few years after I started the cooking school, one of my students, Peter Pacini, a producer at the popular radio station CKFM, invited me to be a guest on the lunchtime show with Judy Webb to discuss a recipe. I chose rice pudding. It resonated so much with listeners that over a two-day period, 450 people called in for the recipe. Back then, they had to mail the recipe to callers and did it for free, but had to change the policy.

They asked me back on the show every week for 10 years.

There are two basic types of rice pudding: creamy, made on the stovetop, and baked rice pudding that sets and can be cut into squares or slices. Although the way I make and serve rice pudding has evolved over the years, I usually prefer it creamy. (One exception to the creamy preference is budini di riso, which are rice pudding tarts that I first tasted in Florence. I love them.) In 2019 our family went to Paris, and one night at dinner at La Régalade, two of us ordered rice pudding for dessert. Out came the others' individual dessert plates with what they'd ordered, along with a giant serving bowl full of rice pudding and a second, smaller (but still very large) bowl of caramel sauce. It came with a ladle and a large wooden spoon to serve, and bowls for everyone at the table. A dream!

CREAMY RICE PUDDING WITH CARAMELIZED BANANAS

Serves 8

We're always trying to dream up new ways to serve rice pudding, and Anna wondered about adding bananas to the caramel sauce. It's become one of our favorites. For the creamiest rice pudding, use whole milk, whipping cream, and Italian carnaroli short-grain rice. It will still work with 2% milk and lighter cream, and the egg yolks are optional, though they add a richness to the pudding, so I like to include them. But I have found that the biggest secret for making creamy rice pudding is to always use short-grain rice. I am also always amazed by how much milk the rice can absorb. The pudding can be made ahead and so can the caramel sauce, but I like to rewarm the sauce and add the bananas just before serving.

continued . . .

Rice Pudding

⅔ cup **Italian short-grain rice** (see note)

1⅓ **cups boiling water**

5 **cups whole or 2% milk**

1 **vanilla bean,** broken in half, or 1 **Tbsp pure vanilla extract**

⅓ **cup granulated sugar**

½ **tsp kosher salt**

½ **cup whipping cream or additional milk**

2 **egg yolks,** optional

Caramelized Bananas

½ **cup granulated sugar**

¾ **cup whipping cream**

¼ **tsp kosher salt**

4 **bananas** (not too ripe), sliced ½ inch thick on the diagonal just before serving

Suggested Toppings

Roasted coconut or almonds

Coarsely crushed ginger-snaps or any delicious crunchy cookie

Shredded halva (sometimes called halva floss)

NOTE: I use Italian short-grain rice to make rice pudding. The easiest ones to find are typically Arborio, Vialone Nana, and Carnaroli.

1. For the rice pudding, in a large, heavy-bottomed saucepan, combine the rice with the boiling water and bring to a boil. Reduce the heat to low, cover, and cook for 10 minutes, or until the water is just absorbed.

2. Add the milk, vanilla bean, sugar, and salt. (If you're using vanilla extract, add it at the end of cooking.) Bring to a boil, stirring often. Lower the heat and cook, partially covered, for 30 to 35 minutes, stirring often to prevent sticking and boiling over. If your rice pudding does boil over (mine has), you'll see why I recommend using a large pot. Keep the heat low, and check and stir often. You are looking for the rice to become tender and thicken to a creamy, pudding-like consistency. You want the milk and the rice to be married, not separated.

3. Add the cream to the rice mixture and stir well. Cook for about 5 minutes longer, or until hot and thick.

4. Whisk the egg yolks, if using, in a medium bowl and whisk about 1 cup of the rice pudding mixture into the egg yolks a little at a time to warm up the yolks. Return everything to the pan and cook very gently for 2 to 3 minutes. Remove from the heat. If you used a vanilla bean, remove it (rinse and dry it well, and keep in your sugar canister). If not using a vanilla bean, stir in the vanilla extract now. Cover the rice pudding with a piece of parchment paper or plastic wrap directly on the surface to keep a skin from forming. Serve warm or cold. It will firm up when cold.

5. For the caramelized bananas, make the caramel by sprinkling the sugar over the bottom of a 10-inch nonstick skillet set over medium heat. Without stirring, let the sugar cook, watching closely for 2 to 3 minutes or until the sugar melts and begins to turn a caramel color (be careful it doesn't burn). When the mixture is caramel, but not at all burnt, remove it from the heat, stand back and add the cream. It will bubble up. Stir well. If the mixture is lumpy, cook over medium-low heat, stirring, until smooth. Stir in the salt. This can be made ahead. It will thicken when cool so simply warm it up just before adding the bananas.

6. Just before serving, reheat the caramel sauce and add the sliced bananas. Heat for about 2 minutes, just to warm the bananas, then spoon the bananas and caramel over the rice pudding. Sprinkle with coconut, nuts, cookie crumbs, or halva.

HAZELNUT CAKE WITH COFFEE BUTTERCREAM, GANACHE, AND PRALINE

Yield: There's never enough

This cake is the result of a compilation of my two favorite birthday cake memories. Years ago, when I was studying Italian cooking with Marcella Hazan in Bologna, it was my birthday and she ordered a hazelnut cake from a famous local bakery that was so delicious, I have been trying to recreate it ever since. And the icing is inspired by my childhood. When I was young, there was one "real" French bakery in Toronto (that we knew of) called Patisserie, and my mom always ordered our birthday cakes from there. It was very expensive compared with other bakeries, and because my birthday was a few days before my dad's, and my sister's was a few days before my mom's, we doubled up and had only two birthday cakes a year. There were many flavors of buttercream, and you could have layers of cake or meringue. We always had cake layers with mocha buttercream, and we loved it so much!

1½ cups **hazelnut flour** (see page 6)

¾ cup **all-purpose flour**

¾ tsp **baking powder**

¼ tsp **kosher salt**

¾ cup **butter,** cut into cubes

1 cup **granulated sugar**

¾ cup **icing sugar,** sifted

4 **eggs**

1 tsp **pure vanilla extract or paste**

½ tsp **pure almond extract or hazelnut emulsion** (see note)

NOTE: Hazelnut emulsion is a hazelnut flavoring that is very similar to an extract, and can be used the same way. It is available online and at some baking specialty stores.

1. Preheat the oven to 350°F. Butter or spray a 9-inch round or square springform pan or deep cake pan, then line with parchment paper.

2. In a medium mixing bowl, whisk together the hazelnut flour, all-purpose flour, baking powder, and salt.

3. In a large bowl using a hand mixer or in a food processor, beat the butter and granulated sugar together until light. Beat in the icing sugar. Add the eggs one at a time, beating after each addition. Add the vanilla and almond extracts. Stir in the hazelnut flour mixture (if you've been using a food processor, transfer the butter mixture to a large bowl before stirring in the flour).

4. Transfer the batter to the prepared pan. Bake for 30 to 40 minutes, or until the cake just starts to pull away from the sides of the pan and the top feels firm-ish when gently touched in the center, and an instant-read thermometer registers between 185°F and 195°F when inserted into the center. Cool completely and refrigerate at least 30 minutes.

Coffee Buttercream

2 Tbsp prepared hot espresso or strong coffee

1 Tbsp instant espresso or coffee powder

½ tsp pure vanilla extract or paste

½ cup butter, cut into cubes

1 cup icing sugar, sifted

Ganache

½ cup whipping cream

4 oz semi-sweet or bitter-sweet chocolate, coarsely chopped

½ cup chopped praline (see note) **or chopped roasted hazelnuts**

5. For the coffee buttercream, combine the hot espresso with the espresso powder, and vanilla extract. Cool completely. In the bowl of a stand mixer fitted with the paddle attachment, or using a hand mixer, beat the butter until light. Add the icing sugar and beat until smooth and creamy. Because coffee varies in strength, add the cooled coffee mixture to the butter mixture slowly, tasting a few times (tough job!) to see if the coffee flavor is strong enough. Remove the cooled cake from the pan and smooth the coffee buttercream overtop. Refrigerate for 2 hours or longer.

6. For the ganache, heat the whipping cream almost to a boil in a small saucepan set over medium heat. Place the chocolate in a small but deep heatproof bowl and pour the hot cream on top. Cover loosely and let the chocolate melt for 4 to 5 minutes. Stir until the chocolate is completely melted and very smooth. Cool until the mixture is room temperature but still pourable.

7. Pour the ganache over the cold iced cake and smooth to the edges, letting the excess run down the sides. Sprinkle with praline or chopped hazelnuts. Refrigerate for at least 1 hour before serving.

TO MAKE PRALINE: Combine 1½ cups granulated sugar and ¼ cup water in a medium heavy-bottomed saucepan and stir until all the sugar is moistened. Cook over medium heat, stirring, just until the sugar dissolves. Stop stirring and cook while swirling the pan occasionally, standing by to make sure it doesn't burn. When the sugar is caramel-colored, stir in 1½ cups roasted hazelnuts (or a combination with roasted almonds). Mix. Spread as evenly as possible on a buttered baking sheet to cool for 1 hour. Break into chunks, and chop or pulverize in a food processor. Freeze what you don't use and sprinkle it on everything.

FLAKY DATE NUT PASTRIES

Makes 24 to 28 pastries

This pastry should probably have a cute mash-up name because it is a cross between North American date squares and the rolled date cookies you find everywhere in Israel. I actually had them like this for the first time at the Aroma Cafe in the Tel Aviv airport. I couldn't believe I was eating something so delicious at an airport. They really won me over.

Filling

¾ lb (1½ cups) pitted dates, cut into pieces (using scissors is the easiest way)

2 cups water or strong tea (such as English breakfast or Earl Grey)

Two 1-inch strips orange peel

⅛ tsp ground cardamom

⅛ tsp ground cinnamon

½ cup chopped roasted walnuts, optional

Pastry

2 cups all-purpose flour

1 cup butter, cold and cut into cubes

8 oz full-fat brick-style cream cheese, cold, cut into cubes

Toppings

1 egg, beaten

¼ cup coarse sugar, optional

1. For the filling, place the dates, water, orange peels, cardamom, and cinnamon in a saucepan and bring to a boil. Reduce the heat to medium-low and cook, stirring often, for 12 to 15 minutes, or until the mixture is thick. Remove and discard the orange peels. Puree with an immersion blender or food processor. Chill until cold.

2. For the pastry, place the flour in the bowl of a stand mixer fitted with the paddle attachment. Add the cubes of cold butter and cut them into the flour until the butter is in little bits. Add the cubes of cold cream cheese and mix just until the dough comes together. If using a food processor instead, be sure to pulse when adding the butter and cream cheese, rather than letting the machine run continuously.

3. Turn the not-quite-formed dough onto a lightly floured work surface and gently knead it together. Divide the dough in half. Shape into two rectangular bricks, about 1 inch thick, wrap with plastic wrap, and refrigerate for at least 30 minutes.

3. Working with one piece of dough at a time, roll out the dough on a lightly floured work surface to a rectangle about 12 × 16 inches. Don't worry if it isn't perfect. Or you can trim the edges and make it more perfect. Repeat with the second piece of dough. Arrange both rectangles on the countertop, with the shorter sides parallel to the edge of the countertop in front of you. Spread half of the date filling over two-thirds of each sheet of pastry lengthwise, leaving the long third of the pastry (to your left/on the left side of the pastry) unfilled. Sprinkle the date section of each sheet of dough lightly with walnuts, if using. Again working with one sheet of pastry at a time, gently fold the unfilled third over the middle section and then the remaining third part gently over the middle. Now you should have three layers of pastry and two layers of dates. Repeat with the second sheet of pastry. You should now have two long pastries, each about 4 × 16 inches.

continued . . .

4. Cut each strip into 12 to 16 irregular or perfect rectangles, or on the diagonal into triangles—your choice, just as long as each pastry has a closed edge.

5. Place the pastries on two baking sheets lined with parchment paper. Cover loosely with plastic wrap and refrigerate for 2 hours or up to overnight. You can also freeze the pastries at this stage on the baking sheets and then transfer to a resealable plastic bag. Bake from frozen (which may take a few extra minutes of baking time).

6. Preheat the oven to 375°F. Brush the pastries lightly with the beaten egg and sprinkle with coarse sugar, if using. Bake for 25 to 30 minutes, or until nicely browned and puffed. Cool on wire racks and store in an airtight container, or freeze.

MOROCCAN CITRUS FRUIT SALAD

Serves 4 to 6

This light and refreshing dessert is perfect after a big meal—or anytime. Sprinkle it with the toppings listed below or with chopped chocolate, sliced dried apricots, or dates. Our editor, Zoe, shared that when she was in Morocco with her husband, Matt, they were served oranges sprinkled with cinnamon after every meal, and they loved it so much that they do it now at home, so you might try cinnamon here too. Or add a few drops of orange blossom water to the accumulated juices for added flavor, as suggested. If cara cara or blood oranges are not available, use pink or red grapefruits.

2 navel oranges, peeled and sliced into rounds

2 cara cara oranges, peeled and sliced into rounds

2 blood oranges, peeled and sliced into rounds (see note)

½ tsp orange blossom water, optional

¼ cup pomegranate seeds

2 Tbsp pistachios, crushed, chopped, or slivered

Dried or fresh rose petals, optional

Sprigs of fresh mint, optional

1. Arrange the navel oranges around the edge of the serving platter. Arrange the cara cara and blood oranges in the center. Or arrange in any way that looks beautiful to you. Combine any juices with orange blossom water, if using, and drizzle over the fruit.

2. Sprinkle with pomegranate seeds and pistachios, dried rose petals, if using, and/or sprigs of fresh mint.

NOTE: To peel and cut oranges or grapefruits for salads, first slice off the tops and bottoms so they stand stable on the cutting board. It's best to use a cutting board with a well around the edge to keep all the juice—to pour it over the fruit afterward. Slice off the peel from the top to the bottom, removing most of the pith. (You can candy the peels so as not to waste them.) Then slice the oranges into rounds. If you have grapefruits or large oranges, you can cut them into suprèmes by cutting the segments out between the membranes (see page 109).

SBRISOLONA

Makes 2 giant cookies!

How can a cookie be so much fun and yet so sophisticated? This crumbly kind of cookie/torta from Mantua, in northern Italy, is hard to describe. You break it apart and it crumbles all over, and you find yourself eating every last crumb. You can use almonds instead of hazelnuts or a combination, and you can add about 1 cup coarsely chopped dark chocolate. Some versions of this recipe include orange peel and/or anise seeds added to the dough. Leftovers make a great cookie-crumb crust for Ruthie's cheesecake (page 226) and ice cream cakes (page 235).

2 cups all-purpose flour

1 cup light brown sugar, pressed through a sieve if lumpy

½ cup fine cornmeal

1 tsp baking powder

½ tsp kosher salt

1 cup butter, cold and cut into cubes

1½ cups roasted hazelnuts, skins removed, coarsely chopped or gently crushed (see page 6)

1. Preheat the oven to 350°F. Butter and line two 9-inch springform pans or cake pans with parchment paper.

2. In the bowl of a food processor fitted with the metal blade or in the bowl of a stand mixer fitted with the paddle attachment and set on low speed, combine the flour with the sugar, cornmeal, baking powder, and salt.

3. Add the cubes of cold butter and process until the mixture starts to hold together. This may take what seems to be a long time—1 to 2 minutes in a food processor, 4 to 5 minutes in a stand mixer.

4. When the dough is starting to come together, add half of the chopped hazelnuts, leaving the larger pieces for the top. Mix to combine.

5. Divide the dough mixture in half and press each half into the prepared pans. Press the remaining nuts into the tops of the dough.

6. Bake for 30 to 35 minutes, or until golden brown and firm-ish in the center. Cool in the pans. Remove gently. Break or cut into pieces to serve.

S'MORES CHOCOLATE BARK

Makes 24 to 30 pieces

There are many recipes and sophisticated variations for chocolate bark, some mentioned below, but I have found over and over again that this riff on s'mores is the one people can't resist. (Not sure if that is good or bad.) The better the quality of chocolate you use, the better the results.

1 lb semisweet chocolate, chopped

1½ cups broken graham wafers

3 cups miniature marshmallows (regular or vegan)

1 cup roasted, salted peanuts

1 tsp flaky sea salt

1. Line a 9 × 13-inch baking sheet with parchment paper, and allow some of the parchment to hang over two sides for easy removal.

2. Slowly melt the chocolate in the microwave in a large glass measuring cup or bowl, or in a bowl set over a pot of simmering water (but not touching the water), until almost melted. Remove from the heat. Cover and rest for 4 minutes, then stir to finish the melting. (See the chocolate primer on page 7.)

3. In a large bowl, combine the graham wafer pieces, marshmallows, and peanuts. Add the melted chocolate and stir to coat everything well.

4. Spread evenly over the lined baking sheet or pan. Depending on how thick you want the bark, it may not take up the entire pan. Sprinkle with flaky sea salt. Refrigerate until set. Lift out of the pan with parchment paper and transfer to a cutting board. With a sharp, heavy knife, cut into pieces. (I like random, uneven pieces, but it's up to you.) Store in the freezer.

VARIATIONS:
1. You can make bark with all bittersweet chocolate, semisweet, milk chocolate, or white chocolate. But be aware that milk and white chocolate melt faster than bittersweet and semisweet.
2. For a more sophisticated bark, mix melted bittersweet or semisweet chocolate with 2 cups chopped roasted almonds and hazelnuts combined.
3. Use bittersweet or semisweet chocolate with 2 cups chopped roasted nuts and dried fruit combined.
4. A beautiful bark can also be made with bittersweet or semisweet chocolate as the base and then topped with chopped pistachios, dried rose petals, and dried cherries. Press in lightly. Chill until set. Sprinkle with pomegranate seeds when serving.

MY FAVORITE SHORTBREAD COOKIES

Makes about 60 cookies

This recipe is very meaningful to me. I have probably made a million of these cookies, and Dely Balagtas, who worked with me (put up with me) for over 20 years, made the other million. These are the cookies we always delivered to neighbors and suppliers at the holidays for the 37 years I had my cooking school, and our freezers at home and at the school were always full of packages for friends and family who stopped by. It is also the recipe I chose to put in my last article after writing a weekly newspaper column for 30 years—the last 17 years of which were at the *National Post*. I have changed the recipe a little over the years. Some people love them plain, and some people love them with chunks of Toblerone chocolate. These are also the cookies that started me baking with salted butter. If you generally prefer to use unsalted butter, for this particular recipe, I strongly recommend using salted instead.

To shape the cookies, I use an old cookie press that Lillian Kaplun, a beloved Toronto cooking teacher, invented many years ago. It was inspired by the pattern on her potato masher. Unfortunately, Lillian's cookie press is no longer available. I took my last one to Israel for someone who contacted me, having seen the pattern in Rose Levy Beranbaum's book *Rose's Christmas Cookies*, where Rose mentioned that I had given her the cookie press on one of her visits to Toronto. That cookie press really got around. You can use the bottom of your potato masher, if appropriate, or the bottom of a glass or a fork to make a pattern all your own.

2 cups salted butter (see intro)

1 cup instant dissolving sugar (see note on page 224)

3¼ cups all-purpose flour

½ cup white rice flour

NOTE: To Anna's delight, we have also made these successfully with Cup4Cup gluten-free flour. If substituting, use 4 cups Cup4Cup total for the all-purpose flour and rice flour. They come out very tender and crisp. Now Anna always has them in her freezer too.

1. Preheat the oven to 300°F and line two baking sheets with parchment paper.

2. Cut the butter into chunks and place in the bowl of a stand mixer fitted with the paddle attachment. Beat the butter for 2 to 3 minutes, add the sugar gradually, and continue to beat until light, 3 to 4 minutes longer.

3. In a large bowl, whisk the all-purpose flour with the rice flour until well combined. Add to the butter mixture and mix on low speed just until the flour is incorporated. This can also be made by hand, beating the butter and sugar together in a large bowl with a wooden spoon and stirring the flour mixture in just until combined.

4. Shape the dough into 1-inch balls. Place on the lined baking sheets. Press down with a cookie press, the bottom of a glass, or a fork. If the cookie press (or whatever you are using) is sticking, dip it into a combination of equal parts flour and sugar.

5. Bake for 25 to 35 minutes, or until very lightly browned but still very pale. Cool on wire racks.

GWEN'S CARAMELIZED NUT COOKIES

Makes about 30 cookies

My good friend Gwen Berkowitz, one of the best cooks I have ever known, died a few years ago but not before leaving me with such delicious memories and recipes. These cookies are a winner—easy to make, very few ingredients, and naturally gluten-free and dairy-free. I used to only make these at Passover but now make them all the time! Serve with sliced oranges, poached pears, or ice cream or sorbet.

2 egg whites

½ cup granulated sugar

½ tsp pure vanilla extract, optional

3 cups sliced almonds (see note) **or coconut chips**

1. Preheat the oven to 350°F and line two baking sheets with parchment paper.

2. In a large bowl, stir the egg whites with the sugar. Do not beat, just stir together well. Add the vanilla and almonds and coat well with the sugary mixture.

3. Use 1 heaping Tbsp of the mixture for each cookie. Mound on the lined baking sheets. Gently flatten the cookies with the back of the spoon (dipped in water if sticky).

4. Bake for 12 to 15 minutes, or until the cookies are browned. For crispier cookies, turn off the oven after baking and let the cookies rest for another 15 minutes with the oven door open.

NOTE: The secret here is to NOT beat the egg whites (which everyone seems to want to do) and to use sliced almonds, which look like flat slices. Slivered almonds are the ones that look like little sticks. I used to always get them mixed up too. You could also use coconut chips or a combination.

THUMBPRINT COOKIES

Makes 40 to 48 cookies

Joyce Milrod was a wonderful baker from Saint John, New Brunswick. She was good friends with my Aunt Celia, who also lived in Saint John. Thumbprint cookies were Joyce's husband's favorite. He was a physician and very concerned with cleanliness. One day, Joyce made a batch of these cookies and let them cool on the countertop while she went to do some errands. When she got back, the jam was missing in every single cookie. She couldn't think of what happened until she saw the cat in the corner licking his lips. Joyce just refilled the cookies and her husband said they were the best ones ever. Everyone in the family knew the story except him. They told this story at Joyce's funeral, and he laughed. And we all cried. You can bake these plain, or dip them in chopped nuts—I usually do some each way. Thumbprint cookies always used to be filled with jam, but lately people have been filling them with salted caramel, chocolate hazelnut spread, lemon curd, or chocolate ganache with a pinch of flaky sea salt on top. And you could use chopped roasted hazelnuts or almonds instead of pecans.

1 cup butter, cut into cubes

1 cup granulated sugar

2 egg yolks

1 tsp pure vanilla extract or paste

2½ cups all-purpose flour

½ tsp kosher salt

2 egg whites, if using nuts

1½ cups finely chopped roasted pecans, optional

½ cup apricot jam (or marmalade, seedless raspberry jam, chocolate hazelnut spread, salted caramel, etc.)

1. In the bowl of a stand mixer fitted with the paddle attachment, or using a hand mixer, cream the butter until light. Add the sugar and beat for 2 to 3 minutes, or until very light. Add the egg yolks. Beat in well, and then add the vanilla.

2. In another bowl, whisk together the flour and salt. Beat into the butter mixture just until combined. Divide the dough into four pieces, shape each piece into a log, and wrap well with plastic wrap. This will make it easier to divide up the dough for the cookies. Refrigerate for at least 1 hour or up to overnight.

3. Preheat the oven to 350°F and line two baking sheets with parchment paper. Cut each log into 10 to 12 pieces, and shape into balls.

4. If coating the cookies with pecans, lightly beat the egg whites in a shallow bowl. Place the pecans in another shallow bowl. Roll the balls in the egg whites and then in the pecans to roughly cover.

5. Place the balls (coated or not) on the lined baking sheets, about 1 inch apart. You should have 40 to 48 cookies, depending on their size. With your thumb or the end tip of the handle of a wooden spoon, make an indentation in the top of each cookie. Bake for 5 minutes. Gently make the indentation again if necessary. Bake for 7 to 10 minutes or longer, or until just starting to brown. Remove from the oven. Repeat indentation. Cool on wire racks.

6. Fill each cookie with about ½ tsp jam or the filling of your choice.

BONNIE'S RUGELACH

Makes 48 cookies

This is my most requested cookie, and the one that I always gave to visiting chefs and teachers who taught at my cooking school. I gave it to Yotam Ottolenghi, and he and Helen Goh included it in their cookbook *Sweet*. I was a little excited, to say the least. It is also the cookie that has traveled the world. Not because I took it around the world, but because I once took an entire suitcase full of my rugelach to Israel to give to friends, but the airline lost the suitcase. It was returned to me 1 week later and I was informed it had traveled far and wide. Certain unnamed parties insisted on still receiving their rugelach no matter what, and reported they were better than ever. I ended up distributing them to everyone on my list, and they also got a story to go with it. Everyone has a slightly different recipe and technique for rugelach, and there are some unique cultural variations. During the pandemic, rugelach went the way of the babka, with all kinds of sweet and savory fillings. This is the recipe I have always used, and while I like to look at the variations from a creative standpoint (e.g., pizza rugelach, everything bagel, smores, blue cheese, pumpkin), from an eating standpoint, I am sticking with these.

Pastry

1 cup butter, cold and cut into evenly sized chunks

2 cups all-purpose flour

8 oz full-fat brick-style cream cheese, cold, cut into evenly sized chunks

Filling

1 cup light brown sugar

½ cup finely chopped roasted pecans

1 tsp cinnamon

½ cup best-quality apricot jam

Glaze

1 egg, beaten

½ cup coarse sugar

1. For the pastry, cut the butter into the flour until crumbly. This can be done in a food processor, in a stand mixer fitted with the paddle attachment, or in a large bowl with a pastry blender. Cut the cream cheese into the mixture until the dough just comes together. Divide the dough into four balls, flatten each to approximately a 4-inch round, wrap in plastic wrap, and refrigerate a few hours or up to overnight.

2. For the filling, in a small bowl, combine the brown sugar, nuts, and cinnamon. Set aside.

3. Preheat the oven to 350°F and line two baking sheets with parchment paper. Remove the dough from the refrigerator about 15 minutes before rolling. Roll each ball into a 10- to 11-inch circle. (Lightly flour your work surface if necessary.) The circles do not have to be perfect—if they aren't as good as you would like them, do not reroll, as in my experience, it never gets better. But you will get better at rolling out the dough with practice. Spread each circle with about 2 Tbsp jam and sprinkle with one-quarter of the brown sugar mixture. Cut each circle into 12 wedges, as if you were cutting a pizza (or 16, if you want them smaller). Roll up each wedge from the outside/wide edge to the middle. Place on the lined baking sheets. The unbaked cookies can be frozen flat on the baking sheets, then transferred to resealable plastic bags once frozen, or you can freeze the cookies once baked. If baking from frozen, they may take a few minutes longer to cook.

4. To glaze, brush each cookie with beaten egg and sprinkle with coarse sugar.

5. Bake for 20 to 25 minutes, or until browned. Cool for about 10 minutes on the baking sheet, then transfer to a wire rack to cool completely. These cookies freeze well.

NOTE: If you are like me and think that more is better and always overstuff things, resist the temptation to do that here. Any extra jam or brown sugar will just ooze out of the rugelach when they bake and could burn. If that happens, you can cut or trim with scissors when cool, or not worry about it.

OATMEAL PEANUT BUTTER SANDWICH COOKIES

Makes about 40 cookies

I spotted these cookies at the Highwheeler Cafe in Baddeck, Nova Scotia, on my way to the ferry for Newfoundland with friends from my Camp Kadimah days. I saved them for the ferry ride, which was unfortunate, because by the time we realized how delicious they were, it was too late to buy more. This is my recreated homestyle version. The funny thing is, years later, Anna called me asking for my advice on what recipe she could use to make homemade pirate cookies. (If you have never heard of pirate cookies, don't worry, neither had I. But apparently, if you know, you know.) Coincidentally I had this recipe. Anna says that at first they seem like a pain to make, then it gets really fun, and, regardless, they turn you into a superstar. They freeze well, and the oatmeal cookies are also delicious on their own.

2½ cups all-purpose flour

2 cups rolled oats

½ tsp baking soda

¼ tsp kosher salt

1½ cups butter, cut into cubes

1 cup light brown sugar

Filling

1 cup peanut butter

½ cup butter, cut into cubes

1½ cups icing sugar, sifted

1 tsp pure vanilla extract or paste

8 oz semisweet or milk chocolate, chopped

1. In a bowl, whisk the flour, oats, baking soda, and salt together. In the bowl of a stand mixer fitted with the paddle attachment, or using a hand mixer, cream the butter with the brown sugar for 2 to 3 minutes or until light. Stir in the flour mixture until it forms a dough. If you're doing this by hand, you may have to knead the dough to bring it together. Divide the dough into eight pieces, form it into balls, and flatten into a disk. Wrap and refrigerate for at least 30 minutes.

2. Preheat the oven to 350°F and line two baking sheets with parchment paper. Working with one piece of dough at a time, roll the dough out between two pieces of plastic wrap or parchment paper, or on a lightly floured work surface, to a thickness of ¼ inch. If the dough is too hard to roll, cover and leave at room temperature for 10 to 15 minutes before trying again. Cut out rounds with a 2-inch cookie cutter. Repeat with remaining dough. (You can reroll leftover pieces of dough once.)

3. Place on the lined baking sheets and bake for 15 to 20 minutes, or until lightly browned. Cool completely on wire racks. You should have about 80 cookies.

4. For the filling, cream the peanut butter and butter together until light. Beat in the icing sugar and vanilla.

5. To make the cookie sandwiches, place 2 tsp to 1 Tbsp filling on the flat side of half of the cookies. Place another cookie on top of each, flat side down, gently pressing to form a sandwich. Refrigerate the sandwiched cookies.

6. Melt the chopped chocolate in the microwave in a glass measuring cup or in a deep heatproof bowl set over gently simmering water (but not touching the water), until almost melted. Cover and let rest for 4 minutes, then stir to finish the melting. Cool to room temperature. Hold one end of the cookie vertically, and dip the other half into the chocolate. Place the cookies on a lined baking sheet and refrigerate until set.

CHUCK'S DOUBLE CHOCOLATE BROWNIES 2.0

Makes about 36 brownies or 72 two-bite brownies

These have been my favorite brownies for many years. And the small updates I've made just increase my love for them. I named these brownies for my nephew Chuck because we sent them to him when he was in Afghanistan with the Canadian Forces. He said they disappeared before he could put them on the table! (I have heard this now happens everywhere you serve them.) I first published the recipe in my cookbook *Friday Night Dinners.* This version has cocoa for an extra chocolate hit, Skor bars for caramel and crunch, and salt on top to make your mouth water. They are great as a brownie on their own, or served warm with ice cream drizzled with caramel sauce (page 236). Anna even once made them as a giant brownie birthday cake, covered in sprinkles for her friend Shana! They freeze well, so I always have some on hand for last-minute gifts. I have started cutting them into squares and then cutting them in half (on the diagonal or straight) because they are rich and for some people two bites are enough (I don't know those people, but I have heard).

10 oz bittersweet or semisweet chocolate, chopped

1 cup butter, cut into pieces

4 eggs

1½ cups granulated sugar

1 Tbsp pure vanilla extract or paste

1 cup all-purpose flour

2 Tbsp cocoa (unsweetened), sifted + more for dusting, optional

1 tsp baking powder

½ tsp kosher salt

1 cup coarsely chopped Skor bars or Skor bits

1 cup coarsely chopped white or milk chocolate (or a combination)

1 tsp flaky sea salt

Caramel sauce (page 236), optional

1. Preheat the oven to 350°F. Butter or spray a 9 × 9-inch baking dish and line the bottom and two long sides with parchment paper.

2. Gently melt the chocolate and butter together in a heavy-bottomed saucepan set over medium-low heat, or in the microwave on high at 30-second intervals. Stir until smooth and cool.

3. Whisk the eggs in a large bowl until light. Gradually whisk in the sugar. Keep whisking until the eggs are thick and pale. Add the vanilla and the melted chocolate mixture.

4. In another bowl, whisk together the flour, cocoa, baking powder, and salt. Stir into the batter until completely mixed. Add the Skor pieces and chopped chocolate. Spread the batter in the baking dish. Sprinkle with flaky sea salt. Bake for 30 to 35 minutes, or until just set (be careful not to overbake). Cool in the pan on a wire rack (if not eating warm with ice cream and caramel sauce). Refrigerate for a few hours, though I like to leave them overnight, as this makes them easier to cut nicely.

5. To remove the brownie slab in one piece for cutting, run a knife around the edges and lift it out with the parchment paper. Trim the edges (give those to the person you love the most, because those are the best part), and cut the slab into pieces the size you like the best. Dust with cocoa, if using.

Drinks

APEROL SPRITZ GAZOZ STYLE

Makes 1 drink

There is a little shop in Tel Aviv called Café Levinsky where they serve the craziest and most beautiful-looking drinks—refreshing, delicious, and one of a kind. They are non-alcoholic, made with homemade syrups of herbs or fruits, spices, vegetables, and gazoz (soda water). Fresh flowers and herbs are used to add flavor, but also beauty and aroma. When you go there, the owner, Benny Briga, asks you whether you like a savory or fruity drink, sweet or sour, and he always comes up with something perfect. He has written a wonderful book about his drinks, called *Gazoz,* with Adeena Sussman. It will inspire you to make his drinks at home just as he inspired me to make this cocktail.

Ice cubes

2 oz Aperol

3 oz sparkling white wine or
soda

3 oz soda water

Tall sprigs of fresh herbs and
edible flowers

1. Place a few ice cubes in the bottom of a tall glass. Pour in the Aperol, sparkling white wine, and soda water, and stir. Beautify with sprigs of herbs and edible flowers.

GUAVA MARGARITA

Makes 3 to 4 cocktails

Fara loves a good margarita. This love has encouraged us to play around with margarita recipes, and we love them too. Here's Ray's version of the delicious Guava Margarita we had in Tel Aviv at the bar in the Mendeli Hotel.

4 oz tequila

2 oz triple sec

1 Tbsp arak

1 cup guava juice (we use Ceres)

2 to 3 Tbsp maple syrup, honey, agave syrup, or simple syrup (see note on page 268)

2 Tbsp fresh lime juice

Ice cubes

Angostura or orange bitters

Rim

Fresh lime juice

Coarse sugar, or a 50:50 mix of coarse sugar and flaky sea salt

Sprigs of fresh mint

Thin lime slices

1. For the rim, take two shallow bowls and put a little fresh lime juice in one and the coarse sugar in the other. Dip the rim of the glasses you'll be using into the lime juice and then into the coarse sugar (or, in coarse sugar mixed with flaky salt) to rim the glasses. This can be done ahead.

2. In a pitcher, combine the tequila, triple sec, arak, guava juice, maple syrup, and lime juice. If making ahead, stir and refrigerate without ice. If serving immediately, add ice cubes and stir. Taste and add more maple syrup if you like your drink a bit sweeter. To serve, place 2 fresh ice cubes in each glass and pour in the mixture. Add 1 to 2 drops of bitters to each cocktail. Add a slice of lime and sprig of mint to each.

RAY'S BOURBON SOUR

Makes 2 or 3 cocktails

Ray is the mixologist of the house and is famous for his Bourbon Sour. When we have company for Friday night dinner, he always welcomes guests with a cocktail, and this is the one everyone (including me) looks forward to most. Sometimes he tweaks the recipe, but what remains consistent is his use of maple syrup. Thank you, Ray, for letting us share your secret. You can also make a pitcher ahead but do not add the ice until you're ready to serve or the cocktail will be diluted.

3 oz bourbon

1 oz freshly squeezed lemon juice (that's my job)

1 oz maple syrup

Ice cubes

1. Place the bourbon, lemon juice, and maple syrup in a cocktail shaker. Add a few ice cubes and shake about 20 times or until the shaker is too cold to handle! Pour immediately into glasses with 1 or 2 fresh ice cubes.

A NOTE ON MAPLE SYRUP: My brother-in-law Wayne Krangle started making maple syrup years ago when his son Chuck came back from Afghanistan after being there with the Canadian Armed Forces. Anna and I had been wanting to go to his maple sugar shack (aka cottage) to learn how to make maple syrup firsthand, and when we finally had a chance a few years ago, we learned that it's hard and time-consuming work, making it easy to understand why maple syrup is so expensive and completely worth it. In Wayne's case, all proceeds from Syrup for Soldiers go to help Canadian soldiers through Wounded Warriors.

BLUSHING ARAK COCKTAIL WITH RED GRAPEFRUIT JUICE

Makes 2 to 3 cocktails

Arak is said to be the very first liquor in the world. It has an anise/licorice flavor. It is quite strong in both taste and potency and therefore is usually served with water and ice. Arak has become very popular, and many new artisanal distilleries are producing it. I once had it served beautifully at a restaurant as a DIY cocktail with a portion of arak, a carafe of red grapefruit juice, a small pitcher of simple syrup, and a glass of ice. At home, I find it's easier to make as cocktails. Whenever I make this, there is always someone who says they won't like it because they don't like black licorice, but I always ask them to give it a chance. After the first two sips, it gets easier. Many countries have a licorice-flavored liqueur—ouzo, sambuca, aquavit, pastis, raki—so if you can't find arak, try one of those.

Red grapefruit suprèmes (see page 109) **or slices**

Ice cubes

3 oz arak

2 oz simple syrup + more to taste (see note)

5 oz red grapefruit juice

1. Place 2 or 3 red grapefruit suprèmes in each of the cocktail glasses and mash coarsely. Add a few ice cubes to each.

2. Place arak, simple syrup, red grapefruit juice, and some ice cubes in a cocktail shaker and shake to combine well, about 20 shakes, or until the shaker is very cold.

3. Pour into the cocktail glasses over the ice.

NOTE: Make simple syrup by bringing equal parts granulated sugar and water to a boil, and cooking gently for a few minutes until the sugar dissolves. Cool and chill well before using. It will keep in the refrigerator for about 1 month.

GOOD HEALTH TEA

Serves 4 to 6

Maybe this should be called "better health tea" because whether you have the flu or a cold or are perfectly healthy, it will still make you feel better. In 2018, Ray and I were in Israel when a bad flu was going around, and we both got it. When I had recovered and started to go out, whenever I went to a café and ordered mint tea, the server would say, "Would you rather have our health tea?" (I guess I still looked a little under the weather!) As a result, I created this recipe, and everyone loves it. (Except for Ray, that is, because it reminds him of having the flu.) I like to serve this from a teapot at the end of dinner, but you can also make it in individual mugs. (It looks great in clear glass mugs or a glass teapot.) When I ordered herbal tea at the end of a meal at Volt, a modern Scandinavian restaurant in Stockholm, they brought a tray of herbs, hot water, and a beautiful glass teapot and let us make our own tea, which is a lovely idea.

1-inch piece fresh ginger, peeled and sliced into thin rounds

1-inch piece fresh turmeric, peeled and cut in half

1 large bunch fresh mint

Peel of half a lemon, in large pieces

1 Tbsp honey or date syrup + more to taste

1 teabag of your choice (black, green, or herbal), optional

4 cups boiling water

1. Rinse your teapot with hot water. Drain the water out.

2. Add the ginger, turmeric, mint, lemon peel, honey, and tea bag, if using.

3. Add boiling water. Let stand for 3 to 5 minutes.

4. Serve the tea with additional honey to taste.

NOTE: If making this in a teapot, leave the ingredients large enough that they don't pour through the spout.

Another Note from Bonnie

What I've Learned from My Daughter

When Anna encouraged me to write this book and offered to help, I don't think either of us realized at that time how much she would become a part of it. It has been a real collaboration. She is a gifted writer with an amazing sense of humor who was able to take my memories and stories and turn them into prose. She is a wonderful cook who tested recipes with me and suggested ways to make them more delicious and easier to follow. I shouldn't have been surprised. She has always had amazing taste. She was a discriminating eater from the time she was very little, meaning, of course, that she was a fussy kid. She always knew when I changed even just one ingredient in a recipe and often that was enough of a reason not to eat it. But working on this project together, as two adults, two cooks, two friends, was an unexpected joy. She is so organized and such an incredible manager that I didn't even realize she was managing me. But I know this book would never exist if it wasn't for her.

Writing this book together was an emotional experience. It's a special gift to meet your child as an adult, see her excel in her field, to see her as a trusted and compassionate friend. I so admire the person she has become—always open to new ideas and challenges. You may think that as a mother, I am prejudiced but if you know her, you know I am being totally objective. It is an honor and blessing to be her mother and her friend. Thank you, Anna, for everything.

Another Note from Anna

What I've Learned from My Mom

Everything. But some things are more relevant to this book, so I'll stick to those.

I'm not the best plan-ahead cook. Whenever I call my mom for cooking advice, she asks, "Did you read through the whole recipe?" The answer is usually no. The next thing she says is, "Okay, don't worry." This conversation usually occurs because I don't have an ingredient and/or did not bring the butter to room temperature. So, in these cases, one of the most-used tips I've learned from my mom is that despite never having buttermilk in my refrigerator, I always have buttermilk in my refrigerator. All you need is milk and lemon juice (see page 178). I've also learned that if you're making a cake or cookies and the butter is not at room temperature, you can cut it into tiny little pieces or grate it and beat it first before adding the sugar—which is only sometimes stated in recipes.

She's taught me that the inspiration for recipes usually comes from somewhere, and that it is so wonderful to be open and explicit about that even if you've changed the recipe. It's part of what makes recipes more than just something to cook. They're stories tied to history, experiences, and relationships.

I've learned to always go ahead and order the French fries when I know they'll be good ones.

I've learned that if you want someone to try a new food, give them the best version of it. I will embarrassingly admit that in my early twenties I had still never tasted a hamburger. They didn't appeal to me. One night she took me as her date to the opening party for Mark McEwan's restaurant Bymark, and mini Bymark burgers were being passed around on platters of hors d'oeuvres. She said, "Anna, if you're ever going to try a burger, do it now." I did, and now I love them all. (I acknowledge the privilege of that first burger, but I hope you know what I mean. I started loving tofu by eating fried tofu. Now I would eat it any which way.)

I've heard my mom tell people often that, if they're cooking for guests, to cook the thing they're most comfortable cooking, and she's so right! Make a roast chicken and vegetables, make the spaghetti and meatballs everyone loves, make anything that you know how to make and won't cause you stress leading up to the meal. And, if anything you make doesn't turn out the way you hoped, don't apologize. You just cooked dinner for everyone! And they may never have noticed anyway.

Not specifically related to cooking, but the most important thing I've learned from my mom is what I would describe as her general ethos—be patient and be kind. She is the most patient and kind person to all of us and to everyone she meets. It can be annoying, because it's true (meaning she's always right). It's always better to be that way. It makes us all love and appreciate her the way we do.

I also want to add two more things I've learned from two other people while writing this book. Tyler Anderson, our incredible photographer, taught me that a histogram is a visual representation of data and asked if I would ever use the word "histogram" again after the shoots were done, and guess what? I just did. And Olga Truchan taught me that food stylists are magical geniuses. Olga, thank you for teaching me the wonders of paper towel and swirls and so much more.

Acknowledgments

The idea for this book came from the understanding that food has the ability to connect us. We feel incredibly grateful to be connected to so many wonderful people in our lives.

This book couldn't have been done without the support of Appetite by Random House. Robert McCullough came to a keynote address Bonnie gave at a cookbook festival a few years back that we had written together and he called Bonnie after with so much enthusiasm and positive feedback, she felt excited to start writing again. Thank you to our editor, Zoe Maslow, who over the years has become an amazing friend to both of us and who never gave up on the idea that one day we'd write this book together. Thank you for being our best cheerleader, and for bringing Matt, Ruby, and Archie into our lives. And thank you also to Judy Phillips for the invaluable copyediting, and Evelyn Ebbs for the detailed index. Kelly Hill—what a brilliant cookbook designer! She took every thought, suggestion, wish, and idea we had seriously and found a way to make this book feel like us. Thank you also to Susan Burns, Carla Kean, Kristin Cochrane, and Anne Collins—your support throughout has meant so much. A special thank-you goes to Scott Sellers, who has become a trusted friend and adviser, and for being Bonnie's partner in the book club for all these years—she couldn't have done it without you. Thank you also to Marian Hebb, Warren Sheffer, and Shelly Tanaka.

Another team was instrumental to putting this book together. We feel particularly indebted to Tyler Anderson, for the stunning photos and being the love of our puppy Clementine's life; Olga Truchan, for agreeing to work with us on this book and being the most wonderful food and prop stylist and friend; and Leonie Eidinger, for always being there at the precise moment she's needed—we would be lost without her help. We couldn't imagine having done this book without the three of you (and still have no idea how we accomplished what we did during a pandemic).

Thank you, Ray, for so many things, including taste-testing recipes even if they had turmeric (although usually without knowing, because we hid it from you). Thank you also for staying calm (or as calm as you were able) when Olga and Tyler turned the entire first floor of the house into a photo studio. You get so many points. But thank you, Ray, for believing in us all, and for making us feel like we can succeed at anything. You've always cared so much about us, your work, and your patients—we know it inspires others to care so much too. To Mark, you are our digital/video/social media/everything creative director. We are so lucky to benefit from your talents. We are in awe of your positivity, remarkable work ethic, and incredible ideas. Your ability to translate concepts into reality is beyond belief, as is your expert whistling. And to Fara, Mark, and Hattie May, your visits to Toronto mean so much to us and are incredibly special. And while travel was not possible, what we've loved about Zoom dinners is feeling so connected to you. Thank you for bringing us Clementine, the giant puppy that joined our family while writing this book and brought more love and joy into our hearts than we thought possible.

Thanks to Jane and Wayne, Heddy, Chuck, Meredith, Jason, and Mersadiz for being our loving immediate family. We are also lucky to be part of big extended families. To the Soltz family, being able to connect twice a year with such a beautiful, vibrant Jewish community is so special. And to Robbie and Ali, and everyone on the Zweig/Tile side, we feel so lucky to be part of your family as well.

Yet family is so much more than those related to you through a family tree. To Mitchell Davis and Nathan Goldstein, there's no one we'd rather cook, eat, shop, laugh, walk, drive, get lost, and everything else with. And that goes for your family as well—Leslie and Judi, Carrie, John and Sophia, Judi and Marcus, Elia, and Oded. And Oded, thank you for being Clementine's guardian angel. Hanoch and Robby, we couldn't imagine our family without you. And Anthony Rose, we love you, your family, and your food so much.

To others whom we love like family: Lynn Saunders and family, Lauren, Dan and the Gutter family, Elizabeth Pizzinato and Richard Paquet, Linda and Joel Rose, Rob Wilder and Jackie Rothstein, Patti and Earl Linzon, Andrea and Jorge Iceruk, Anita and Mike Gravelle, Susan and John Devins, Julie and Bernard Lewis, Richard Rottman and Ellen Greenblatt, Judy and Jack Winberg, Ann Sharp and Vernon Shaw, Marsha Werb and Ed Hamer, Elyse Goldstein and Baruch Sienna, Daphne Smith, Myrna Yazer, Sarah Sergio, Ruthie Ladovsky, Nathan Ladovsky, Irene Tam, Eric Kirzner and family, Jacquie Altman,

Fran Berkoff, Jayne Cohen and Howie Spiegler, Luis Fagundes and Marco Moniz, Michael and Marilla Wex, and Jonathan Guss and Leslie Milrod. Thank you also to our Clementine family: Maria Fine, Angelique Miller Stelnick and the team at Spinks Veterinary Clinic.

Thank you to the cooking school family: Maureen Loller, Jenny Cheng Burke, Francine Menard, Leonie Eidinger, Linda Stephen, Dely Balagtas, Letty Lastima, Anne Apps, Jennifer Mahoney, Valerie Seto, Rhonda Caplan, Melissa Mertle, Larissa Vitorino, Peter Tsiligiannis, Josef Rogovsky, Jonathan Rapoport and Stan Clapp. To Lorraine Butler, thank you for organizing Bonnie's life. And to Stephen Alexander and Cumbrae's, Hart Melvin and Gelato Fresco, Ararat, Avenue Seafood, Fresh Harvest Foods, Marvellous Edibles and all the farmers and farmers' markets for having incredible quality products and for always being consistent and reliable.

Bonnie's trips to Israel have had a huge influence on her and on her cooking. Through these trips we've developed an Israeli family, including those who have come on Bonnie's tour and those who make the tours so wonderful: Judy and Bob Goldman, Janna and Ilan Gur, Gil Hovav, Danny and Nomi Halperin, Adeena Sussman and Jay Shofet, Erez Komarovsky, Nof Atamna-Ismaeel, Uri Scheft, Tina Scheftelowitz, Jacob Ladovsky, Naama Shefi, Yossi Elad, Moshe Basson, Ronit Yam, Bill Shinman, Hedai Offiam, Ronit Vered, Ika Cohen, Laura Pollack, Idit Papular, and Janice Snider.

There are so many other incredible chefs who have had an impact on us both, and on Bonnie in particular, through their involvement with the cooking school, visiting and teaching for 37 years. They shared more than knowledge and recipes— they shared their stories and how to adapt cooking to locally available ingredients and individual tastes. They imparted the importance of under-standing that when cooking from cultures other than your own, we must appreciate what food represents and means beyond just a tasty dish. Our hope is that you know the recipes brought to you in this book are being presented with the utmost respect for where they've come from. Thank you Madhur Jaffrey, Rick Bayless, Jacques Pépin, Nina Simonds, Nick Malgieri, Madeleine Kamman, Hugh Carpenter, Jim Dodge, Martin Yan, Vikram Vij, Mark Bittman, Elizabeth Andoh, Diana Kennedy, Chris McDonald, Lucy Waverman, Arpi Magyar, Jonathan Gushue, Jacques Marie, Clive Adamson and Suzanne Rannie, Joanne Weir, Sarah Villamere, Mark McEwan, Jamie Kennedy, Michael Stadtlander, David Cohlmeyer, David McMillan, Fred Morin, Simon Thibault, Mary Risley, Leah Koenig, Alison Fryer, Lesley Chesterman, Helen Goh, Darina Allen, Susur Lee, Adam Sachs, Gabriella Gershenson, Shelagh Rogers, Elizabeth Baird, Monda Rosenberg, Jeffrey Yoskowitz, Alanna Fleischer, Brian Cheng, Barbara-Jo McIntosh, Matt Duffy, Hubert Aumeier, Evelyn Zabloski, Pati Jinich, Hidekazu Tojo, James Chatto, and so many others.

On a trip together in 2010, we went to Copenhagen but stopped in London on the way. This was the first time we ate at Ottolenghi and met Yotam and Sami. They opened the world to the flavors of the Middle East and had everyone, not just vegetarians, looking at vegetables differently. When we got to Copenhagen, we ate at Noma and met Rene Redzepi. Rene made Copenhagen a culinary destination, and gave chefs, no matter where they were, the confidence to cook with local ingredients and traditions, and he is currently encouraging change in the hospitality industry to make it sustainable. All three of them were so incredibly kind and inspiring, and we felt so lucky to meet them. Like what Marcella Hazan did for Italian cooking, Madhur Jaffrey did for Indian cooking, and Jacques Pepin and Julia Child for French cooking, looking back now, they were so clearly forging the future.

Additional thanks from Anna: Thank you to Julia Sharp and Jay Lubinsky, Shana and Michael Peiser, Lauren and Gabriel Granatstein and Dara and Brad Gottleib—I love you all so much and being included as part of your families means the world to me. Thank you also to Carmen Garcia, Ashleigh Wishen, Sara Lass, Talia Leszcz, Bhairavi Vijayakumar, Miriam Balsam, Kelly Jory and Anne Matthews—for a million things but especially for the love, laughter, and support you've brought to my life. Thank you, Wesley Normington, for your support and for loving the chicken cake. Thank you to my team and colleagues at the George Hull Centre. In particular, Kim Curran, for your constant support, and who, along with Diane Bartlett, Leticia Gracia, and Susan Chamberlain, have given me incredible opportunities and meaningful work, and have taught me so much. And to Isobel Vallely and Dian Bent for always lending your ears and hearts. I tell anyone who will listen that my best career and life advice is to maintain relationships with your mentors and people who you think are brilliant, and no one has made that more true for me than Ian Roth and Antony Duttine. Thank you also to Mark Cole, Martin Knapp, and Valentina Iemmi, all academic mentors, for believing that I had the potential to do things I had no idea I could do. Finally, thank you to Elisse Peltz, Leslie Davis, and Faye Doell, who over many years have had a tremendous impact on helping me figure out who I am and work toward who I want to be.

Lastly, thank you to everyone we miss so much: Gwen Berkowitz, Ed Weil, Helen Kirzner, Sydney Bacon, Paul Soles, Peter Gzowski, Arlene Zweig, Norm Saunders, Bernie Glazman, Nathan Fong, Charles Greco, Guiliano Bugialli, Biba Caggiano, Marcella Hazan, Simone Beck, Lillian Kaplun, Norene Gilletz, Anita Stewart, Julia Aitken, Pearl Rupert, Jack Rupert, and Maxie and Ruthie Stern.

Index